(Continued from front flap)

starting point, makes him guide extraordinary to a new completeness in Christian thinking. The author not only explains how Whitehead's system makes tenable the personal God that many philosophical systems reject, but draws out the great philosopher's thought in theological contexts.

Chapter I introduces the reader to Whitehead's total scheme of thought. Chapter II analyzes his ideas on the nature of man which relate to theological anthropology. Chapter III summarizes Whitehead's theories of value and draws deductions for ethics. Chapters IV and V trace the development of his thought about God and suggest a systematic doctrine of God dependent upon Whitehead's philosophy but nevertheless differing from some of his explicit statements. Chapter VI breaks new ground in the interpretation of various religious experiences in Whiteheadian terms. Chapter VII explicates the nature of philosophy and theology and compares them as methods.

This book is a necessity — not only for students of theology and philosophy, but for any minister or Christian layman who would try to communicate with the estranged intelligentsia . . . to combat nihilism with knowledge, to convey the possibility of an organic view of the universe with a Christian God at center.

THE AUTHOR

John B. Cobb, Jr., an ordained Methodist minister, was born in Kobe, Japan, the son of missionaries. He studied at Emory University, Atlanta, Georgia; the University of Michigan; the Divinity School of the University of Chicago. He is Associate Professor of Systematic Theology at Southern California School of Theology, Claremont, California.

A
CHRISTIAN
NATURAL
THEOLOGY

Books by
John B. Cobb, Jr.
Published by The Westminster Press ®

A Christian Natural Theology:
Based on the Thought of Alfred North Whitehead

Living Options in Protestant Theology:
A Survey of Methods

Varieties of Protestantism

A CHRISTIAN NATURAL THEOLOGY

BASED ON THE THOUGHT OF ALFRED NORTH WHITEHEAD

by

John B. Cobb, Jr.

Philadelphia
The Westminster Press

Grateful acknowledgment is made to The
Macmillan Company for permission to quote
from *Adventures of Ideas* (1933); *Modes of
Thought* (1938); *Process and Reality* (1929);
Religion in the Making (1926); and *Science
and the Modern World* (1926); to Little,
Brown and Company for permission to quote
from *Dialogues of Alfred North Whitehead*
(copyright 1954 by Lucien Price); and to
Houghton Mifflin Company for permission
to quote from Colin Wilson, *Religion and the
Rebel*.

LIBRARY OF CONGRESS CATALOG CARD NO. 65–11612

PUBLISHED BY THE WESTMINSTER PRESS®

PHILADELPHIA, PENNSYLVANIA

PRINTED IN THE UNITED STATES OF AMERICA

To Charles Hartshorne:
To whom I owe both my understanding
and my love of
Whitehead's philosophy

Contents

Key to References

Footnote references to Whitehead's books use the following abbreviations. Numbers after the abbreviations in the footnotes refer to pages unless otherwise indicated.

AI   *Adventures of Ideas.* The Macmillan Company, 1933.

CN   *The Concept of Nature.* Cambridge University Press, 1920.

Dial   *Dialogues of Alfred North Whitehead,* as recorded by Lucien Price. Little, Brown and Company, 1954.

ESP   *Essays in Science and Philosophy.* Philosophical Library, Inc., 1947.

FR   *The Function of Reason.* Princeton University Press, 1929.

Imm   " Immortality," in Schilpp, ed., *The Philosophy of Alfred North Whitehead.* See " Schilpp " below.

MT   *Modes of Thought.* The Macmillan Company, 1938.

PNK   *An Enquiry Concerning the Principles of Natural Knowledge.* Cambridge University Press, 1919; second ed., 1925.

PR   *Process and Reality.* The Macmillan Company, 1929.

RM   *Religion in the Making.* The Macmillan Company, 1926.

SMW   *Science and the Modern World.* The Macmillan Company, 1926.

Works about Whitehead are listed in the first footnote entry by author and title. Subsequent entries are usually by author only.

Blyth   John W. Blyth, *Whitehead's Theory of Knowledge*. (Brown University Studies, Vol. VII.) Brown University Press, 1941.

Christian   William A. Christian, *An Interpretation of Whitehead's Metaphysics*. Yale University Press, 1959.

Ely   Stephen Ely, *The Religious Availability of Whitehead's God*. The University of Wisconsin Press, 1942.

Hammerschmidt   William W. Hammerschmidt, *Whitehead's Philosophy of Time*. King's Crown Press, 1947.

Johnson   A. H. Johnson, *Whitehead's Theory of Reality*. Beacon Press, Inc. 1952.

Kline   George L. Kline, ed., *Alfred North Whitehead: Essays on His Philosophy*. Prentice-Hall, Inc., 1963.

Lawrence   Nathaniel Lawrence, *Whitehead's Philosophical Development*. University of California Press, 1956.

Leclerc   Ivor Leclerc, *Whitehead's Metaphysics: An Introductory Exposition*. The Macmillan Company, 1958.

Leclerc   (Ed.) Ivor Leclerc, ed., *The Relevance of Whitehead*. The Macmillan Company, 1961.

Lowe   Victor Lowe, *Understanding Whitehead*. The Johns Hopkins Press, 1962.

Palter   Robert M. Palter, *Whitehead's Philosophy of Science*. The University of Chicago Press, 1960.

Schilpp   Paul Arthur Schilpp, ed., *The Philosophy of Alfred North Whitehead*. Tudor Publishing Company, 1951.

Sherburne   Donald W. Sherburne, *A Whiteheadian Aesthetic*. Yale University Press, 1961.

Preface

This book is a Whiteheadian Christian natural theology. The formal description and justification of this enterprise is attempted in section 1 of Chapter VII. But even in this brief preface, there is a place for a less rigorous and more personal explanation for the reopening of the work of natural theology and specifically for the appeal to Whitehead.

In *Living Options in Protestant Theology,* I argued the need for a Christian natural theology primarily by analysis of the bases on which major recent theologies have sought to justify their affirmations. I tried to show that even those theologies which explicitly repudiate natural theology have had assumptions or developed implications that should, in fact, be recognized as belonging to the sphere of natural theology. In the case of those theologies which affirm natural theology, I argued that the natural theology in question has specifically Christian character. If this is the case, it is reasonable to propose that we take the problem of constructing a natural theology with utmost seriousness, while not supposing that in doing so we are employing a rationality itself unaffected by our Christian commitments.

I suggest further that many of the problems with which theologians now wrestle arise out of assumptions formed for them by more or less consciously accepted ideas of a philosophical sort. To turn attention away from these ideas because they are philosophical is to allow them a tyranny over theological work that can be dispelled only by critical and self-conscious reflection about them. That means that it is only by facing the task of natural theology directly that the Christian theologian may hope to achieve his appropriate freedom.

It must be stressed at the outset that serious concern with natural theology does not militate against serious concern for the other tasks of Christian theology. My original intention had been to include attention to some of these tasks in this volume, but this proved impractical. Hence this book deals almost exclusively with natural theology. If I postpone for some years publication of equally serious study on such topics as Christology and soteriology, I hope that will not give the impression that I view these topics as of less importance. The sequence from natural theology to Christology, however, is significant, for it correctly reflects my view that it is not possible to formulate a Christology without the employment of a conceptuality requiring clarification in natural theology. This does *not* mean that faith in Christ requires such prior clarification. The priority of natural theology applies *only* to doctrinal formulation. Apart from faith in Christ, the problem of a Christian natural theology would not arise any more than would the problem of Christological formulation.

My argument is not that faith can never proceed directly to Christological formulation. Clearly it can do so, and clearly much of the greatest theology has followed this procedure. My argument is that even when it does so, a great deal is assumed that is not directly validated by faith itself. Where these assumptions — about the nature of language, of reality, of history, or of nature — are widely accepted, and where they are congenial to the task of doctrinal formulation, their uncritical acceptance is harmless. But if, as I believe, this is not now the case, if the diversity of assumptions inhibits communication, and if many of the assumptions militate against any adequate expression of the gospel, then the frontal assault on natural theology becomes the systematically prior task of adequate theological construction.

Thus far I have argued for serious attention to natural theology on the grounds of the situation within the theological discipline. I believe there is also reason to renew the enterprise of natural theology for the sake of faith itself.

It is widely recognized that we live in a time when the categories in which the Christian message has traditionally been presented have lost all meaning for major segments of the population. This could be illustrated at many points. At some of these points it could be shown that the change is much like that experienced by every generation, that the translation of the gospel into the vocabulary of the day is a perennial task which should cause us no special problem. However, at some other points, I am convinced, one cannot thus relativize our problem.

The crux of the matter has to do with the concepts of man and of God. To simplify the present discussion, I shall limit it to treatment of the latter. For much of the culture that is growing up about us and within us, " God " has become an empty sound. This is no longer a problem only for those Christians trying to communicate with a special segment of the intelligentsia estranged from the church. It has become the problem of the suburban pastor in his dealing with his most sensitive church leaders and youth. Perhaps most of all it has become the problem of the perceptive minister in dealing with himself and his own understanding of his ministry.

In reacting to this situation, most of the theologians who have been opposed to natural theology have taken the position that this cultural phenomenon must be treated as of no fundamental importance for the gospel. Some have thought it a matter of indifference — or a positive gain — on the grounds that false ideas of God are thus destroyed, and that the opportunity for the encounter with the truly transcendent God known only in Jesus Christ is heightened. This view is commonly associated with an attitude of contempt for the kind of piety actually characteristic of our churches. Others have thought that the emptiness of the term " God " makes it clear that we must either cease to use this word or redefine it in terms of categories that are meaningful to modern man — love, the depth dimension, creative interchange, authentic life, or *Mitmenschlichkeit*. From this point of view " God " in any other sense has no essential place in the gospel.

The alternative reaction is to try to restore the term " God " to meaningful discourse in some real continuity with its historic use. In my judgment such restoration is both useful and possible. Indeed for my own spiritual existence as a Christian it is a matter of life and death that the reality of the referent of " God " be a part of my intellectual conviction. I realize that others do not share my sense of the importance of such intellectual conviction. Those who understand faith as a gift of God that is in no way dependent upon any spiritual or intellectual openness toward faith on the part of man can reasonably object that the intellectual approach to God is pointless or worse. In Biblical and Christian history, however, I find little justification for the view that God acts in such radical independence of intellectual and cultural history. On the other hand, those who believe that the gospel requires no reference to God in any sense other than a special mode of human existence or togetherness seem to me not to have realized that the same cultural and intellectual forces that have militated against the meaningfulness of the word " God " operate also against most of that which they continue to affirm.

In any case, whatever the alternatives may be, I must speak for myself. To me it appears that the struggle to restore the meaningfulness of the word " God," which means to justify the horizon in which this word can have its appropriate reference, is a matter of ultimate importance for the health, even for the survival, of Christian faith. It need hardly be pointed out that the evaporation of meaning from this crucial term has occurred, not as a function of that theology which is the expression or articulation of faith, but as a function of that cosmology which has destroyed the horizons within which early Christian, medieval, and early modern man understood his existence. For this reason it seems equally evident that the restoration of meaning to this term requires direct consideration of those forces which have destroyed it as well as the continuation of that proclamation and that theology which presuppose its meaningfulness. This means that natural theology in our generation is not to be seen as a dubious luxury of the systematician but as foundational to proclamation and to the realization of faith as well.

That natural theology is possible as well as needed presupposes that the destructive forces of modern cosmology are not rooted with any final necessity in the intellectual situation of modern man. Discussion in general terms of such a thesis is impossible here. The book as a whole must constitute the argument. Implicitly this argument will be that a cosmology lacking the destructive implications of much modern cosmological thought is not only possible but also more adequate to the modern situation than its competitors.

The philosophy by which I am myself grasped, and on the basis of which I propose to develop a Christian natural theology, is that of Alfred North Whitehead. In his work there is a fully developed alternative to the nihilistic tendencies of most modern thought. No one else in the twentieth century has attempted so impressive a synthesis of that knowledge which forces itself upon the attention of the honest and open mind. In recent years there has been a marked renewal of interest in his work, and we may expect that the days of his greatest influence lie in the future.[1]

---

[1] Cf. Lowe, *Understanding Whitehead*, p. v; and Lowe, "Whitehead's Philosophical Development," Schilpp, ed., *The Philosophy of*

The effort to develop a Christian natural theology based on Whitehead's thought presupposes the philosophical excellence of that thought. For this presupposition no proof can be offered. For myself I am persuaded that he ranks with Plato, Aristotle, and Kant as one of the greatest creative thinkers of all time. I regret that from the use I will make of his work in this book the reader is unlikely to receive any adequate sense of Whitehead's genius. The fundamental adequacy of his analysis and comprehensive synthesis I must ask the reader to test for himself through careful study or else, for the present, to take for granted.

Not to prove my case as to Whitehead's excellence, but only to show that he sometimes arouses admiration in surprising quarters, I offer the following tribute from the English existentialist Colin Wilson, who also wrestled without personal satisfaction with the problem of writing a summary introduction to Whitehead's thought. I concur with, and would make my own, all that Wilson says.

"Whitehead's thought is extremely difficult, and his prose style is not always all that could be asked; consequently, the foregoing [in my case, following] summary is

Alfred North Whitehead, p. 124. The objective evidence for the claim of probable increase in the influence of Whitehead lies in the increased volume of published work about his thought and the growing number of dissertations being written about him. The recent belated recognition of the great importance also of the work of Charles Hartshorne is closely connected with this. See Schubert Ogden, "Theology and Philosophy: A New Phase of the Discussion," The Journal of Religion, Jan., 1964, pp. 1–16. More subjective is the judgment that the approaches to both philosophy and theology that have been dominant in recent decades and that have militated against attention to the work of both Whitehead and Hartshorne are running dry and that new vitality can be attained best in both disciplines by serious dialogue with Whitehead. Still more subjective is my opinion that even in the physical sciences there is a dawning awareness of the need to wrestle again with the questions on which Whitehead cast so much light. This is suggested by the work of Milic Capek, The Philosophical Impact of Contemporary Physics (D. Van Nostrand Co., Inc., 1961), and Adolf Grünbaum, Philosophical Problems of Space and Time (Alfred A. Knopf, Inc., 1963).

bound to seem puzzling. I am also conscious that I have not succeeded in making Whitehead's thought seem attractive to readers who approach it for the first time. Nevertheless, it is my own conviction that he will one day be regarded as the outstanding philosopher of the twentieth century; and the attempt to present him in summary had to be made. England is always singularly unfair to its thinkers; if Whitehead had been a German, he would have had a special department of some university dedicated to expounding his thought.

" What is surprising — even in view of the English indifference to metaphysics — is that no one has noticed that Whitehead has created his own kind of existentialism; and that it is fuller and more adequate than that of any Continental thinker. He was his own Hegel and Kierkegaard rolled into one. *Science and the Modern World* is the *Unscientific Postscript* of the twentieth century — with the additional advantage of being readable." [2]

Despite my keen interest in Whitehead's philosophy as philosophy and my conviction of its great value in that context, this book is about Christian natural theology. This means that it is a treatment of questions of importance for Christian theology in which the criteria of philosophical excellence determine what can be said. The argument presented asks to be judged in terms of its philosophical merits, but the selection of topics and the focus of inquiry are determined by theological passion.

Ultimately the book expresses my own convictions. In some sections it deals with topics untreated by Whitehead, and in others it presents a position that deviates from his. Nevertheless, I am so profoundly and overwhelmingly indebted to him for the fundamental structure of my thought, and I begin my own reflection on each topic so deeply influenced by my understanding of his philosophy, that the book is also a book about Whitehead. I have tried

[2] Colin Wilson, *Religion and the Rebel* (Houghton Mifflin Co., 1957) , p. 317.

to indicate carefully in the text where exposition of his position ends and my own ideas are introduced. In some instances I have presented, as my own, ideas that may well also have been Whitehead's. I have not done this out of special eagerness to claim originality, for I am much more comfortable when I can claim his authority. But I have wished to keep the book relatively free of any scholastic discussion as to which of the interpreters of Whitehead is correct on disputed points.[3] For this reason, where there can be serious doubt as to the agreement of my own views with his, I have assumed responsibility.

The book as a whole can make no sense apart from a basic understanding of some main features of Whitehead's philosophical position. There are several excellent volumes explanatory of his thought, most of them published quite recently. For a brief introduction I recommend Ivor Leclerc's *Whitehead's Metaphysics: An Introductory Exposition*, Part I of Victor Lowe's *Understanding Whitehead*, or the first eighty-eight pages of Donald Sherburne's *A Whiteheadian Aesthetic*. A somewhat older work, still useful and recently reprinted, is A. H. Johnson's *Whitehead's Theory of Reality*. William Christian's *An Interpretation of Whitehead's Metaphysics* offers a much more exhaustive discussion of many features of Whitehead's thought.[4]

I make no effort in this book to provide a competing introduction to Whitehead. However, I cannot assume that my readers will have read one of these books or will have adequate firsthand acquaintance with Whitehead's writing. Hence in Chapter I, I do attempt to introduce the

---

[3] Many of the best recent critical and expository essays on Whitehead have been published in book form. See Kline, ed., *Alfred North Whitehead: Essays on His Philosophy;* Leclerc, ed., *The Relevance of Whitehead;* Schilpp, *op. cit.; Studies in Whitehead's Philosophy* (Tulane Studies in Philosophy, Vol. X. Tulane University Press, 1961).

[4] A reader preferring to tackle Whitehead directly is advised to begin with *Adventures of Ideas,* especially Part III.

reader to Whitehead's perspective and to give him some clue as to the meaning of some of the essential terms. The appeal must be to intuition, but hopefully an apt example may facilitate such intuition.[5] I have kept this material very brief in the hope that most of the essential concepts can be clarified for the reader as he follows the argument in the following chapters. I have placed Whitehead's technical terms in quotes where I first introduce them in a context that I hope will communicate their meaning.

Chapter II presents a number of features of Whitehead's doctrine of man that have bearing upon theological anthropology. To my knowledge there has been little previous work done on this aspect of Whitehead's thought. Chapter III summarizes major features of the value theory developed by Whitehead. In addition it introduces reflections on the specifically ethical situation of man that go beyond anything to be found in Whitehead. It is my hope that this ethical theory is fully compatible with Whitehead's value theory and general philosophy, but for much of what is said I assume full responsibility.

Chapter IV surveys the development of the thought about God in Whitehead, primarily through three of his books. Although the question of Whitehead's methodology is discussed, the presentation is generally descriptive rather than critical. Chapter V returns to some of the themes of Chapter IV, this time raising systematic problems and developing solutions that appear to me most fully consonant with the essential philosophical demands of Whitehead himself. This at some points leads to conclusions definitely not accepted by Whitehead and at other points settles

[5] I do not mean that Whitehead came to the formulation of his problems in the way suggested in Ch. I. For a lucid account of the actual genetic development of Whitehead's thought from the foundations of mathematics and logic to the principles of natural science and to comprehensive cosmology, see Lowe, "Whitehead's Philosophical Development," Schilpp, pp. 15–124. This is revised, expanded, and republished in *Understanding Whitehead*, pp. 117–296.

issues left unsettled by him.

Chapter VI is an attempt to understand religion in Whiteheadian terms. It includes a discussion of Whitehead's own thought on this subject but also considers quite independently how Whiteheadian philosophy can account for types of religious experience not reflected upon by Whitehead himself. Here too, to the best of my knowledge, I am breaking new ground.

Chapter VII is an attempt to explicate that understanding of theology and its problematic nature which underlies the whole book. Some reference is made to Whitehead, but in this chapter it is my own understanding of the nature of philosophy and theology that is under discussion. The reader with strongly methodological interests may wish to turn to this chapter before he reads the first six.

The book as a whole belongs in a peculiar way to Prof. Charles Hartshorne, to whom also it is dedicated. It was he who introduced me to Whitehead's philosophy and fired my enthusiasm. It is he also who has already developed from Whitehead a natural theology of first importance for Christian theology. In the discussion of God in this book there is little that is not inspired directly or indirectly by Hartshorne's work. My failure to give credit in detail is due to my desire to avoid complicating the text by discussion of the ideas of a third man. Let it simply be said that what is philosophically valid and valuable in my proposals for developing Whitehead's doctrine of God is due chiefly to Hartshorne. Of course neither he nor those whose help is acknowledged below are responsible for my formulation in detail, and such confusion and error as is to be found in my work is entirely my own responsibility.

Professor Hartshorne read an earlier essay of mine on Whitehead's doctrine of God and gave me valuable criticisms and still more valuable encouragement. I received similar help from Thomas Altizer, Nels Ferré, Ivor Leclerc, and Donald Sherburne. I want to take this opportunity to express again to each of them my sincere appreciation. I presented the earlier material on God as well as some fragments on Whitehead's doctrine of man to my students in a Whitehead seminar. For their patience, their questions, and their objections, I am grateful.

Other graduate students have helped me. Chief of these is Larry Rose, who, in addition to much detailed checking, editing, and indexing, read the manuscript without prior familiarity with Whitehead to check its intelligibility and suggest means of improvement. In quite a different way I am indebted to Delwin Brown, who is currently engaged in writing a dissertation on Whitehead's doctrine of God. He has read and criticized the entire manuscript. Furthermore, at a number of important points my present understanding of Whitehead has grown out of conversations with him that preceded the writing of this book. James Catanzaro and James Goss have also read portions of the manuscript and made helpful suggestions. Without the encouragement and assistance of President Ernest C. Colwell, I could not have completed my project.

Finally and most important, I would express my gratitude to my family and especially to my wife. Their tolerance, understanding, and support are the *sine qua non* of my study, reflection, and writing.

I

An Introduction to Whitehead's Philosophy

1. WHITEHEAD'S PHILOSOPHY AND THE PROBLEM OF DUALISM

The central question for traditional philosophy is to determine the kinds of things that are and how they are related to each other. In answering this question, we have two main types of clues. We may look at the world of sticks and stones, mountains and trees, animals and human bodies, and we may intuit some notion of matter or substance. On the other hand, we may reflect on the nature of our own conscious experience and intuit some notion of mentality. Of course, notions of matter and mind vary widely, and there are other possibilities as well, but much philosophy can be illumined by this simple duality.

Given this duality, one confronts the question of the relationship of material things and mental things. Are they fundamentally different from each other, such that there is no more-inclusive understanding of what the reality is that serves to explain both? This seems reasonable, but it leads to acute philosophic problems. Our mental experience seems to be highly correlated with the movements of material things both within our own bodies and beyond. How can this be? Can minds influence material bodies if they are completely different from matter? This would mean that the cause of the motion of matter could be something of a wholly different order from matter, and that seems inherently strange and unrelated to what the physical scientist discovers. Or conversely, it would mean that minds are determined in their behavior by causes of an entirely nonmental sort.

This dualism has played a large role in common sense, but most philosophers have tried to overcome it. This can be done in one of three main types of ways. First, one can understand matter as an appearance to mind. The justification for this view is that when we consider carefully the basis of our notion of matter it turns out to be entirely a function of sense experience. But we know that sense experience is fundamentally mental, that is, it belongs to mentality to have conscious experiences. Hence, the notion of matter should be reduced to the notion of a togetherness of sensuous qualities.

Despite its philosophic plausibility, common sense and the science of the seventeenth, eighteenth, and nineteenth centuries largely ignored this proposal. People were quite sure they had to do with something other than their own experience, and this something other seemed to be material. The second solution to the problem posed by dualism took this materiality as its clue and held that minds are functions of matter. Minds may be held to be epiphenomenal. The real causes of all things are seen in the behavior of matter, and subjective experience is regarded as a product of material forces with no independent influence upon them.

But total materialism is as difficult to accept as total mentalism. Even if mental experience is epiphenomenal, it still seems to *be,* and to us humans it seems to be quite important. It seems to be our minds, for example, that are inquiring about their relations to matter. Even if it should prove that all our mental states are caused by material states, this still does not tell us what mind is or how this cause operates. Hence, a third alternative commends itself; namely, to subsume the duality under some more-comprehensive unity. This might mean that some kind of reality underlies our subjective mental states as well as that which seems objective to them; it might mean that all reality participates in both mentality and materiality without in fact being either. This attempt to find a single type of reality explanatory of both what we call mind and what we call matter has taken many forms. Whitehead's philosophy is one of them.[1]

In the twentieth century the physical sciences have become open to the idea that the notion of matter is, after all, not illuminative of that which they investigate. This has happened in several ways, but it will be sufficient to note one of these by way of illustration. As long as what we call atoms were regarded as the ultimate stuff of the universe, the notion of matter seemed appropriate. Atoms seemed to function as little lumps of impenetrable stuff. They could be viewed as having definite location and as moving continuously through space. On the whole, mechanical models could be employed to understand them. Other phenomena that could not be understood in this way could be imaged as being like the waves on the ocean. Some medium such as air was compressed and extended or undulated. An appropriate medium for the transmission of light, for example, was posited as extending through all space and was called ether.

However, when the atom was discovered to be not ultimate but, rather, composed of electrons, protons, and "empty space," problems arose. At first one tried to understand these new entities as particles of matter, and for some purposes this imagery worked well. However, in other respects they turned out to function not as particles but more like waves. Evidence for a similar duality in the functioning of light that had long puzzled investigators also became more insistent. It seemed that the ultimate entities of which the world is composed are able sometimes to function as particles and sometimes as waves. To this disturbing fact was added the fact that they seemed also to be able to move from one place to another without passing

[1] *AI* 245; *MT* 205.

through the intervening space. Further, it became clear that electrons and protons are not things that carry electric charges, as a material model would require, but rather they themselves *are* electric charges. It seemed that something happens, now here, then there, with definite connection between one event and the next, but without continuous movement between them. Things happen in bursts or jerks rather than in an even flow. One might think of the motion picture, which in fact is only a succession of discontinuous pictures.

Due to these and other even more perplexing mysteries, many scientists gave up the idea that the human mind can frame any notion as to the nature of things. The effort to picture reality was widely abandoned. New theories were advanced which are completely baffling to our intuition but nevertheless are successful in explaining or predicting the results of experiments. On the whole, philosophers gave up the attempt to answer the questions of traditional philosophy and devoted themselves to the study of language. But some refused to acknowledge the ultimate unintelligibility of the universe and continued to seek models in terms of which to understand its strange functioning. One of these philosophers was Whitehead.[2]

Neither the usual notion of matter nor the usual notion of mind helped in understanding these discontinuous events that seem to be the ultimate entities of the natural world. But there were other ideas of mind, or rather of human experience, that were more suggestive. William James, for example, had argued that human experience grows by buds or drops rather than developing as a smooth, undivided process.[3] In a single second there are a series of such occasions of experience.[4] This can suggest that

[2] Cf. *MT* 185–186.

[3] Whitehead acknowledges the influence of James at this point. (*PR* 105–106.)

[4] Whitehead suggests that there may be from four to ten such occasions of human experience in a second. (*AI* 149, 233; *MT* 220.)

there may, after all, be something common to the human mind and the entities found in nature by physical science.

In one way or another any model by which we attempt to understand reality or any part of it must arise from human experience. There is simply nowhere else to turn. But the things given in the flow of sense experience suggest no other models than those of particles and waves already found inadequate by science. The only hopeful model, then, is the human experience as such. Furthermore, philosophical problems that are insoluble if we insist that human experience and physical nature are of radically different character are far more manageable if we can find some common genus to which both belong. Our modern conviction that human beings and their mentality have evolved through long ages from simpler and still simpler natural forms also suggests that there is some family connection between human experience and the entities of the natural world.[5] At any rate, Whitehead launched boldly forth on the speculative possibility that human experience as such is a clue to the ultimate nature of things. Electronic events are to be thought of as occasions of electronic experience. Their disconnectedness can be conceived as being like the disconnectedness of successive human experiences.

Whitehead never suggested that electronic experiences are like human ones in any inclusive way. They have no sense experience, no consciousness, no imagination. If "experience" necessarily implies all those things, then surely a more general term would have to be found; but Whitehead thought the notion of experience could itself be made to serve. After all, men speak of their unconscious experience.

The suggestion that the entities in nature are to be thought of as belonging to the same category of existence as human experience would have little value if it did not lead to further explanation. If the first speculative conjec-

[5] *FR* 11; *AI* 237.

ture has merit, then the philosopher must proceed to the exhaustive analysis of how human experience occurs. He may be able to find at its most primitive level factors that can be generalized so as to be illuminative also of the ultimate entities in the physical world.[6] This process of analysis is worked out by Whitehead in amazing detail and is productive of numerous suggestions as to how specific physical phenomena are to be understood. It also provides a basis for understanding space and time and the many geometries with which the modern scientist approaches his world. It is, further, rich in its suggestiveness for aesthetics, ethics, and religion. Indeed, there are few areas of human interest on which Whitehead's analysis fails to shed some light.

2. THE ANALYSIS OF AN ACTUAL OCCASION

Whitehead brought to his task great distinction as a mathematician and logician, but his procedure was not what we might expect on the basis of a usual understanding of these disciplines. We might call his procedure phenomenological except that at no time did Whitehead dismiss from his thought the relevant knowledge about physics, physiology, and psychology. It would be best to say that he began with human experience as we all know it, and as we further understand it in the light of science, and then presented the question as to what must be the case in order that this experience can occur.

We have noted that what must be assumed, in order that human experience (and the ultimate particles of nature) can be understood, are successive " actual occasions of experience." [7] Rather than being a continuous flow, experience comes to be in discrete and indivisible units. These

---

[6] PR 29, 172; AI 239, 284; MT 231–232.

[7] PR 33, 113. The complete phrase, " actual occasion of experience," is not characteristic of Whitehead. In PR he usually speaks of " actual occasion " and in AI he writes of " occasion of experience." The referent is the same.

momentary occasions succeed each other with a rapidity beyond any clear grasp of conscious attention. The direct analysis of a single occasion of experience is impossible.[8]

The difficulty or impossibility of focusing attention upon an individual occasion does not prevent us from carrying out an analysis of what these occasions contain, for we may assume that whatever qualities we are aware of experience as having at all obtain also in individual occasions. The only exception is change, since this is the difference between successive momentary experiences each of which in its own being must be changeless.[9] We can take a simple experience of a second or so; we can analyze what it contains other than what depends on temporal successiveness; and we can assume that one or another of the occasions within that second — and perhaps all — had those qualities or characteristics. Let us take an example.

Suppose I am looking at a green tie and wishing it were brown.[10] Let us analyze the ingredients in this experience. Sense experience plays a considerable role, but at the outset we must be clear that for Whitehead it does not play the foundational role.[11] He shows that the assumption that sense data alone are given in experience is disastrous for philosophy. Certainly it would put an end to any possibility of finding aspects of human experience attributable also to electrons, for it would be absurd to suppose that subatomic particles enjoyed vision or touch. There is, of course, the experience of the patch of green. But there is also the experience of some thing that is green and that occupies a region of space in a particular geometric rela-

---

[8] Whitehead shows that no occasion can be conscious of its own satisfaction. (*PR* 130. See also *PR* 387.)

[9] *PR* 52, 92.

[10] For readers interested in a more technical discussion, it may be noted that this involves the contrast of a conscious perception and an imaginative feeling. Sherburne's account of these higher phases of experience is excellent. See *A Whiteheadian Aesthetic*, pp. 55–69.

[11] The comparative superficiality of sense experience is a main theme of *MT*. See, e.g., pp. 41, 152, and 181.

tion to my body. This experience of thingness, Whitehead insists, is not dependent on a process of learning. We do not first experience only sense data and then later learn by experience that these represent entities. The simplest animal acts as if it were aware of being among things and not simply sensa.[12] The sense of there being a reality other than our experience given to us in the experience is absolutely primitive. Indeed, our knowledge of physiology shows us, if immediate introspection does not, that sense experience is the secondary and not the primary factor in experience.

According to physics and physiology, we know that a train of light coming from the molecules in the tie strikes our eye and activates certain cells there which in turn relay this impact to the occipital lobe. It is only after all this has occurred that we experience the green patch somehow projected back onto roughly the region of space where those molecules are located. Whitehead insists that we must take this knowledge seriously and employ it in the understanding of what is occurring in any occasion of experience.[13] In this way the seeing of the green tie is revealed to be a matter of considerable complexity. It originates in a complex and indirect process in which the molecules in the tie make an impression on the experiencing subject. The experiencing subject most immediately experiences the events in his brain, but these relay to him the events in the eye which in turn point beyond themselves to their cause. Thousands of events have occurred, each having causal efficacy for its successor. All this represents the physical impact of the world upon the occasion of experience. Whitehead calls it the " physical pole "[14] of experience, that by which we experience ourselves as related to, and our experience as derivative from, events in our recent past.

The physical pole of our experience can be analyzed into

---

[12] *MT* 154. [13] *MT* 166. [14] *PR* 49.

" physical prehensions " or " physical feelings." [15] Each physical prehension is the feeling by one momentary occasion of another momentary occasion. It is of utmost importance for the understanding of Whitehead's philosophy to note that the occasion that is felt is always in the past of the occasion that feels it. Cause always precedes effect. The relation of prehension is always asymmetrical. The earlier occasion has " causal efficacy " [16] for the later. The later occasion " prehends " [17] the earlier. These terms cannot be reversed. In other words, there is no causal relation between contemporary occasions.[18] The deeply ingrained commonsense view that cause and effect are often, if not always, simultaneous is derived from experiences at the macrocosmic level and does not apply to the world of microcosmic entities. At the macrocosmic level it seems that the pressure I exert on the pen causes movement of the pen simultaneous with the exertion of pressure rather than subsequent to it. At this level Newtonian mechanics seems quite adequate. But the inability of models derived from our experience of objects like pens to deal with the microcosmic world is precisely the cause of the collapse of the old world views. Further, at least in retrospect, we can see that acute philosophical problems were always entailed by the concept that cause and effect are simultaneous, for in that case our whole sense of the influence of the past upon the present is rendered unintelligible. Yet without memory of the past, which is surely an important influence of the past upon the present, no knowledge whatsoever would be possible. In any case, in studying Whitehead, we must always remember that physical prehensions are

[15] The only difference between " feeling " and " prehension " in Whitehead's technical vocabulary is that only positive prehensions are called feelings. Since the idea of negative prehensions can be omitted from this discussion, the two terms are treated as equivalent. See *PR* 35, 66.

[16] *PR* 125.

[17] *PR* 28–29.

[18] *PR* 95, 188, 192.

only and always prehensions of the past, chiefly of the immediate past. The events in the eye succeeded the events in the space between the tie and the eye, and these in turn succeeded the molecular events in the tie. The events in the nerves leading to the brain succeeded the events in the eye and were in turn followed by the events in the brain and finally by the impact upon the conscious human occasion of experience. Thousands of successive physical prehensions were required for the molecular events in the tie to have their efficacy mediated to the human experient.

What ordinarily deceives us is that in conscious experience the green patch is presented to us as though it were simultaneous with the experience that sees it. Whitehead calls this dimension of our total experience " presentational immediacy." [19] Whenever we try to focus our attention clearly and distinctly, our physical feeling of the past (experience in the mode of causal efficacy) fades into the background, and elements of our experience in the mode of presentational immediacy predominate. The most prominent aspects of experience in this mode are sense data. This has led philosophers concerned for clear and distinct ideas to treat these sense data as primary. But when we reflect more profoundly on experience, we realize that we constantly assume that real things and not sense data constitute our environment and are causally effective for experience. We must take seriously the scientific account of how this causal efficacy operates. When we do so, the problem is to understand, in our example, how the patch of green comes to dominance in presentational immediacy — that patch so different from the myriad of molecules that bounced the light off in the direction of our eyes.

The only immediate source for that patch of green must be the events that took place in the eye and in the brain. These contributed their multiplicity of data to the human experience. Some quality present in those data must be

19 *PR* 189 ff.

abstracted from them and transformed (Whitehead says "transmuted" [20]) into what we call greenness. It is then projected back onto a contemporary region of space outside the body, roughly that region in which the molecules reflected light to the eye. This is an immensely complex process, but we will omit here most of the details. The main point is that this process of transforming the many received data into one patch of green is a mental operation. It involves the introduction of some quality not present in the data. That is, the consciously experienced visual quality of green can hardly be supposed to be enjoyed by the brain cells in just that way. There must be some quality, somehow analogous to greenness, that they do possess and contribute to the experience, but the human occasion is here introducing an element of novelty. This originality of the occasion of experience which is not derivative from the thing experienced but is contributed by the experient, Whitehead calls the "mental pole" [21] of the occasion. This originality plays a role in sense experience as here indicated, but it also plays a role in more primitive levels of experience. Its most striking role is in imaginative thought.

In this example I am conceiving the possibility of the tie being brown instead of green. Let us assume that I am not at the moment seeing any brown object. I am remembering some brown object I saw earlier, or rather, I am remembering just its color. This means that some past occasion of my experience is also contributing something to the present experience. Since this past occasion is an entity other than the becoming one, this is another physical feeling by the new occasion. Yet the quality of brownness was part of that earlier occasion's mental experience. Whitehead calls the physical prehension of what was mental in the prehended occasion a "hybrid prehension." [22] The prehension of brownness, derived from this hybrid prehension, is now held in contrast with the green-

[20] *PR* 40.   [21] *PR* 165.   [22] *PR* 163.

ness that is part of this occasion's mentality. The comparison or contrast of the two colors is another more complex part of the experience, and the idea of the *tie* as brown, which Whitehead calls a " propositional feeling," [23] is still another. All this complexity belongs to the mental pole of the experience.

But there is more to the experience than this. Each aspect of what has been described above is accompanied by an emotional tone. The sheer it-ness [24] of the tie conveys its emotional tone, the patch of green another, the memory of brownness a third, the idea of the tie as green a fourth, the idea of the tie as brown a fifth. All these emotional tones Whitehead calls the " subjective forms " [25] of the prehensions that are the experiences of the entities in question. Some of the prehensions have as their objects other actual occasions, and these, as we have seen, Whitehead calls physical prehensions. Other prehensions are of forms, relations, or qualities in abstraction from any particular embodiment. Whitehead calls the entities felt in these prehensions " eternal objects." [26] Eternal objects are not actual entities like the occasions of experience. They are pure possibilities for realization in any experience at all, conceived quite apart from any such realization. Every actual occasion is the realization of some limited number of such possibilities. When we entertain such a possibility without reference to where it has been met in embodied form, we have an instance of what Whitehead calls a " conceptual prehension." [27] A conceptual prehension is a prehension of an eternal object as such. Just as physical prehensions comprise the physical pole of each actual occasion of experience, so conceptual prehensions constitute the mental pole.

---

[23] *PR* 391 ff.
[24] *AI* 336–338. See also *PR* 394, 398; *AI* 327.
[25] *PR* 35, 326, 362, 378, 391, 399.
[26] *PR* 69–70.
[27] *PR* 35, 49.

We have still far from exhausted the complexity of the occasion of experience. For one thing, the whole experience is governed by some purpose. Probably I would not wish the tie brown unless I had some use in mind. Perhaps I intend to dress for the evening and want to put on a new suit. Some end is in view, and it is partly in the light of that end that the prehensions have the particular force they have and the subjective forms that are associated with them. This purposive element Whitehead affirms as present in every occasion and is what he calls its " subjective aim." [28]

In addition, we recognize how very much we have abstracted from the concreteness of any experience when we describe it only as wishing that a green tie were brown. I have already suggested that some idea of putting on a suit contrasted with some other possibility of not being able to wear that particular suit, a still dimmer reference perhaps to the plans for the evening which would require enormously complex analysis in terms of the memories that combine to make such expectations possible, numerous other present sensory experiences besides that of the tie, bodily feelings, perhaps of hunger or vague discomfort, and a penumbra of memories from the past — all these play their roles in each moment of experience. All of them can be analyzed into the data from which they arise, physical and conceptual, and into the complex patterns formed from these data and their subjective forms. Perhaps more important than all of them is the immediate continuity with the preceding moment of experience which is another physical prehension with its subjective form and aim largely repeated in the present. The occasion of experience as a whole is a synthesis of syntheses of syntheses of the simple elements out of which it is composed. This final momentary synthesis Whitehead calls its " satisfaction." [29] Yet if we ask how long it takes for such an experience to occur, we know that everything I have described may

<hr/>

[28] *PR* 37, 130.   [29] *PR* 29, 38, 129.

happen in the first moment my eye lights upon the tie. A fraction of a second suffices.

This is an analysis of a rather ordinary human experience. In detail it will differ from every other experience, but in its most general structures, Whitehead suggests, we may have a clue to the nature of experience in general. There is a reception of influence from the past, or what Whitehead calls physical prehension. This involves the causal efficacy of the whole past for the new occasion, largely mediated by the adjacent occasions but finally reflecting the whole course of past events. There is some subjective form of these prehensions which may be little more than a repetition of the way in which the past occasions felt. There is some reenactment of the data received from the past with the possibility of deviation or novelty in the conceptual prehension. And all this is governed by a subjective aim at achieving some satisfaction that will have value for the occasion itself and an appropriate influence on the future. In these most general terms, Whitehead believes, all occasions of experience are alike.

In the description of this simple human experience I have used the relatively neutral term " events " to characterize the other occurrences on which the human occasion of experience depends for most of its content. We have already seen in our earlier discussion of the mind-matter problem that the only clue we have to the notion of microscopic events appears to be human experience as such. We are now ready to consider whether this analysis of a human occasion of experience is in fact capable of illuminating the notion of microscopic events. If so, we must consider the hypothesis that these events in nature are in fact also actual occasions of experience.

Of course, when the description of the general structures of the human occasion of experience is applied to the realm of subatomic entities, all the terms employed must be divested of any suggestion of consciousness. But this is true already in the human occasion. We are not conscious of our prehensions of the events in our brain. We are not conscious of the individual feeling tones that constitute the subjective forms of those prehensions or of the individual elements that go into the composition of our mentality. We are only conscious of the very high-level syntheses of these simple data that are effected in the advanced phases of the becoming of the occasion.[30] At this point the vast multitude of individual prehensions has been simplified into a comparatively few general contrasts and synthesized into unity. An occasion of experience that never goes beyond the reception of data, their reproduction and their communication to the future, would of course remain totally unconscious.

Whitehead shows that the vector transmission of energy through discrete, successive occurrences can be explained in terms of physical prehensions.[31] He shows that when we understand entities as actualizations of experience, both their particle-like and wave-like characteristics can be accounted for.[32] He shows how the actual occasions can be seen to be grouped together in societies [33] of varying degrees of organization and unity and why it is that physical laws have a statistical character as a function of such societies.[34] But I am not competent to comment further on the detailed applicability of his categories to the interpretation of physical phenomena.[35] This should suffice, nonetheless, to suggest the intimate relationship between our human experiences and microscopic occurrences.

The one concept this analysis is intended to illumine is that of the actual occasion of experience, for this is the key

[30] PR 246.
[31] PR 177 ff.
[32] PR 53–54.
[33] See section 3 below for discussion of what Whitehead meant by societies.
[34] PR 305 ff.
[35] For discussion of the application of Whitehead's philosophy to physical science, see Robert Palter's *Whitehead's Philosophy of Science.*

to Whitehead's cosmological formulation. This concept, referred to indiscriminately as actual occasion or occasion of experience, is equivalent to " actual entity." [36] The only distinction Whitehead makes between actual occasion and actual entity is that he uses only the term " actual entity " when he refers to God.[37] Wherever in the book I deviate from Whitehead's practice in this regard I shall try to make my usage clear. The actual entities are the finally real things, the ultimate individuals. Apart from them there is nothing at all. The whole of the philosophy is an analysis of such entities and their relations with each other.

Each actual occasion comes into being against the background of the whole past of the world. That past is composed of innumerable actual occasions that have had their moment of subjective immediacy [38] and have " perished." [39] As perished, they have not become simply nothing. Rather, they have their own mode of being, which Whitehead calls " objective immortality." [40] That means that they are effective as objects to be prehended by new occasions. They are the efficient causes explaining why the new occasions embody the characteristics they do in fact have. If, for example, someone wants to explain my experience, he must point to my past experiences and to the immediately past events that have been transpiring in my environment and in my body.

The influence of this past in determining what I become in the present is so vast that many psychologists are inclined to suppose it is complete. Some believe that if they could know every detail of my past experience, the force of the wider past embodied in my heredity, and all the influences now impinging upon me, they could predict

[36] PR viii–ix.
[37] PR 135.
[38] PR 38. For clarification of this term, see below, p. 44.
[39] PR 126.
[40] PR 89, 94.

exactly what my experience must be. But Whitehead holds against this the universal practical assumption that we are free. We may not be able to focus a particular act of freedom vividly in our consciousness, but that is no different from the situation with respect to physical prehensions. Our vague and persistent experience is that we are both determined by our past and also free. That is, the determination by the past is real but not absolute. What I have been in the past, and what the world as a whole has been, may narrowly limit what I can become in this next moment. But within those limits it is still my decision in that moment as to how I shall react to all these forces impinging upon me.[41]

Once again, this freedom is not a matter of consciousness. The freedom or self-determination of the occasion occurs first. In the human occasion there may or may not be some consciousness of it. Clearly-conscious decision would be a very special case of decision generally. Some element of self-determination or decision Whitehead attributes to all occasions whatsoever. In vast numbers of occasions this freedom is used only to reenact the past. But there are signs in modern physics of an ultimate spontaneity at the base of things. Not only is it clear that in principle man can never predict the behavior of individual electrons, it is also clear that the reason for the success of his predictions when he deals with larger entities is that so many of the ultimate actual entities are involved. Where enough individuals are involved, even pure chance or spontaneity on the part of each individual can allow for great precision in predicting the behavior of the group. There is no basis for exact prediction about individuals. For this reason, Whitehead's assignment of freedom as well as the vast causal influence of the past even to such minute entities as electrons seems to be in accord with the world revealed to us by science.

[41] *PR* 41–42. See also below, Ch. III, sec. 1.

3. SOCIETIES OF ACTUAL OCCASIONS

The final indivisible entities of which the world is made up are actual occasions of experience. But these occasions exist only momentarily, enjoying a fleeting moment of subjective immediacy before passing into the past. These individual occasions are only detectable either by intense introspection or by scientific instruments. None of the entities of which we are conscious in common experience are individual occasions [42] and only rarely do these appear even in the sciences. For the most part, our conscious experience is concerned with entities that are groupings of occasions rather than individual occasions.

Any group of occasions characterized by any real interconnectedness at all is called a " nexus," [43] however loose the connectedness may be. When a nexus is characterized by some common trait exemplified by each of its members in dependence on some of the others, the nexus is called a " society." [44] There may be societies of any degree of organization or specificity.

Whitehead does not deduce the existence of more special types of societies from the general idea of occasions and societies. The universe might be composed of a nexus of occasions lacking even in social order, or it might have some tinge of social order and no more. The only reason for affirming that there are more special types of social order is that we do, in fact, encounter entities that have such order.

[42] Whitehead writes, "It is only when we are consciously aware of alien mentalities that we ever approximate to the conscious prehension of a single actual entity." (PR 387.)

[43] AI 258.

[44] AI 261. Our cosmic epoch, Whitehead tells us, is a vast electromagnetic society (PR 147), and it is the ideal of mathematical physics to systematize into laws the characteristics of this society. But the electromagnetic society as such would provide "no adequate order for the production of individual occasions realizing peculiar 'intensities' of experience unless it were pervaded by more special societies" (PR 150).

Consider, for example, a molecule. If there existed only more or less random occasions, we could not speak of a molecule at all, but, in fact, we are able to identify a single molecule through a long period of time as the same molecule. Indeed, we are so impressed by its self-identity through time that it requires considerable scientific and philosophic reflection to persuade us that it is not a blob of changeless matter undergoing changing relations with an external world. Whitehead has taught us that indeed it is nothing more than a succession of molecular happenings or occasions, but he must still account for the fact that there is a special connection between these occasions, such that we may identify a single molecule as an " enduring object." [45]

An enduring object is a society of actual occasions that are temporally contiguous and successive. Whitehead describes such societies as having serial or personal order.[46] In such a society no two occasions exist at the same time, but at each moment one such occasion occurs, prehending all the preceding occasions in the society, reenacting the defining characteristic of the society, and mediating this pattern to its successors.

The molecule is typical of enduring objects in the extreme similarity of the successive occasions that make it up. Whitehead shows that this is caused by the overwhelming preponderance of the physical pole or physical feelings. Each occasion feels and reenacts the preceding occasion's feeling and reenactment of its predecessor, and so on indefinitely. The successive occasions are comparatively little affected by other past occasions and the novelty of the new occasion is both trivial in itself and ineffective for the future. Enduring objects provide the things of the world with stability.

We have already noted that in ordinary life we have little to do with individual occasions. Now we must recognize that we do not have much to do with individual

[45] *PR* 51–52.　　　　　[46] *PR* 51.

enduring objects either. We have to do with tables and stones. These objects, we know, are made up of numerous molecules which in turn are intimately interrelated. Bodies of this sort, analyzable into enduring objects, Whitehead calls "corpuscular societies." [47]

However, we must be careful not to think of these classifications of societies as in any way rigid. A society may be composed of many actual occasions of which some are and some are not organized into enduring objects. According to the predominance of one or the other type of occasion, the society will be more or less corpuscular. Furthermore, enduring objects vary as to the importance of their defining characteristics and the decisiveness of their inheritance from previous members of the enduring object in question. There is an infinite variety of degrees of order among which the two instances of the enduring object and the corpuscular society stand out with a certain simple clarity.

Perhaps the most important society that does not fit into either of these categories is the living cell. Within the cell there are enduring objects such as molecules. But there is also much space not occupied by enduring objects. This space is often called empty, but in this "empty space" occur those occasions which constitute the life of the cell.[48] At first sight this association of life with "empty space" may seem strange; hence some explanation is in order.

As we have seen, for Whitehead every occasion has both a physical and a mental pole. That means that every occasion prehends both past occasions and eternal objects or possibilities. This prehension of eternal objects introduces the possibility of novelty, that is, the possibility that the becoming occasion will embody some quality not received from its past world. To the degree that this possibility is actualized, the germ of life is present. But in the molecular occasions, as in occasions composing enduring objects generally, novelty is and must be trivial. Repetition is re-

[47] PR 52.   [48] PR 161.

quired for endurance. It is these enduring objects and the corpuscular societies composed of them that are subject to investigation through our sense organs and through instruments. Where such societies are not present we can detect nothing. Yet we know that important events transpire in " empty space," so we must reckon with occasions there also.[49]

Now there is far more life in the cell than in the molecules found within it. Therefore, this life must be found in the space not occupied by these molecules, and specifically in the occasions located there. These occasions must be characterized by much more novelty and much less continuity than the molecular occasions. The cell as a whole, then, combines the stability of the enduring objects and the life of the primarily mental, and therefore not physically detectable, occasions within it.

Cells in their turn are organized into complex societies of cells, such as vegetables and animal bodies. Once again there is no sharp line of division between these great families of living things. Nevertheless, there are important differences between the more fully developed members of each class. Vegetables, Whitehead tells us, are democracies, whereas animals have ruling, or presiding members.[50] In vegetables no single member of the society is essential for the well-being of the society, whereas in animals one such member does exist. This member Whitehead calls the " dominant " occasion.[51] The dominant occasion in our own bodies is that which we know most immediately in conscious introspection.[52] It will be discussed at considerable length in Chapter II.

The distinction between individual actual entities and

[49] PR 269.

[50] AI 264; MT 38.

[51] Whitehead uses a variety of terms to refer to what I am calling the dominant occasion. "Dominant" appears in PR 156, 182; AI 264; "presiding" in PR 167; "final percipient" in PR 516.

[52] PR 164. See also PR 74; MT 231.

their groupings into different types of societies prepares us to understand Whitehead's creative contribution to the question of the subject-object schema, so much criticized in recent philosophy. Whitehead believes that the subject-object schema is fundamental to experience.[53] Every occasion of experience is a subject in relation to other entities that are objective to it.[54] However, several features of Whitehead's analysis set it sharply in opposition to traditional interpretations of the subject-object schema.

In the first place, an exhaustive analysis of the actual entities experienced as objects reveals that in their own nature they also are subjects.[55] The difference between a subject and an object, as long as we are focusing upon individuals and not societies, is only that the subject is present and the object is past.[56] The actual occasion of experience now enjoying " subjective immediacy " [57] will cease in a moment to have such subjectivity and will become an object for new occasions of experience. In this moment the objects it is experiencing are themselves nothing but past subjects. If we keep clearly in mind that causal efficacy is always the efficacy of the past, and that as past an occasion is no longer a subject, we can see that causes are always objects for effects that are always subjects. The correctness of the epistemological analysis of experience according to the subject-object schema must not be allowed to lead to an ontological view of objects as different in kind from subjects in any way other than the difference between past and present.

In the second place, Whitehead shows us that the true objects of experience are not the presented sensa or the contemporary entities in the regions on which we project the sensa. Most traditional thinking about objects has made the mistake of thinking of them as contemporary with subjects and as given in sense experience. This error has been at the root of much of the difficulty with this subject-

[53] AI 225–226.   [55] PR 89, 443; AI 226–227.   [57] PR 38; AI 227.
[54] PR 38, 336 ff.   [56] AI 229.

object schema. The correct recognition that the world of the sensa belongs in and with the world of the subject has erroneously led to the conclusion that experience has no object at all.[58] Whitehead is able to do justice both to the objectivity of the real world and to the wholeness of the self-in-the-world experience of presentational immediacy.

In the third place, Whitehead shows that our understanding of subjects and objects has been confused by our failure to distinguish actual individuals from societies of such individuals. Philosophers have been especially prone to treat corpuscular societies as if they were individuals. Since we correctly resist the idea that sticks and stones as such have subjectivity, we have been driven either to deny them any status independent of our experience or else to regard them as objects in an ontological sense. Whitehead shows us that they are societies of subjects. The society as a whole has no subjectivity, but this is because it has only the individuality of a particular form or pattern, not that of a truly individual entity. The inertness and passivity of the stick or stone as a corpuscular society gives us no grounds for positing a similar inertness or passivity on the part of the protonic and electronic occasions of which the society is composed. It is to these and not to the sticks and stones that Whitehead refers as subjects in their moment of immediacy and as objects for new subjects when that moment is past. Our experience of societies is ultimately derived from this primal experience of individual past occasions of experience.

With this brief introduction to Whitehead's philosophy I conclude the chapter. My chief concern has been to communicate some notion of what Whitehead means by actual entities or actual occasions of experience, how they are related to each other, and how they are grouped together in societies. Many important aspects of Whitehead's

[58] See Whitehead's critique of "the subjectivist principle" (*PR* 238 ff.). He describes his own position as a "reformed version of the subjectivist doctrine" (*PR* 288).

philosophy have been wholly omitted from consideration. Some of them are indispensable for understanding the discussions in later chapters, and I will try to explain them as they arise. Further, I hope that the topics introduced in this chapter will become gradually clearer and more meaningful as the subsequent discussion unfolds.

II

The Human Soul

1. THE SOUL AS SOCIAL

Whitehead is remarkable among recent philosophers for his insistence that man has, or is, a soul. Furthermore, he is convinced that this doctrine has been of utmost value for Western civilization and that its recent weakening systematically undercuts the understanding of the worth of man. The understanding of the human soul is one of the truly great gifts of Plato and of Christianity, and Whitehead does not hesitate to associate his own doctrine with these sources, especially with Plato.[1]

Nevertheless, Whitehead's understanding of the human soul is different from those of Platonism and historic Christianity and is one of his most creative contributions for modern reflection. If we are to understand any aspect of Whitehead's doctrine of man, we must begin by grasping his thought on this subject.

Perhaps the most striking differentiating feature of Whitehead's doctrine of the soul is that it is a society rather than an individual actual entity. A moment's reflection will show that this position follows inevitably from the distinction between individuals and societies explained in the preceding chapter. Individuals exist only momentarily. If we identified the soul with such an individual, there would be millions of souls during the lifetime of a single man.

[1] *AI*, Ch. II.

But when we speak in Platonic or Christian terms, we think of a single soul for a single man. If we hold fast to this usage, and Whitehead basically does so,[2] then we must think of the soul as that society composed of all the momentary occasions of experience that make up the life history of the man. The soul is not an underlying substance undergoing accidental adventures. It is nothing but the sequence of the experiences that constitute it.

In contrast to some Christian views of the soul, it should also be noted at the outset that Whitehead's understanding of the soul applies to the higher animals as well as to man. Wherever it is reasonable to posit a single center of experience playing a decisive role in the functioning of the organism as a whole, there it is reasonable to posit a soul. For the soul is nothing but such a center of experience in its continuity through time. The use of the term " soul " carries no connotation in Whitehead of preexistence or of life after death. There is no suggestion that the soul is some kind of supernatural element which in some way marks off man from nature and provides a special point of contact for divine activity. The soul is in every sense a part of nature, subject to the same conditions as all other natural entities.[3]

Nevertheless, the soul is a very remarkable and a very distinctive type of society, and among souls the human has still further remarkable distinctiveness. In this section we will attend to the peculiar character of the soul in general, and in the following section we will focus on the distinctiveness of the human soul in relation to subhuman souls.

The soul is remarkable, first, because it is a society com-

[2] MT 224. However, since for Whitehead identity through time is an empirical question, he allows for the possibility of a plurality of souls in a single organism. See below, p. 72.

[3] Although this is Whitehead's usual terminology in his later writings, in such earlier works as CN and occasionally in his later writings he speaks of nature in a more restricted sense. See below, pp. 60–61.

posed of an extraordinary type of occasion. This type of occasion was barely introduced near the end of the preceding chapter.[4] Whitehead calls it the presiding or dominant occasion of a complex animal organism. In vegetables and perhaps in very simple animals no such dominant occasion occurs, but in the higher organisms, especially where a fully developed central nervous system and brain is found, there is strong indication of centralized control of many aspects of the animal's behavior. We find such centralized control present in our individual human experience, and we have immediate introspective awareness of the conscious experience that functions in this control.[5] There is every reason to suppose that the higher animals have similar immediate enjoyment of themselves as centers of experience.[6]

The dominant occasions of experience are extraordinary in that they are almost certainly the only occasions of experience that are conscious. Consciousness Whitehead identifies as a factor in the subjective form of some prehensions or feelings.[7] But it must be remembered that it occurs only where a high level of mentality or originality is present. Further, it depends upon a complex integration of conceptual and physical feelings involving highly developed contrasts.[8] No other type of occasion of experience would appear capable either of so high a level of mentality or of such complex integration of conceptual and physical feelings.

The dominant occasion can rise to such heights of experience only because the entire body is so organized as to make this possible. It is so constructed that there is a constant flow of novelty from all its parts to the brain. In the brain there are many living occasions which in turn contribute their novelty to the dominant occasion located among them.[9]

[4] See above, p. 43.
[5] *PR* 164. See also *PR* 74; *MT* 231.
[6] *PR* 164.
[7] *PR* 246.
[8] *PR* 369–372.
[9] *PR* 166–167, 516.

In the case of humans, and presumably of the higher animals as well, these dominant occasions are so ordered as to constitute enduring objects. Enduring objects are societies in which only one member occurs at a time.[10] This arrangement of occasions can be spoken of as serial order or personal order.[11] But the enduring objects composed of dominant occasions, that is, souls, are extremely different from other enduring objects, such as the molecule that has been our example heretofore. The molecule maintains itself through time by endless repetition, by trivializing of novelty or mentality, and by thus existing in an almost totally physical form. By contrast, the most striking feature of the soul is its aliveness or mentality.

Just as decisive is the contrast of the soul with the living occasions previously encountered in the empty space of the cell.[12] These occasions lack all continuity and even social relatedness. They constitute, Whitehead tells us, a nonsocial nexus within the cell.[13] The dominant occasions of the animal, on the other hand, have serial or personal order of the kind definitive of enduring objects, thereby maintaining a high degree of continuity through time.

This synthesis of endurance and life leads Whitehead to employ a distinct term, " living person."[14] A living person is a soul.[15] It is a type of enduring object, but I will follow Whitehead's usual practice of using the latter term to refer to the far more numerous societies that achieve endurance by the sacrifice of life. We must ask, then, what makes endurance possible without sacrifice of novelty, life, and mentality.

This problem will be treated at some length below in section 4. However, a brief introduction is needed here.

[10] See above, p. 41.

[11] *PR* 50–51.

[12] See above, p. 43.

[13] *PR* 152.

[14] *PR* 163.

[15] *AI* 271. The term " soul " rarely appears before *AI*, but there and in *MT* it is frequent.

To explain the peculiar way in which continuity is maintained without sacrifice of originality, we must introduce a distinction between two types of "simple" physical feelings.[16] A simple physical feeling is one in which a single actual occasion is felt. Such an actual occasion must be prehended by the new occasion in terms of some selected eternal object embodied in it. When the eternal object selected for this purpose was embodied in the physical pole of the actual occasion felt or prehended, that is, when it expresses how that actual occasion prehended its predecessors, then the simple physical feeling is "pure."[17] But when that eternal object is embodied in the mental pole, that is, when it expresses some novelty in the self-determination of the actual occasion prehended, then the prehension is "hybrid."[18] In ordinary enduring objects hybrid prehensions play almost no role. In living persons hybrid prehensions are decisive.[19]

Hybrid prehensions preserve for the future the flashes of novelty that have occurred in the past. The new occasion adds its own novelty, thus compounding the richness of the inheritance of successive occasions. With some peculiar completeness each member occasion of the living person sums up the past of the society,[20] contributes its own novelty and passes away.

In the identifying of the soul, the emphasis has been placed upon the special connectedness of the successive dominant occasions in the animal organism. This is proper, and we must return later to the difficult question of the self-identity of the soul or person through time.[21] It is

---

[16] PR 355, 375.

[17] PR 375–376. Unfortunately, Whitehead also speaks of pure feelings as those not involving both physical and conceptual feelings. Such double use of terms adds to the difficulties experienced by the student.

[18] PR 376.

[19] PR 163.

[20] PR 244, 531.

[21] See below, sec. 4.

equally important to note the profound involvement of the soul with the body [22] and its relationship with other souls.

The body, and specifically the brain, is the immediate environment of the soul.[23] Because of the apparent primacy of the sense data perceived outside of the body, this immediacy of the bodily environment is sometimes neglected. Actually, what the soul immediately experiences or prehends are the occasions of experience of the entities immediately adjacent in the brain. These in turn prehend other contiguous occasions and so on throughout the body. This experience of the body is the primal datum for the soul.

This contribution of the feelings of the body to the soul is a major part of what Whitehead calls causal efficacy. The causal efficacy of the body for the dominant experience is always dimly in the background of that experience. But within the body there are organs designed to give the soul needed information for adjusting the body to its environment. These are the specialized sense organs. Their experiences also have causal efficacy for the soul, but to a distinctive degree they lead to a special kind of activity within the soul. In the introduction, we saw how sensuous experience of the external environment (in the mode of presentational immediacy) arises out of physical prehensions by the soul (in the mode of causal efficacy) of contiguous events within the brain.[24] Thus the body mediates to the soul a knowledge of the outside world, but even here the information is fundamentally about the body and its states, and only secondarily about the more distant sources of the bodily stimuli.

The doctrine of the two modes of perception, causal efficacy and presentational immediacy,[25] has immense im-

---

[22] *PR* 182 ff.; *AI* 241–243; *MT* 218–219.
[23] See below, sec. 6, for discussion of the locus of the soul.
[24] See above, pp. 31–32.
[25] Cf. *PR* 255 ff.

portance for Whitehead's philosophy. Through it he jus-
tifies an ontological realism rare in our day. He synthesizes
our knowledge of physiology with the immediate deliv-
erances of experience and shows the many ways in which
error can enter our judgment. He also brings the scientific
vision of a world of electrons and molecules into intelligible relation with the world given us in visual experience. All this, however, is beyond the scope of the present
work. The point here is to show how seriously Whitehead
takes the relation of the dominant occasions, which constitute the soul, to the organism over which they preside,
while refusing simply to identify or merge soul and body.

In addition, Whitehead is open to the evidence that there
may be relations among souls not mediated by occasions
spatially between them. For example, if there is empirical
indication of mental telepathy, Whitehead sees no philosophical difficulty in incorporating such relations into his
system. The general philosophical principle is that every
new occasion takes account of every occasion in its past.
So far as this principle is concerned, every past occasion,
near or far in time or space, might be directly prehended
by every becoming occasion. Factually, however, in our
cosmic epoch, this does not seem to occur. Rather, physical
influences are brought directly to bear on the new occasion
only by those immediately contiguous to it. To state this
in more technical terms, simple physical feelings of the
pure variety are limited to contiguous occasions. These,
in turn, mediate the physical influence of other occasions.
This is, however, only a probable, and in any case contingent characteristic of our world to be affirmed on the basis
of scientific inquiry. It affords no basis for either affirming
or denying that the mental aspect of noncontiguous occasions can be directly prehended. Whitehead's own judgment is that there are, in fact, immediate prehensions of
the mental poles of noncontiguous occasions. He gains
empirical support for this judgment both from " peculiar
instances of telepathy, and from the instinctive apprehen-

sion of a tone of feeling in ordinary social intercourse." [26] He thinks that the inevitable mixing of these hybrid prehensions of other souls with the mediated experiences of the same souls explains why it is so difficult for consciousness to focus on clear instances of unmediated prehensions.

The soul is, then, in immediate contact with some occasions of experience in the brain and with the mental poles of the experiences of other souls. (Presumably the mental aspects of other types of occasions might also be directly prehended, but this would be trivial.) Indirectly, but intimately, the soul also prehends the whole society that constitutes its body and still more indirectly, but still very importantly, the wider environment that is the whole world. At the same time, the soul contributes itself as an object for feeling by other souls, the contiguous occasions in the brain, and indirectly by the whole future world.

Whitehead's understanding of the relational character of the soul is still more radical than this suggests. One could understand all that has been said thus far to mean that the soul is first something quite definite and then receives the influence of its world. But the soul, or rather each occasion of its life, like every other actual occasion of experience, is relational or social in its essence.

An actual occasion *is* a new synthesis of its past. Everything that it is, except its own sheer actuality and subjectivity, it receives from beyond itself. It *becomes* only in this receiving.[27] The more it receives, the more it can become. Insofar as it is closed to its world, it impoverishes itself. The multiplicity of the other occasions entering into the composition of the new occasion is so great that the problem in understanding an actual occasion is not so much how it as an individual enters into social relations but how all the relations that make it up achieve the unity

[26] PR 469.

[27] Whitehead makes this point forcefully by stressing that an actual occasion is as much a "superject" of its prehensions as a subject. (PR 43.)

of subjective immediacy and satisfaction.

This point is sufficiently important to an understanding of a doctrine of man to justify further elaboration. If we begin with the idea of self-contained entities, relations are necessarily accidental or external. The entity can be characterized first, and then we consider how it is related to other entities. This is a natural procedure when we are thinking of the corpuscular societies around us, such as tables and chairs. The table seems to be a self-contained entity, enduring through time and only externally affected by being moved to another part of the room. This is an exaggeration, but for common purposes we get along very well with this point of view. However, modern science has shown us that the table is not finally understood as a single entity but rather as a society of entities exceedingly different in character from the smooth, hard, passive, still, impenetrable surface we seem to experience. It is these actual entities to which Whitehead directs our attention in his philosophy. These entities, he tells us, must be thought of as happenings, occurrences, or occasions rather than as lumps of inert matter. Furthermore, each of these happenings seems to reflect the whole state of the universe as it impinges upon that happening and then to become a part of the universe impinging upon subsequent happenings. Each occasion is a synthesis of the universe as it is grasped from that perspective and contributes to the universe its own definiteness of synthesis or satisfaction. Such occasions cannot be understood as first occurring and then being in relation. They are constituted by their relations to the occasions in their past.

The question is whether we should understand the soul after the pattern appropriate to our common dealing with the things of our world or after the pattern appropriate to our understanding of actual occasions as the ultimately real entities of the world. Whitehead's answer is unqualifiedly in the latter direction. In each of its momentary occasions the soul *is* one of these ultimately real entities of the world. It absorbs into itself in each new occasion of its life the total impact of its universe from its special perspective. It differs from other entities in the vastness and complexity of what it can receive from its world and synthesize in its own novel becoming.

In Whitehead's view, therefore, the soul is not at all like a substance undergoing accidental adventures in time. It is constituted by its adventures. It can attain richness and depth only through the variety and quality of the entities it encounters and its own willingness and ability to be open to what they can contribute.

This does not mean, of course, that sheer quantity of stimuli is important or that the soul has no use for privacy. A part, and a very important part, of the relations by which each new occasion is constituted is its prehension of its own past, that is, of past occasions in the life of the same soul. Ultimately, those occasions received their richness of life from beyond the occasions of that soul altogether. Hence, the individual depends radically upon the society of other souls. But provisionally there may be every reason to retreat from the complexity of the environment into one's own interior life so that one may better be able to be enriched by the larger world.[28]

2. THE DISTINCTIVENESS OF THE HUMAN SOUL

Thus far, although the human soul has been the prime example, all that has been said may apply also to the souls of the higher animals. That this is so is certainly significant for Whitehead's doctrine of the soul. The idea that men can be distinguished from other animals by their possession of souls gains no support from him. Wherever there is evidence of some centralized dominance in the animal organism, he assumes that a dominant occasion is present; and to whatever degree such dominant occasions have sig-

---

[28] Cf., e.g., Whitehead's passage on the role of withdrawal in which occurs his famous definition of religion as " what the individual does with his own solitariness." (*RM* 16-20.)

nificant serial order, they jointly constitute a soul. The gulf between a soul, any soul, and living occasions not organized into living persons is vast, but it must not be confused with the gulf that separates man from the rest of the world.

Our question therefore is, What is distinctive about the *human* soul? To answer this question, we must get some sense of the kinds of gradations that can be found among souls.

One way of distinguishing among souls is according to the significance to the individual dominant occasions of their serial connectedness with each other. Just as among enduring objects the uniting characteristic may be more or less important, so also with living persons or souls. Consider, for example, what may be the case with some very low-grade animal organism. Much of the time such an organism may function essentially as a vegetable. Now and then, however, there may be need for some unified coordination of its behavior. The society may communicate to its brain some special richness of feeling making possible the emergence of a dominant occasion. This occasion may fulfill its function and cease to exist. Subsequently, another need may produce another occasion, but in the extreme case this new dominant occasion may inherit nothing of special importance from its predecessor. If we were to speak of a soul at all in this extreme case where effective continuity between the dominant occasions is lacking, we would recognize an absolute minimum of significance of this term. There would be dominant occasions, but they would not be socially ordered to any relevant degree.

Even in more highly developed organisms, it may be that most of the connection between successive dominant occasions is mediated by the central nervous system. One experience may leave its mark upon the brain which then in turn affects a later dominant occasion. Perhaps some insects might be understood in this way. Many persons seem to suppose that all experience of our own past is mediated in this way, that we directly experience only our brain. Whitehead disagrees. In our memory of our immediately preceding experience, we have direct intuition of that experience actively forming the present.[29] Nevertheless, part of our relation to past experience is undoubtedly mediated by the brain, and to that degree, the ordering that constitutes the society of occasions as the soul has less to do with the outcome.

We may also distinguish between souls according to the relative importance of fresh organic stimuli and past experiences. In general, animals seem to be more fully absorbed in the present than are adult humans. This would suggest that the role of past occasions of their soul in determining the present occasion may be less than the role of fresh occurrences in the bodily environment of the soul. To whatever degree that is the case, the relationship among the dominant occasions that constitutes them conjointly as a soul is less marked and significant.

It is my assumption that along these lines one can argue with Whitehead's tacit support that soul is more fully developed in men in general than in animals in general.[30] Presumably, however, there would be exceptions if we were to contrast a mature high-grade animal with a human infant or with an extremely retarded child. These exceptions are not important except to caution us that whatever we say of the difference between men and other animals must be affirmed in terms of gradations and with empirical warrant.

The second and more important basis for comparing men and other animals has to do with the quality of the occasions constituting their souls. Once again we must recognize the extreme range of experiences that can belong to dominant occasions of animal organisms. Even within human experience, we can note wide differences between mo-

[29] *AI* 233.

[30] Cf. *AI* 267. " It is not a mere question of having a soul or of not having a soul. The question is, How much, if any? "

ments of intense alertness and moments of drowsy semi-consciousness shading off into unconsciousness. It is difficult on this line to indicate a precise point at which animal consciousness reaches its apex and beyond which only human consciousness can go. Nevertheless, it is clear that very great differences exist. Whitehead recognizes that all such differences are matters of degree, but that where degree achieves a certain magnitude, the difference amounts, for practical purposes, to one of kind.[31] Both a chipped rock and an IBM machine are tools, but the difference of their complexity and capabilities is so vast that for most purposes we properly regard them as quite different types of objects.

When we ask specifically what distinguishes man from the other animals, the single clear answer is language.[32] According to Whitehead, language and the human mind in its distinctiveness are correlative. We may say either that the human mind has created language or that language has created the human mind.[33] It is language that makes possible thought of any degree of complexity as well as the progressive cumulation of the fruits of thought.[34] In addition to language, Whitehead notes that morality and religion are distinctive of man. But even here he hedges, for he believes that something like morality can also be observed among the higher animals.[35]

These efforts to distinguish the human from the animal soul are not of special importance in their details. The important point is that Whitehead is open to affirming whatever difference the evidence warrants our affirming. He does not allow any a priori affirmations of human distinctiveness. There is no kind of entity present in man that is

---

[31] *MT* 38.
[32] Even here we may assume that there is no *absolute* discontinuity between animal and human communication.
[33] *MT* 57.
[34] *MT* 49.
[35] *MT* 39.

not present in animals. There is only a peculiarly powerful and complex development of ontologically similar entities. This view of difference within unity is characteristic of Whitehead's thought throughout. There are categories descriptive of every entity whatsoever. These are metaphysical categories, and insofar as one succeeds in grasping one of these he has a genuinely necessary truth. But these metaphysical categories are exemplified in an unimaginable diversity of modes. Whitehead has characterized some of the particular forms and structures important in this cosmic epoch and on the surface of our planet. Among the most important of these are enduring objects. Thus, when we note that the soul, like the molecule, is an enduring object, we are saying something important about the identity that underlies their diversity. Yet we are not minimizing their diversity. Likewise, when we show that in animals as well as in men the dominant occasions are grouped together as souls, we have stated something of great significance about the kinship of men with the other animals, but we have left open for further consideration the differences that may or may not exist between them.

The distinctiveness of man is often formulated today in terms of the antithesis of history and nature. We may consider briefly whether Whitehead allows this distinction and how it would apply. We know in advance that there can be no ultimate distinction, for both must be understood as participating in a more inclusive unity.

"Nature" is not a consistently used technical term in Whitehead. Sometimes it is used as an inclusive term for all that occurs.[36] In this sense, of course, not even a provisional duality would be possible. History could be conceived only as some portion of nature; for example, that part in which life or mentality plays a significant role, or as still further limited to the events in which consciousness, or some special form of consciousness, is decisive. Any such definition is possible.

[36] *AI* 99, 237; *MT* 214.

On the other hand, Whitehead sometimes defines nature in terms of that which is typically investigated by the natural scientists.[37] In these terms, nature may be sharply contrasted with history, for Whitehead shows the virtual irrelevance to human events of the physicist's analysis.[38] The natural scientist abstracts from the meaning, purpose, and subjectivity of things. He thereby distorts, Whitehead believes, even the physical objects that he treats.[39] The effort to treat nature as a mere object of the scientist's investigation must finally break down, even in the scientist's own province. When it does, the deeper underlying unity of the reality of physical objects and of historical events can be grasped without minimizing the decisive differences that also obtain.

In concluding this discussion of the distinctively human, we may ask whether there is such a thing as human nature and how it is related to history. If the term " human nature " is used meaningfully, it must point to characteristics common to all human souls and absent from all other animal souls. We are asking now not simply how the human soul differs from the animal soul, but whether in its distinctiveness it is marked by common structures. It is rather clear that if we are demanding some common factor actualized in all human souls, we must be disappointed, for the exceptional case in which that factor is lacking can always be found. If, however, we ask for distinctive potentialities, then something positive can be said.

In the light of the preceding discussion, we can say that language is the fundamental distinctive common mark of the human.[40] Presumably the larger brain and other bodily differences underlie this new dimension of the human.

---

[37] *SMW* 171; *MT* 100, 174. See also *AI* 265 for an identification of " nature " as " a complex of enduring objects."

[38] *SMW* 265; *MT* 185.

[39] *FR*, Ch. I.

[40] Whitehead makes the striking statement, "Speech is human nature itself." (*MT* 52.)

Language, in turn, introduces many other possibilities into human life which are remote from that of animals. But language is not a property of the human soul such that the soul possesses it by virtue of its nature. Rather, what the human soul possesses by virtue of its rich inheritance from the body is the potentiality for learning and using language. The actualization of this potentiality and of the further possibilities it opens up for men depends upon social relationships. Human nature then, in the first instance, is simply the common potentiality of men (where there is no serious bodily deformation) for language.

It may be, further, that the process of actualizing certain human potentialities always exhibits some common structures. Clearly, in specific terms the actualization varies almost infinitely. The potentiality for language does not include any predisposition toward one language rather than another. There does not seem to be such a thing as a natural language, beyond perhaps a few sounds made by infants. But at a level of sufficient abstraction, it is still possible to discuss structures common to all languages. In a similar way in the area of ethics, for example, as its distinctively human development is made possible by language, almost any act regarded as right in one culture may be regarded as wrong in another. It is idle to appeal to human nature to settle disputes about matters of this kind. Yet at a level of sufficient abstraction there may be some common structures. The question of whether such structures exist and what they are is always an empirical question, but whatever they may be, in their transcendence of what man shares with the animal they may be thought of as part of human nature.[41]

Human nature, then, is the set of unique potentialities of the human soul with whatever formal structures may be necessarily involved in their actualization. When we turn from potentiality to actuality and from highly abstract structures to the concrete particularity of actual things, we

[41] See below, Ch. III, esp. secs. 3 and 4.

turn also from human nature to human history. Most of
what is distinctively human is extremely diverse in its human manifestations. This diversity is a matter both of the
extent to which the potentialities are developed and of the
form which they take in their parallel development. To
understand a particular man is not to understand what he
has in common with *all* other men, or even with all other
equally developed men. It is to understand how he has
been formed and has formed himself in his historical existence. The decisive characteristic of human nature is his-
toricality, man's potentiality for being formed by history.[42]

3. LIFE AFTER DEATH

One of the questions to which the similarity and difference of animal and human souls is relevant is that of their
existence after death. Whitehead dealt with this question
only rarely, and then very briefly. The most important passage on the subject can be quoted.

" A belief in purely spiritual beings means, on this metaphysical theory, that there are routes of mentality in respect to which associate material routes are negligible, or
entirely absent. At the present moment the orthodox belief
is that for all men after death there are such routes, and
that for all animals after death there are no such routes.

" Also at present it is generally held that a purely spiritual being is necessarily immortal. The doctrine here developed gives no warrant for such a belief. It is entirely

[42] I recognize the altogether inadequate character of these brief
remarks on history and the historical character of human existence.
It is my intention to discuss this much more fully in a subsequent
book on history and Christ. Whitehead's major discussion of history
is found in *AI*, Part I. A brief treatment of history is found in *MT*
22–27. That Whitehead understood the historical character of human
existence is clearly indicated in his correlation of civilizations and
languages (*MT* 49) along with the identification of human nature
with speech (*MT* 52) already noted. See the whole discussion of the
relation of man to animal and of speech and written language in relation to civilization. (*MT* 38–57.)

neutral on the question of immortality. . . . There is no reason why such a question should not be decided on more special evidence, religious or otherwise, provided that it is trustworthy. In this lecture we are merely considering evidence with a certain breadth of extension throughout mankind. Until that evidence has yielded its systematic theory, special evidence is indefinitely weakened in its effect." [43]

Whitehead never returned to a positive treatment of this question, largely because his own interest focused on quite a different conception of immortality.[44] Hence, if we are to discuss this aspect of his doctrine of man, we must lean heavily upon this single fascinating passage. A number of points are clear. First, with reference to the topic of the last section, it seems that Whitehead is doubtful that so sharp a line can be drawn between animals and humans that there is real warrant for affirming total extinction of all animals and survival of all humans. Here again we see the insistent rejection of a priori and absolute distinctions. Second, Whitehead explicitly and forcefully denies that the existence of the soul is any evidence for its survival of bodily death. On the other hand, it is clear that he regards his philosophy as perfectly open to the possibility of immortality and that relevant evidence might in principle be obtained. Third, Whitehead recognizes that our response to evidence of this sort depends upon a wider structure of conviction that either opens us to the likelihood of that which is being affirmed or closes us to it.

The passage quoted is found in *Religion in the Making* and uses terminology slightly different from that employed in this book which depends on his later writings. In terms of the analysis offered above, we may put the question quite simply: Can the soul exist without the body? Can it have some other locus than the brain and some other function than that of presiding over the organism as a whole? In other words, can there be additional occasions in the living person without the intimate association with the body in which the soul or living person came into exis-

[43] *RM* 110–111.   [44] *Dial* 297.

tence? To these questions Whitehead answers yes.[45] However, the philosophical *possibility* that this occurs is no evidence that it in fact occurs. Furthermore, it might occur
for some minutes or days or centuries and then cease.
Whitehead's private opinion was probably that it did not
occur at all.

Nevertheless, in our day the philosophical assertion of
the *possibility* of life beyond death is sufficiently striking
that we will do well to consider the grounds of this openness. Since in faithfulness to Whitehead it cannot be argued that there *is* such life, I will only try to show why the
usual philosophical and commonsense arguments for the
impossibility of life after death are removed by his philosophy. These arguments stem both from anthropology and
from wider cosmological considerations. They are treated
below in that order.

The basic form of the anthropological argument against
the possibility of life after death has already been answered
in what has gone before. This argument fundamentally is
that man *is* his body, or his body-for-itself,[46] or the functioning of his body, in such a sense that it would be strictly
meaningless to speak of life apart from the body. The
body-for-itself obviously shares the fortunes of the body in
general, and certainly the functioning of the body cannot
continue without the body. Others, more correctly (from
Whitehead's point of view), state that man is a psychophysical organism. Clearly a psychophysical organism cannot survive the death of the physical organism. From this
point of view, whatever might survive could not in any case
be the man.

Whitehead recognizes that language does commonly refer to the entire psychophysical organism as the man.[47] In
this it bears testimony to the extreme intimacy of the
interaction between body and soul. However, he himself

---

[45] Whitehead even speculated as to the existence of other types
of intelligences in far-off empty space. (*Dial* 192.)

[46] Sartre.

[47] *AI* 263–264.

ordinarily identifies the man with the soul.[48] It is the soul that is truly personal, the true subject. The body is the immediate environment of the person. Hence, the continued existence of the soul or the living person would genuinely be the continued existence of the life of the man. That there is a soul or living person, ontologically distinct from the body, is the first condition of the possibility of life after death. This distinct existence has been established in Whiteheadian terms in the preceding sections of this chapter.

The secondary anthropological objection against such life Whitehead himself probably found more weighty. This is that we have no experience of souls apart from the most intimate interaction with bodies. It is by bodies that the causal efficacy of the universe is mediated to them, and it is as the controlling forces in bodies that they have their basic functions. But whatever significance Whitehead may have attached to such considerations, he knew they were far from decisive. The soul in each momentary occasion prehends not only its environing brain but also its own past occasions of experience and the experiences of other souls.[49] These prehensions are not mediated by the body.

[48] *PR* 141.

[49] Most important of all is the prehension of God, omitted from the text because of my effort here to limit myself to what can be said of man without reference to God. Attention will be devoted to God and to man's experience of him in Chs. IV to VI. Insofar as Whitehead himself speculated about the separability of the soul from the body, the relation to God was uppermost in his mind. Note the following passage, *AI* 267: " How far this soul finds a support for its existence beyond the body is: — another question. The everlasting nature of God, which in a sense is non-temporal and in another sense is temporal, may establish with the soul a peculiarly intense relationship of mutual immanence. Thus in some important sense the existence of the soul may be freed from its complete dependence on the bodily organization." Whether Whitehead actually had in mind in this passage the kind of life after death of which I am speaking or the kind of immortality in the consequent nature of God that was his usual concern I do not know.

Hence there is no evidence that they could not occur apart from the body. The extreme vagueness with which other souls are prehended directly in this life [50] might be replaced by clarity when the mediating influences of the pure physical prehensions are removed. Such speculation makes use of no materials not directly provided by Whitehead. But it affords no evidence that the soul does live beyond death. It simply supports Whitehead's statement that his philosophy is neutral on this question.

Even if it is accepted that the soul is such that it *could* exist in separation from the body, we are likely to object that there is no " place " for this existence to occur. The days when heaven could be conceived as *up* and hell as *down* are long since past (if ever, indeed, they were present for sophisticated thinkers) . In the Newtonian cosmology, disembodied souls seemed thoroughly excluded from the space-time continuum. But souls, or mental substances, fitted so ill in this continuum at best, even in their embodied form, that it did not seem too strange to suppose that beyond the continuum of space and time there might be another sphere to which human souls more naturally belonged. Those who believed that somehow the soul could also be explained in terms of the little particles of matter that scurried about in space and time could not believe in any such other sphere. But for those who were convinced that mind could never be explained in terms of the motions of matter, the duality of matter and mind pointed quite naturally to the duality of this world and another, spiritual world in which space, time, and matter did not occur.

Gradually, however, the sharp line that separated matter and mind gave way. Evolutionary categories brought mind into the natural world, involving it in space and time.

---

[50] *PR* 469. " But of course such immediate objectification [of other living persons] is also reinforced, or weakened, by routes of mediate objectification. Also pure and hybrid prehensions are integrated and thus hopelessly intermixed."

Even if this forced the beginning of the abandonment of the pure materiality of the natural world, it also undermined the justification for conceiving of any sphere beyond this one. If minds have emerged in space and time, it is to space and time that they belong. A nonspatiotemporal mental sphere seemed no more meaningful or plausible than a nonspatiotemporal material sphere. There seemed no longer to be any " place " for life to occur after death.

Theology responded to this new situation by reviving the ancient doctrine of the resurrection of the body. If heaven could not be another sphere alongside this one, then it must be a transformation of the spatiotemporal sphere which will come at the end of time. The Pharisees, it appeared, had more truth than the Orphics. But the belief in an apocalyptic end was hard to revive, and even among the theologians who used its language, there were many who regarded the resurrection of the body more as a symbol of the wholeness of the human person, body and mind, than as a reliable prediction of the future. Outside of conservative ecclesiastical circles, the doctrine of the resurrection of the body continued to appear anachronistic. Natural theology, at any rate, could not be asked to attempt to make any sense of such a theory.

But in our situation, in which the mind or soul has been naturalized into the spatiotemporal continuum, can natural theology suggest any " place " for any kind of life after death? I am not sure that in any positive sense it can, and I am sure that I am not capable of the kind of imaginative speculation that would be required to give such a positive answer. Yet something may be said in a purely suggestive way to indicate that our commonsense inability to allow a " place " for the new existence of souls is based on the limitations of our imagination and not on any knowledge we possess about space and time. We will turn to Whitehead for the beginning of the restructuring of our imagination, on the basis of which further reflection must proceed.

The first point that must be grasped and held firmly is

that we are not to think of four-dimensional space-time as a fixed reality into which all entities are placed. Space-time is a structure abstracted from the extensive relationships of actual entities. So far as what is involved in being an actual entity is concerned, there is no reason that there should be four dimensions rather than more or fewer. The world we know is four-dimensional, but this does not mean that all entities in the past and future have had or will have just this many dimensions. Indeed, it does not mean that all entities contemporary with us must have this number of dimensions, although there may be no way for us to gain cognition of any entity of a radically different sort.

Our four-dimensional space-time is the special form that the universal extensive continuum takes in our world. Every actual entity participates in this extensive continuum. But even this is not because the extensive continuum exists prior to and is determinative of the occurrence of actual entities. The extensive continuum is necessary and universal only because no actual entity can ever occur except in relation to other actual entities. Such relations may not be such as to allow for measurement, as they do in our four-dimensional world; certainly they may not have the dimensional character with which we are familiar. But some kind of extensiveness, Whitehead believes, is a function of relatedness as such.

If we try to imagine what it would be like to have no intimate relations with a body or with an external world as given to us in our sense experience, we seem to be left with a two-dimensional world. There is the dimension of successiveness, of past and future. We have memory of the past and anticipation of the future. In addition, there remains the direct experience of other living persons in mental telepathy. These persons are not experienced as related to us in a three-dimensional space but only as being external to ourselves, capable of independent, contemporary existence. Shall we call this a one-dimensional spatial relation?

Let us suppose, then, that the life of souls beyond death

occurs in a two-dimensional continuum instead of the four-dimensional continuum we now know. Is it meaningful to ask " where " this two-dimensional continuum exists? Such a question can only mean, How is it related to our four-dimensional continuum according to the terms of that four-dimensional continuum? And perhaps, in those terms, no answer is possible. However, if there are relations between events in a two-dimensional continuum and events in a four-dimensional continuum, then those relations too must participate in some extensive character. Perhaps, therefore, in some mysterious sense, there is an answer, but I for one am unable to think in such terms.

For the speculations I have just outlined, I can claim no direct support from Whitehead. He does make clear that the relation of an occasion to the mental pole of other occasions does not participate in the limitations that I take to be decisive for our understanding of a three-dimensional space.[51] He does affirm that even now there may be occasions of experience participating in an order wholly different from the one we know.[52] He repeatedly emphasizes the contingency of the special kind of space-time to which we are accustomed.[53] But beyond this the speculation is my own.

Even if my speculations are fully warranted by Whitehead's understanding of the extensive continuum, it should be clearly understood that these considerations argue only for the *possibility* of life after death, not at all for its actuality. There is nothing about the nature of the soul or of the cosmos that demands the continued existence of the living person. If man continues to exist beyond death, it can be only as a new gift of life, and whether such a gift is given is beyond the province of natural theology to inquire.

[51] *SMW* 216; *PR* 165, 469; *AI* 318.
[52] *MT* 78, 212. Whitehead anticipates the gradual emergence of a new cosmic epoch in which the physical will play a lesser role and the mental a larger one. (*RM* 160; *ESP* 90.)
[53] *SMW* 232; *PR* 140, 442.

4. PERSONAL IDENTITY

Another objection to the possibility of meaningfully affirming life after death may be raised. Whereas in the preceding cases we saw that Whitehead's way of understanding man and space took the sting out of the objections, this objection is directed specifically at his own position. It is pointed out that life after death would be meaningless on his terms because that which would then live would not be identical with what had died. After death, there would be a quite new set of occasions, numerically different from those which had occurred before death. Whitehead's own reflections on meaningful preservation may have been affected by this kind of thinking. He became much more interested in considering how each occasion's values might be preserved than in speculating on the occurrence of additional occasions.[54]

The objection rests upon the fact that Whitehead attributes total unity or self-identity only to individual occasions. All other things are built up of these units. They are societies of occasions rather than individual actual occasions. Some of these societies have a special order which Whitehead calls personal. These are the enduring objects and living persons. But even here an ontologically discrete entity is present at each moment. There is no absolute self-identity through time.

This lack of absolute self-identity through time does indeed pose problems for any doctrine of life after death. It poses many other problems as well. Our ordinary moral and legal practice presupposes personal identity. If there is no such personal identity, all justification for rewards and punishments seems to vanish. It would seem that there is no particular necessity to accept responsibility for our past acts, since they were performed by a numerically different entity. Gratitude would seem to be misdirected

[54] See below, Ch. IV, pp. 161 ff. for a discussion of the consequent nature of God, and Ch. VI, sec. 1, for a treatment of Whitehead's religion.

when expressed after the moment of the beneficent act. Past promises would not bind. The list of consequences is endless and disastrous.[55]

Whitehead himself was troubled by the apparent conflict of his doctrine and the universal intuition and practice of mankind. He shared the intuition, and again and again he returned to the topic, seeking to shed light upon it.[56]

The most obvious commonsense basis for asserting the identity of a person through time is the continuity of the body of whose dominant occasions that living person or soul is composed. When we are dealing with the same body, we almost always assume that we are dealing with the same person. This is surely part of the normal meaning of personal identity.[57] If it were the only meaning, the doctrine of life after death would be nonsensical. However, quite apart from this consequence, the understanding of personal identity in terms of the identity of the body has at least two limitations.

First, our bodies change. If two points of time are sufficiently remote, we are told that no enduring object earlier present in the body will be there at the later time. Of course, the gradualness of the change is such that we have no difficulty in identifying the body as the same from birth to death. Nevertheless, it is highly questionable that we would correlate closely the identity of the person and the actual identity of the body. Second, Whitehead affirms that a single body may house dominant occasions ordered in competing societies. He believes that this is the case where split personality occurs.[58] If so, it is clear that the identity of the body would not guarantee the identity of the soul.

[55] Paul Weiss frequently criticizes Whitehead to the effect that he allows for no such responsibility. Sherburne in his response, " Responsibility, Punishment, and Whitehead's Theory of the Self," in Kline, seems to agree. However, Whitehead did not himself take this line. See *Imm* 690.

[56] *AI* 210, 240; *MT* 129–130, 221–222; *Imm* 689–690.

[57] *MT* 222.

[58] *PR* 164.

Whitehead sometimes answers that the identity of the person through time points to the inheritance of a common character through the successive occasions.[59] This is an application to the special case of the soul of the general principle by which social order is defined.[60] It should be noted that it contains two aspects: the insistence on a common character, and the transmission of this character from member to member of the society. It will be worthwhile to consider the two elements separately to determine their individual relevance.

It is certainly clear that commonness of character in itself provides no basis for personal identity. Twin boys at six months of age are likely to be very much alike, whereas if we compare one of those boys of six months with the man of twenty he later becomes, we will be more impressed by the great differences. Yet we never suppose that the twins are the same person, whereas we do assume that there is a personal identity of the child of six months and the man he grows to become. However, granting that commonness of character alone helps us very little, we must ask whether it is indeed commonness in what is inherited that causes us to judge personal identity. There is some evidence in our ordinary speech in favor of this view. If a person has changed greatly, we may say that he is a new person, or if the change is unfavorable, that he is not his old self. Whitehead's account would illuminate such language.

Nevertheless, Whitehead is in error if he intends to explain the common intuition of personal identity in this way. If pressed, the persons who use phrases such as those just suggested will insist that the person in question is really the same person, only changed. An exception may be made in the case of split personality or total amnesia, but mere change of personality will not lead to the conclusion that personal identity is gone. Furthermore, if the change leads to heightened sensitivity and responsibility, the per-

[59] This note is primary in *Imm*. See pp. 688–691.
[60] *PR* 50–51.

son himself may take more rather than less responsibility for obligations undertaken before the change. Men will take it as a mark of bad character rather than enlightenment if, after the most drastic alteration in personality, a man refuses responsibility for all earlier commitments.

It is a perplexing fact, and perhaps an indication of some desperation on Whitehead's part, that he fell into the trap of describing personal identity in terms that refer to a common character. He was himself quite aware that the decisive feature of life is novelty and not the repetition of past patterns. When considering the status of a living cell and the living occasions within it, he rejected the suggestion that they be considered as enduring objects on the grounds that " ' endurance ' is a device whereby an occasion is peculiarly bound by a single line of physical ancestry, while ' life ' means novelty." [61] Since the cell is alive, we should not regard it as an enduring object just because the special feature of enduring objects is that they continue a common character through successive occasions. How then, when we come to the soul, which is even more alive than the cell, can we appeal to the inheritance of a common character to explain its identity through time?

If this were Whitehead's only answer, or the only answer his categories would allow, the philosophy would be in serious trouble. Reflection upon our normal understanding of our self-identity makes it quite clear that it is not in virtue of similarity of character that we affirm our identity through time. The whole burden of Whitehead's case must fall on the fact of inheritance, for as he himself fully recognized in discussing the cell, commonness of character is not the distinctive mark of life. But in that case, the distinction must be made in terms of a distinctive mode of inheriting, since otherwise, personal identity would relate every occasion to every other occasion in its past.

On several occasions, Whitehead stressed the fact that personal identity depends upon a special mode of inherit-

[61] PR 159.

ing rather than upon a common pattern inherited. He wrote, " We — as enduring objects with personal order — objectify the occasions of our own past with peculiar completeness in our immediate present." [62] And again, " An enduring personality in the temporal world is a route of occasions in which the successors with some peculiar completeness sum up their predecessors." [63] In these quotations, the enduring objects and enduring persons are what we have called, in dependence on other passages in Whitehead's writing, living persons and souls.

Unfortunately, Whitehead did not adequately develop what he meant by peculiar completeness, and the theory of personal identity that follows goes beyond his explicit statements. However, I believe it to be the only satisfactory approach to personal identity allowed by his system and to correspond closely with my own intuition as to what constitutes my own identity through time. Furthermore, I consider it the only way to take seriously the statements of Whitehead just cited.

My sense of personal identity with my past seems to me to depend upon memory. I think of myself as remembering my own past experiences but not as remembering the past experiences of other persons or of any other entities. I may remember something *about* those experiences, but only my own are directly remembered as such. If, indeed, I remembered any experience, I would affirm that it was my own, and if I were persuaded that I could not have had that experience, I would be extremely perplexed. Likewise, I find it very difficult to identify myself as the subject of experiences of which I have no memory whatsoever, such as experiences I am told I had while under ether. I incline to view those experiences as belonging to my body but not to me. Also, I have a very limited sense of identity with the infant who, I am told, I was. I view that infant, in my imagination, from without rather than remembering his experiences from within.

[62] *PR* 244.   [63] *PR* 531.

Now I recognize that much of what I have forgotten and which is seemingly beyond recall could be recovered to memory under hypnosis or even on an analyst's couch. Hence, I extend my sense of identity beyond my actual ability to recall. I assume that in my unconscious even now there is a relation to past experiences, also influencing my present conscious experience, that binds them to me " with some peculiar completeness."

My understanding of my future self-identity with my present runs along the same lines. If I could suppose a future condition, in this life or another, in which the occasions then occurring had no peculiar mode of inheritance from those I now am, I would not identify myself with them in imagination. To be told that there might be some underlying substance that would be the same then as it is now would not affect my judgment. Neither would Whitehead's doctrine of inheritance of a common character. Only memory can serve in my self-understanding to determine self-identity through time.

I have made this statement quite independently of Whiteheadian terminology to pose the question as to whether, after all, Whitehead's philosophy allows an explanation of this peculiar phenomenon of the sense of personal identity. If the inheritance from previous occasions in the soul is different only in quantitative ways from other routes of inheritance, then I believe it does not, and the consequences must be accepted or the philosophy itself altered or abandoned. But, in fact, I believe that we can make sense of the " peculiar completeness " of this inheritance, and that not only in quantitative terms.

In an enduring object of the ordinary physical variety, each occasion can directly prehend only the immediate predecessor occasion. This is because it objectifies its predecessor by the physical pole, and such prehensions are only of contiguous occasions. The influence of earlier members of the enduring object must be mediated through the more recent ones. In a living person, on the other hand, the mental poles of the past occasions are of primary importance for their objectification.[64] Prehensions of the mental poles of occasions do not depend upon contiguity. Hence, there may be immediate objectification of many, perhaps of all, of the past occasions in the living person. In this way, a peculiar completeness of summing up would be accounted for and the question of common characteristics would be seen as entirely secondary. Also, my own experience of personal identity as described in non-Whiteheadian terms would be explained. I do experience immediate prehensions of former mental experiences, sometimes with considerable vividness. This experience does assure me of my personal identity, not of course of numerical identity, with that earlier occasion of experience.

We need not make personal identity in this view dependent upon the unmediated prehension of *all* past occasions in the person in question. So long as all those past occasions of experience are potentially available for such recall, whether spontaneously or under hypnosis, the peculiarity of the sense of identity can be explained. Whether or not in the unconscious dimensions of our experience they are continuously effective is a factual question best left to the depth psychologists.[65]

This understanding of personal identity explains our sense of responsibility for our past acts. We remember, or can remember, those experiences from the " inside." Hence we identify ourselves with them. If, in fact, I am entirely unable to remember some past act attributed to me and am persuaded that the relation of that acting occasion to me is not like those of occasions I can remember, I can feel no responsibility for that act whatever others may say. The sense of responsibility is a function of that kind of identity determined by the possibility of memory in this sense, in Whiteheadian terms, the possibility of the unmediated prehension of the mental pole of a past occasion.

This understanding of personal identity is also adequate

[64] *PR* 163; *AI* 271–272.   [65] See below, sec. 5.

for explaining the hope for life after death. That hope will be satisfied if there exist occasions that have to each other and to my present occasions this relationship of memory. Their character may be quite different. The fact that personal identity in this life depends so little upon the relation to a common body and so much upon unmediated hybrid prehensions of past occasions of the soul's life strengthens the plausibility of the claim that continuity may occur after bodily death. In no sense does it prove that this will occur.

I believe this to be an account of personal identity fundamentally loyal both to Whitehead and to normal human intuitions. I regret to note that in my own view it is still not entirely satisfactory.

The analysis I have given would serve to exhibit personal identity with full discreteness except for one point. Whitehead's philosophy and some empirical evidence point to the possibility of having in relation to other souls experiences like those I have described as memory. In mental telepathy there seems to be an unmediated prehension of the mental pole of another person's experience. Experiences have been reported in which occasions of experience in the distant past have been " remembered " in this way. If personal identity is *defined* as I have defined it, then all mental experiences subject to being prehended unmediatedly must be included in the living person. We can solve the problem definitionally by appealing to the fact that the living person is serially ordered, but the deeper question remains. It can be pointed up by a wild hypothesis.

If the dominant occasion in my body began to " remember " the past dominant occasions of another body and to fail to remember its own, my definition would require that it be regarded as a continuation of the other person. This would seem proper to common sense also, if we may appeal to common sense in this realm of fantasy. But what if successor occasions continued to occur in the other body in a quite normal fashion? Would these two strands of occasions then be the *same* living person?

An analogous difficulty can be posed with respect to the suggested possibility of life after death. Suppose that after my death there is a set of serially ordered occasions that enjoy unmediated memory of all the occasions of my life. Is it not possible still to wonder whether those occasions will be " me "? If so, it is clear that the definition of personal identity I have offered does not really exhaust the common intuition of self-identity. That intuition remains mysteriously unformulable.[66] It may be an illusion, but I suggest that it is a persistent one which remains baffling in the light of any existing philosophy.

Meanwhile, so long as the eccentric possibilities I have mentioned are never actualized, the account I have proposed is quite satisfactory for practical purposes. It is that personal identity obtains whenever there is a serially ordered society of primarily mental occasions (a soul) in which each occasion actually or potentially prehends unmediatedly the mental poles of all its predecessors.

5. THE UNCONSCIOUS

The discussion of personal identity has raised the question of unconscious experience. This topic is obviously of great importance in our day for the understanding of man. When Whitehead spoke of the soul, he focused attention upon consciousness, but his philosophy also points up the very large role of unconscious experience. " Consciousness," Whitehead tells us, " presupposes experience, and not experience consciousness." [67] Most actual occasions of experience enjoy no consciousness at all. Where consciousness occurs, it appears as the subjective form of some part of the higher phases of experience. It presupposes a complex process of comparison of earlier and simpler phases of

[66] Whitehead also speaks of " the mystery of personal identity," and says that " in respect to such intuitions . . . our powers of analysis, and of expression, flicker with our consciousness " (*AI* 210).

[67] *PR* 83.

experience which can never enter into consciousness. It depends specifically upon negation, upon the contrast of what is with what might be.[68]

The occurrence of consciousness is of immense importance. Apart from it, no high form of animal life would be possible. Apart from conscious enjoyment, all value would seem trivial. All our thought presupposes consciousness, as does all our effort to consider the unconscious dimensions of experience. Nevertheless, Whitehead's philosophy agrees with the depth psychologists in emphasizing the priority and greater massiveness of what is unconscious. Clear consciousness focuses itself upon the appearances immediately surrounding our bodies. Very dimly it suggests that there is another mode of relation to our bodies and their environment in which their reality is effective in us. But this awareness of the world in the mode of causal efficacy fades away before close attention. We can grasp the massiveness and complexity of what is present in our unconscious experience in relation to the relative simplicity and superficiality of our consciousness by considering what we, in fact, are experiencing in each occasion in comparison with that which we can bring into focus with some conscious clarity.[69]

Consider again Whitehead's basic doctrine that each occasion prehends every occasion in its past. This has been stated again and again, but it remains an idea utterly staggering to the imagination. It means that a virtually infinite number of discrete entities are each playing some role, however trivial, in each moment of my experience. Of course, the vast majority of these influences are mediated through contiguous occasions. But somehow, Whitehead insists, their distinctive efficacy is therein preserved.

Even if we limit our consideration to occasions immediately contiguous to the soul, the contents of our experience are quite amazing. In each occasion we are immediately

[68] PR 372.
[69] Cf. Whitehead's discussion of consciousness, e.g., MT 166–171.

prehending numerous occasions of experience in the brain. We are totally incapable of becoming conscious of these prehensions, although it is through them that we receive the eternal objects that we project upon the environing world as sensa. All of our most immediate experience of other occasions remains unconscious, qualifying consciousness only with a vague sense of derivation from the body.

In addition to this, consider the prehensions of past occasions of the soul's life. Let us assume that these are, as Whitehead says, summed up with some peculiar completeness in each new occasion of the soul. Let us assume further, as I have suggested above, that they are all immediately felt at all times as well as being mediated by proximate occasions. In this instance, we can indeed become conscious of some fragments of these feelings. Most of the time I am not conscious of my immediately precedent experiences, but by a focusing of attention I can become so with considerable vividness. Similarly, many occasions of the more distant past can be recalled with varying degrees of conscious vividness. But since consciousness presupposes experience and not experience consciousness, we must reckon with the possibility that *all* of them are, in fact, prehended at all times — hence, with an immense richness of unconscious experience.

Beyond this are the prehensions of other persons. Here too there seem to be exceptional occasions in which these prehensions can be lifted into conscious awareness. But clearly, the vast majority of such prehensions remain totally unconscious. Furthermore, these prehensions need not be limited to the recent experiences of those prehended. Past experiences, even remote past experiences, are not excluded. There may be immediate feeling of every past experience of the race insofar as mentality functioned significantly therein.

These last ideas are not necessitated by Whitehead's doctrine, but they seem to be a reasonable interpretation. Whitehead affirms only that the present occasion prehends its entire past either mediately or immediately. Where past occasions are objectified by their physical poles, all that are not contiguous are mediated through the contiguous occasions. Where they are objectified by their mental poles, contiguity is not necessary. Since primarily mental occasions are presumably most often objectified by their mental poles when prehended by other primarily mental occasions, immediate prehension of all of them seems indicated.

This idea is certainly fantastic, although no more so than many that have been made commonplace by modern physics. Moreover, depth psychology seems to provide some evidence for its truth. Mysterious concepts like that of the racial unconscious, quite inexplicable as they are usually presented, become fully intelligible in the context of Whitehead's philosophy. Whether all past occasions of experience of human souls are directly prehended in each new occasion is indeed a factual question, but insofar as evidence of the influence of the past upon our psychic life is uncovered, it tends to confirm the natural speculations issuing from Whitehead's philosophy.

6. THE LOCUS OF THE SOUL

The soul is located in the brain. Perhaps it would be best to leave the question of location at that point. However, Whitehead gave an explicit suggestive answer, and against this answer I would like to propose an alternative. I believe that my alternative makes better sense than Whitehead's suggestion, but it does so only if we accept a special view about the relations among the regions that constitute the " standpoints " of occasions.[70] By the standpoint of an occasion, Whitehead means that unique extended locus it occupies in the total spatiotemporal continuum. The argument in favor of my view of the locus of the soul requires a considerable excursus.

Whitehead's answer to the question of the place of the soul is that it is to be found in the " empty spaces " in the

[70] *PR* 435.

interstices of the brain.[71] Here it wanders from place to place according to the richness of the stimuli received at these places. Wherever it goes, it must be surrounded by living occasions,[72] presumably of the variety found also in the empty spaces of the cell.

In opposition to Whitehead's view, I suggest that the soul may occupy a considerable region of the brain including both empty space and the regions occupied by many societies. This proposal assumes that it is possible for the region that constitutes the standpoint of one occasion to include the regions that constitute the standpoints of other occasions. To the defense of that view I shall return shortly. First, however, I want to offer my arguments for the superiority of this interpretation as against that of Whitehead himself.

First, the inheritance along the route of presiding or dominant occasions is more intelligible if there is continuity in the regions occupied by these occasions. If the dominant occasion is now here and now there, the degree of continuity and identity actually experienced is surprising. It is true that if the successive occasions are united only by prehensions of the mental poles of their predecessors, then such contiguity is not essential. But its occurrence would help greatly to explain the clear difference almost always felt between prehensions of one's own past experiences and those of other persons and thus tend to solve the still mysterious problems of personal identity.[73] This argument could be countered by suggesting a permanent location of the soul in one particular interstice of the brain. But Whitehead does not think in these terms, for he recognizes that diverse portions of the brain make the major contributions to our experience at different times. There is no indication that one segment of the brain is the unchanging seat of consciousness.

[71] *PR* 161, 516. Cf. the more open statement in *AI* 290.
[72] *PR* 163.
[73] See above, sec. 4.

Second, Whitehead's view seems difficult to reconcile with the apparent joint immediacy of inheritance from many parts of the brain. Hearing, seeing, remembering, and calculating seem to occur concurrently in one dominant occasion. If these functions are most intimately related with diverse portions of the brain, then it seems necessary to suppose that the dominant occasion is present at the same time at all these diverse places.[74] The alternative is to appeal again to the independence of hybrid prehensions from the need for contiguity. However, it is doubtful that we should regard *all* the prehensions constituting the dominant occasions as hybrid. Furthermore, if this argument is pressed, there seems no necessity that the dominant occasion be located in the human body at all! Whitehead certainly thought that it is located contiguously to occasions in the brain from which it inherits.

Third, Whitehead's doctrine of straight lines would be far more plausible if we adopt the view here advocated. Whitehead believed it important for geometry and physics to demonstrate that our understanding of straightness does not depend upon measurement. He shows, therefore, that our intuition of straightness can be explained if we posit pairs of points located in the region of the dominant occasion, the connections between which are projected out into the environment of the body.[75] If the region of the dominant occasion is of microscopic size, as suggested by Whitehead's account, its projection of straight lines on a macroscopic scale is remarkable. However, since even the tiniest region contains an infinity of points, this argument is not decisive. More important is the fact that we can detect no shifting from one part of the head to another in the center from which projections of direction take place, whereas if

[74] This is Hartshorne's view as shown by his question to Whitehead in "Whitehead's Idea of God," Schilpp, p. 545.

[75] *PR* 492. In *AI* 277, the segment of line is in the brain rather than in the percipient occasion, but I assume that the theory depends upon the line's presence in that region in which the percipient occasion (hence the soul) is present. This suggests the advantage of my theory.

the dominant occasion does move from place to place such a shift must, in fact, occur.

In view of arguments of this sort, why did Whitehead himself limit his few references to the standpoint of the soul to the view of a shifting locus in the interstices of the brain? A possible answer is that Whitehead may have conceived of all actual occasions as microscopic in size. Furthermore, he conceived of all space as occupied and considered what we regard as empty space simply as space in which the occasions are not organized into enduring objects. These occasions may be highly original in character. Just as such mental or living occasions are located by him in the empty space of the cell, so others may be conceived as occupying the empty spaces surrounding the brain cells. These would provide a peculiarly favorable environment for that most mental of all occasions, the dominant occasion of the animal organism.

My counterview proposes that we think of the region of the soul in its relation to the regions of both the brain cells, and the occasions in the interstices of the brain as Whitehead thinks of the cell in its relation to the molecules and empty spaces within it. I believe I have shown that this view would have a number of substantial advantages. It would, however, require the doctrine that the region constituting the standpoint of one actual occasion can include the regions constituting the standpoints of other actual occasions. Whether or not Whitehead himself thought this relationship possible, he made no explicit use of it and never dealt with the special problems it would raise. We may conjecture that he either rejected its possibility or failed to consider it seriously. Yet I believe his metaphysics allows for this understanding and that his cosmology, not only with respect to the problem now at hand — the locus of the soul — but at other points as well, is more intelligible if we affirm this principle.[76] Because of its importance for my own vision of the cosmos, I shall argue this point

[76] See below, Ch. V, sec. 3, for my discussion of God and space in these terms.

at some length. Since one of Whitehead's ablest interpreters has argued the impossibility of such relationships in the context of his thought, some of the argument will be directed implicitly against his objections.[77]

Fundamentally, the unity of an actual occasion is the unity of its subjective immediacy culminating in its satisfaction. Its unity does not derive from the specificity of its standpoint or region. The region determines for the actual entity just what other actual occasions are in its past and hence, causally efficacious for it.[78] It determines, further, which occasions are contiguous and hence immediately effective for it physically. But the region the occasion occupies could have been actualized by several actual occasions instead of one, or could have been part of a larger region, or could have been parts of several regions rather than united as the actual standpoint of a single occasion. It is the occasions in their concrete immediacy which provide the principle of unity, not the standpoints.

Thus far there is no dispute. My contention is, however, that if the unity of the occasion does not reside in its standpoint, then a single region may be included in the standpoints of more than one occasion without affecting the discrete individuality of the occasions in question. This means that the inclusion of one region by another would *not* entail inclusion of one actual occasion by another.

This idea that a particular region of space-time may be occupied by more than one entity without reducing the relation of those entities to that of part to whole is so strange to our common sense that further explanation is needed. If we think of the entities with which we have to do in ordinary life, we can gain no analogy. For example, a page in a book occupies a space also occupied by the book as a whole, but we immediately see that this is because the

[77] Christian argues that any relation of overlapping or inclusion among standpoints of actual occasions is impossible. *An Interpretation of Whitehead's Metaphysics*, pp. 93–104.
[78] *PR* 434–436.

page is part of the book. In the macroscopic world, to occupy a part of the region occupied by something else is
virtually definitive of the relation of part to whole. If I
insert a sheet of paper between the pages of the book, the
space occupied by that sheet of paper is no longer occupied
by the book precisely because the paper is not part of the
book.

We must remember, therefore, that the entities with
which we are now dealing are not like books and pages.
They are not primarily to be conceived of as objects at all,
but rather as subjects. The unity of objects (in the sense
of corpuscular societies prehended from without) is in-
separable from their spatial unity. Objects such as books
can be cut in half, and each half will have physically much
the kind of unity the book as a whole previously had. But
subjects are indivisible. The regions they occupy are divisible, but the subject either has unity as subject or is not
a subject at all. It is my contention that if we understand
this very different kind of unity possessed by subjects, we
will be able to understand that location within the region
of another subject does not make a subject simply part of
the larger subject. Indeed, it is meaningless to speak of one
subject as part of another. As subjects, each is strictly an
individual and is indivisible.

This relationship can be further explicated in Whitehead's terms by discussing the way in which these entities
would prehend each other. One of Whitehead's cardinal
cosmological principles is that contemporaries occur in
mutual independence.[79] They do not directly prehend each
other. Consider, then, actual occasion A, whose standpoint
is entirely included in the region constituting the standpoint of actual occasion B. At the time A originates, B has
not reached its satisfaction. Therefore, A does not prehend B. Likewise, at the time B originates, A has not
reached its satisfaction. Hence, B does not prehend A. The
two occasions will have much in common because of the

[79] PR 95.

similarity of their standpoints. However, their standpoints are not identical. Some occasions contiguous to B will not be contiguous to A. Furthermore, the occasions contiguous to both may not be objectified in the same way. A may objectify the past entirely through pure physical feelings, whereas B may objectify it primarily through hybrid feelings. The inclusion of the region of A in B does not entail that B include in its objectification of a common past the eternal objects by which A objectifies that past. Certainly it will not include the subjective form, the subjective aim, the subjective immediacy, or the satisfaction of A. The radical discreteness numerically and qualitatively, of A and B is not affected by the peculiar relation of the regions they occupy.

If A and B are occasions in the historic routes of enduring objects, then subsequent occasions in each route will prehend the earlier occasions in the other route. Moreover, we may speculate that the special regional relationship will enter into the subjective form of this prehension in some way. But fundamentally, these past occasions of the regionally included enduring object will be included in the later occasions of the including enduring object just as all past occasions are included — not in any special sense as part to whole.

The idea of the inclusion of one regional standpoint by another calls attention to another point that may require some adjustment of common sense. A region is a perspective on the world. Every perspective, it may be thought, must ultimately be reducible to that of a point. For example, the causal efficacy of a contiguous past occasion would seem to affect that part of the becoming occasion that is contiguous *before* it affects other parts, if the becoming occasion is extended. But then we would have to introduce physical time into the interiority of the occasion. So long as we can think of the occasion as sufficiently minute, this problem does not seem acute, but when we start to speak of occasions large enough to include others, our imaginations are bothered by this problem.

The answer, however, is that the principle of the ex-
tendedness of the regions of actual occasions is absolutely
crucial to Whitehead's thought, and that once the principle is accepted, the size of regions is irrelevant. The physical prehensions of the becoming occasion may indeed be
correlated with the several portions of the region, but the
subjective unity of the occasion is equally related to the
whole region indiscriminately.[80] Portions of this subjectivity do not first arise in one part of the region and then
get communicated to others. They are omnipresent
throughout the region, whether that region be large or
small.

Although Whitehead did not deal with the question of
regional inclusion, some of his cosmological statements,
taken at face value, seem to imply it. Thus far we have
considered, as our chief examples of enduring objects,
molecules [81] and souls. These are among Whitehead's examples. But Whitehead also gives others. Specifically, he
identifies corpuscles of light,[82] electrons,[83] protons,[84] and
probably subelectronic particles [85] as enduring objects. For
the sake of simplicity we can focus our attention on just
two of these examples — molecules and electrons.[86]

Now, molecules and electrons as enduring objects must
be composed of serially ordered occasions which we may
refer to as molecular and electronic occasions. On the
basis of physics, it is clear that there are electrons *inside*

[80] *PR* 434–435.

[81] *PR* 124–125, 151.

[82] *PR* 53.

[83] *PR* 139–141.

[84] *PR* 141.

[85] *PR* 152. This is by inference from the fact that he says electrons and protons are probably structured societies.

[86] It is, of course, possible that Whitehead did not mean to have
all his examples taken literally or seriously. Hence, although I believe the burden of proof should be on those who deny that he
meant what he said, I do not regard the following as proof that he
intended to allow regional inclusion.

of molecules. This would seem to mean, in Whiteheadian terms, that the regions occupied by some electronic occasions are entirely included in the regions occupied by some molecular occasions.

The alternative explanation of the relation of molecular actual occasions to electronic ones would be that the molecular actual occasion is really a dominant occasion in the society of occasions constituting the molecule. It could then be located in the empty spaces within the molecule alongside of the many other occasions in the society.

This interpretation is a possible one, although it receives no direct support from Whitehead. His understanding of dominant occasions is entirely associated with living societies, specifically, animals. He speaks of animal bodies as corpuscular societies, whereas he speaks of molecules, quite directly, as enduring objects. The molecule is also, it is true, a structured society, but it is not a living society. Hence, this interpretation must be regarded as imposed upon Whitehead's language on the assumption that the more natural reading is impossible. Since I see no impossibility in the more natural reading, I regard it as some support for my own speculative development of Whitehead's thought. However, the fundamental issue is that of the *possibility* of regional inclusion and not whether this relation obtains between molecular and electronic occasions.

The cosmological vision made possible by this principle has been much more fully articulated by Charles Hartshorne. It is undoubtedly because it was he who first introduced me to Whitehead's thought that I have been strongly inclined to interpret Whitehead as having been open to this view. Hartshorne sees the universe built up of compound individuals.[87] At each level of individuality, the electron, the atom, the molecule, the cell, the person, new

[87] Hartshorne, "The Compound Individual," *Philosophical Essays for Alfred North Whitehead.* (Longmans, Green, and Company, 1936) , pp. 193–220.

social relations obtain, and hence new laws must be formulated. The individuality of the compound individual in no way militates against the individuality of the individuals of which it is compounded. Hartshorne himself gives Whitehead much of the credit for this cosmology. Given this understanding of Whitehead's philosophy, we can conceive of the soul occupying generally the region of the brain, receiving the causal efficacy of every portion of the brain at once, and experiencing its own synthesis of all these influences in its own unified subjective immediacy.

III

Man as Responsible Being

1. FREEDOM AS SELF-DETERMINATION

Whitehead recognized that the idea of moral responsibility presupposes personal identity through time.[1] Society holds men responsible for their past acts on the assumption that they are the same persons who have performed the acts. It recognizes, of course, some limits to this identity and hence to the responsibility, but personal responsibility remains basic. Also, as individuals we accept such responsibility for our own pasts. This problem was dealt with in the preceding chapter, and the solution proposed will be assumed to be adequate despite its acknowledged limitations.

However, if we are to make sense of the notion of moral responsibility, a notion that Whitehead certainly affirms, much more must be established. First, we must show that men are free, so that the ultimate cause of their actions cannot be placed outside their own self-determination. What a man is simply compelled to do is not a morally responsible action. Second, we must show that there are objective distinctions of better and worse, such that it matters how a man exercises his freedom. If every consequence of action were intrinsically equal in value, or equally lacking in value, or if the question of better and worse were simply a matter of whim, moral responsibility would be

[1] *Imm* 690.

meaningless. In the third place, we must raise the question of the distribution of value. Many of the questions normally recognized as ethical occur here. What about the relation of self-interest to altruism, of immediate enjoyment to prudential concern for the future? In the fourth place, we must ask how the discussion of values and their distribution relates to the question of obligation. On what basis do we finally settle the question as to our obligation? These four topics will constitute the first four sections of this chapter.

The question of freedom has proved to be a peculiarly perplexing one in the history of thought. The intuition of freedom has expressed itself so deeply in the language and customs of mankind that its outright denial seems self-contradictory. If the denial of freedom is itself the expression of a metaphysical necessity, why should we take it more seriously than the equally necessary affirmation of freedom? Paradoxes of this sort abound.

On the other hand, the affirmation of freedom proves peculiarly difficult to sustain. If we do not employ the doctrine of causality at all, then we have only descriptions of various patterns of feeling and behavior. Freedom is rendered meaningless. If we include the idea of cause, then we must seek the cause of the free act. That cause we will presumably find in the decision. Then by what is the decision caused? By the attractiveness of the good it wishes to attain? And is not that attractiveness, in turn, caused by the psychological state of the decider, the condition of his organism, and the structures and relations present in his environment? And if we deny this and say that the decision is caused by the man himself, does this not mean by the state of the man in the moment preceding the decision? And was not that, in turn, caused by its predecessors, and so on? If we take still another tack and say that by a free decision we mean one that is not caused at all but is purely spontaneous, it would seem that we are speaking of a purely chance event rather than of any kind of responsible human freedom. Freedom must mean self-determination, and self-determination must be in a single moment, for otherwise the self that determines is not the self that is determined, and the vicious regress begins again. But how can a self determine itself in a durationless instant? Does decision occur in such an instant?

So rarely have men faced the full range of questions demanding answer if human freedom is to be affirmed, that in our day philosophers and their critics alike have declared that the idea of freedom is not capable of being expressed in philosophic terms.[2] Whitehead, however, does not agree. For him, freedom is one of the fundamental metaphysical categories, and its character is such as to warrant man's sense of moral responsibility.[3] It is essential, therefore, to pay close attention to his argument.

If we are to understand human freedom in Whitehead's terms, we must begin by considering the kind of freedom that human experience shares with all the other occasions of experience. Whitehead believes that freedom is a universal or categorical feature of all actual entities whatsoever; [4] so human freedom must be viewed as a special case in this wide context.

Once again, if we are to have any imaginative grasp of what is being said, we must shift our attention away from the tables and stones and books that we so often employ as illustrative of the things in the world. The point is not at all that objects of that sort have freedom. They are corpuscular societies, and such freedom as can in any sense be attributed to them is, in fact, the property of the individual entities of which they are composed. These entities are very different in kind from the corpuscular societies as a whole and, Whitehead is convinced, have

[2] Cf. my article, "The Philosophical Grounds of Moral Responsibility: A Comment on Matson and Niebuhr," *The Journal of Philosophy*, July 2, 1959, pp. 619–621.

[3] *PR* 74, 339, 342, 390.

[4] *PR* 41, 75, 130, 135.

much more kinship to the actual occasions of human experience.

When freedom is affirmed of these microscopic entities, it must be understood that this is freedom within limits — ordinarily very narrow limits. The notion of freedom as such, unqualified freedom, is nonsensical. Freedom must always be freedom within some settled conditions. These settled conditions are the totality of the world as it has been down to the moment of the becoming of the new occasion. The new occasion must occur in just that world and it must take some account of all that has occurred in that world. The causal efficacy of the past for the new occasion is just as important for Whitehead's view as is the freedom of the new occasion. The new occasion must take account of every occasion in its past.[5] Its freedom lies in its own self-determination as to just *how* it will take account of all these occasions.

It is not sufficient simply to declare that every occasion is free to determine *how* it will take account of the universe. We quite properly want to know by what criteria it will decide this. The apparent orderliness of the universe indicates that each occasion is not simply random in its decision. How could a molecule endure for centuries if each molecular occasion were radically indeterminate as to how it would take account of its predecessors?

Whitehead's answer is that each occasion determines how it will take account of its predecessors according to its subjective aim.[6] This aim is given to the occasion in its initial phase along with its " initial data " which are the occasions in its past.[7] These occasions are objectified, alternative possibilities are entertained, and a new synthesis is reached according to the subjective aim of that occasion. This aim is always in accord with what is possible in that

---

[5] *PR* 66, 366.
[6] *PR* 41. See above, p. 35.
[7] *PR* 230, 361. The source of the aim is discussed below, pp. 154 ff., and 179 ff.

situation and with what will enable that occasion not only to enjoy its own satisfaction but also to contribute to the narrower and wider societies of which it is a part.[8]

But now in order to explain the order in the universe, we seem to have lost the freedom. If the subjective aim in terms of which the occasion selects from its past for fresh synthesis is given to the occasion in its origin, then the decision seems in fact to be made *for* the occasion rather than *by* the occasion. Freedom seems, after all, to be a fraud.

Whitehead's reply is that we must distinguish between the initial phase of the subjective aim (also called simply the "initial aim"[9]) of the occasion and the later phases of the subjective aim. The initial aim is given to the occasion. It points that occasion toward an ideal possibility for its satisfaction. But it does so in terms of gradations of possible realization. The actual occasion is not compelled to actualize some one of these possibilities. In their close connection with each other they already provide a principle of selection for the actual occasion in terms of its relation to its past. But during the successive phases of the occasion's self-actualization, as it compares and harmonizes the data it has received from the world, it also modifies and adapts its subjective aim.[10] This self-determination of its own aim is the final locus of freedom within the limits of causal force as determined by the settled past and the principle of order inherent in its initial aim.

Freedom in the human occasion of experience is not ontologically different from that in any other occasion. Nevertheless, the great differences between human and other occasions in all other respects also have their importance in the area of freedom. Man's actions, insofar as they are genuinely his actions, are determined by his purposes. His purposes are given for him to a large degree by his situation. Yet they are not simply given. A man may freely modify his own goals. He may refuse to actualize

<hr />

[8] *PR* 130.   [9] *PR* 372.   [10] *PR* 74, 342–343, 375.

the highest possibilities he confronts. Indeed, men seem widely to experience a difference between themselves and some ideal for their lives, an ideal partly participated in but also partly missed.[11] If we ask how this difference arises, and if we press our question fully, we find that the answer is that in each occasion of human experience there is a decision determining the subjective aim of the occasion which may deviate from the full ideal offered the occasion in its initial phase.

In most occasions, the universally present element of self-determination has nothing to do with morality as ordinarily understood. Decisions are normally regarded as moral and immoral only where consciousness is present. Even the decisions made in conscious occasions are not generally of any moral significance inasmuch as the consciousness is usually focused upon the objective world and not upon the process of decision-making. Only where consciousness eventuates in self-awareness and self-awareness comes to include awareness of a choosing among alternatives do we arrive at clear instances of moral choice. Whitehead thinks such instances may occur at times among the higher animals, but for practical purposes we may consider man to be the distinctively moral animal.[12]

One may object that men rarely or never achieve consciousness of the process of decision occurring in a single occasion of experience. If these occur, as Whitehead suggests, perhaps ten times in a single second,[13] rare indeed are the occasions when we fasten upon them in their individuality. This is certainly correct. Our consciousness blurs the lines separating the occasions of experience as it obliterates the lines separating the molecules of paint on the surface of a wall. But we are aware of a process of making decisions in terms of seconds and even fractions of seconds. Our awareness of this process in turn affects the process, heightens the range of freedom in the successive occasions, and intensifies consciousness. All these dimensions of com-

11 *RM* 60–61, 66. 12 See above, p. 59. 13 *AI* 49, 233.

plexity, dimensions that raise the moral question to crucial significance, are distinctively human potentialities.

2. INTRINSIC VALUE AS BEAUTY

Freedom would be entirely meaningless unless there were some good at which to aim. It could at best be mere randomness, mere chance. There would be no responsible conduct because there would be no better and worse. All sense of purpose would evaporate. There are those in our time who believe that this is indeed the situation in which modern man finds himself. Whitehead is not one of their number.

In Whitehead's view, there is a definite oughtness in life. We may speak of this oughtness in terms of moral obligation.[14] The fulfillment of such obligation is of essential importance, and to this topic we will return. However, obligation in its turn would be meaningless apart from some good which ought to be aimed at. If all states of affairs were intrinsically at the same level, there would be no valid reason for aiming at the achievement of one rather than another. Morality presupposes the objectivity of values. Until we know what is valuable in itself, apart from all considerations of further consequences, we have no basis for morality and no meaning for life.

In dealing with this question, we must recognize its double character. We must distinguish between the question as to what kinds of things possess value in themselves and what features of these things constitute them as valuable. We can then go on to an analysis of the basis on which comparisons of alternative values can be carried out.

Value theorists have suggested a variety of answers to the question as to what kinds of things can possess values in themselves. Some attribute value to objects or to qualities. However, objects can be valuable only in some relation to subjects, and qualities in abstraction from the things qualified by them are nonexistent. We may state,

[14] This is not a characteristic term for Whitehead.

therefore, with little fear of dispute, that the kinds of things that are valuable are states of affairs.

At this point ontology enters in. What are states of affairs? In Whitehead's terms they may be either " events " or "actual occasions." " Event " is a general term for a happening of any degree of complexity or extension through space and time. My striking a key on my typewriter is an event. So is a Presidential campaign. There are certainly values involved in such events, but one cannot speak of the event as such as having a certain determinate value in itself. Consider the simpler of the two events suggested, the event of my striking the typewriter key. This apparently unified occurrence is actually extremely vague, and when rendered precise, turns out to be either quite abstract or quite complex.

The event in question may refer to that which an observer sees as he looks in my direction at an appropriate moment. It may include also what he hears and even involve other organs of sense. It may further include his experience in the mode of causal efficacy. But in none of these cases would the event actually constitute the totality of his experience during the moments involved. Necessarily it would abstract from that totality some fragment bearing a more or less important role in his consciousness. Furthermore, the value of the event for him would depend upon other aspects of his experience at that time. The sound might jar him out of a train of thought he had found very satisfying, or it might indicate to him his success in finally getting me down to work on a project in which he took great interest.

The event may refer to an aspect of the experience of any number of observers. It may refer to the possibility of such experience even in the absence of such observers, that is, it may refer to what *would* be seen by a favorably situated observer. It may refer to my own experience of striking the key. It may refer to the physical occurrences in my body, in the typewriter, and in the paper on which

I am typing. It may refer to a very complex nexus of occasions somehow involved in my striking the key, a nexus with indeterminate limits fading off toward infinity.

In this analysis, I have employed the term " event " in the loosest way to refer to any conceivable kind of happening or occurrence with or without clear boundaries. Whitehead himself used the term in this looser way in some of his earlier writings. However, in *Process and Reality* he clearly defined event in relation to actual occasion. " An event is a nexus of actual occasions inter-related in some determinate fashion in some extensive quantum: it is either a nexus in its formal completeness, or it is an objectified nexus. One actual occasion is a limiting type of event." [15]

Once the distinction between event as nexus and actual occasion as individual entity is clearly grasped, it is evident that the locus of value must lie ultimately in the latter. A nexus in its formal completeness has no other value for itself than the values of the occasions that compose it. An objectified nexus is always objectified by some actual occasion and has its value for and in that occasion. Intrinsic value is the value of individual occasions of experience.

Furthermore it must be in the subjective immediacy of the individual occasion that intrinsic value is to be found. Once the occasion has perished, it becomes an influence upon the future and has value for that future, but it is no longer a value in itself. Its value is instrumental to the values of later occasions, but it is those occasions in their subjective immediacy that are the bearers of intrinsic value.

We are now ready for the second question. What factor in an actual occasion constitutes its value? A common answer to this question has been that the pleasure-pain continuum is the basis for the comparative values of experiences. The problems with this view, however, are notori-

[15] *PR* 124.

ous. If we take pleasure and pain as highly specific aspects of experience, we find that, in fact, we often view the value of experiences in ways that do not conform to the calculus of pleasures. An old example is that many of us would prefer to share with Socrates an experience of pain than to share with a pig the experience of contentment. To be told that we *ought* to prefer the experience of the pig is sheer dogmatism. Values must be correlated with reflective preferences, or assertions about them are meaningless and arbitrary. If, in view of this problem, we define pleasure broadly as equivalent to preferred modes of experience, we solve the problem at the expense of speaking tautologically. Such a definition illumines nothing and functions only as an obstacle to further clarification.

Whitehead uses the term " beauty " to refer to that which gives value to actual occasions of experience.[16] This too can be confusing, but Whitehead is quite clear as to his meaning. In most of our minds, beauty first suggests a property of objects such as paintings and sunsets. Whitehead says that these objects are " beautiful." [17] That means that they have the potentiality of contributing a particular character to actual occasions of experience that are affected by them. This character is " beauty " which is then a property of the experience and not as such, directly, of the things experienced.[18] It is this character that Whitehead generalizes.

When we describe objects as beautiful, we usually mean that they participate in a certain harmony of proportions and relations. Colors and shapes or sounds are so related with each other that each contributes to the whole in such a way that the whole in turn accentuates its parts. Of course, we know that if we are, in fact, speaking of the painting or the sunset as a mere object, we cannot attribute any such harmony to it. The molecules of paint or of moisture are incapable of this kind of prehension of each other or of the whole nexus of which they are parts. The

[16] *AI* Ch. XVII.   [17] *AI* 328–329.   [18] *AI* 324.

harmony is one that is contributed to the human observer. As he views the painting or the sunset, a certain important part of his experience enjoys harmony or beauty.

At the same time, his total experience may be quite disharmonious. He may be worried or a toothache may make it very difficult for him to attend to the beautiful object. The total value of his experience may, therefore, be trivial or even negative. But if we ask by what the value of the experience as a whole is to be judged, we must answer, by its comprehensive harmony or beauty. This harmony or beauty can be facilitated by beautiful objects, but it may also obtain quite independently of them. Beauty may be achieved just as well in experiences dominated by thought or love as in those dominated by sensory elements.

Every occasion achieves some measure of harmony out of the data provided it for its synthesis. In this sense, every occasion has some positive value. However, in some occasions discord may be more prominent than harmony. The occasion may feel elements that it is not able to harmonize and then feel also their mutual destructiveness. This discordant feeling is intrinsically evil, and to the extent that it is predominant, we may speak of the occasion as a negative value. Physical pain and mental suffering are alike positive evils of this sort.[19]

However, when we compare the values of occasions, we find that they do not correlate simply with the scale running from harmony to discord. Against such a view we would have to raise the same objections as noted above against the pleasure calculus. The pig may enjoy more harmony than does Socrates in pain! Harmony may be achieved by the elimination of incompatible feelings in such a way that a very low level of harmonious feeling is attained. It may be perfectly harmonious, but its beauty is trivial.[20]

Compare, for example, the beauty of a wall painted entirely in one pleasant color and a great painting. There is

[19] RM 95–96; AI 330.   [20] AI 331–332.

no discord in the wall. It is perfectly harmonious. But we hesitate to describe it as beautiful because this trivializes a powerful idea. The painting, on the other hand, works into its final harmony a multiplicity of elements potentially capable of discord, but in this case effectively harmonized. The painting is far more beautiful than the wall because it incorporates into itself a far larger number of discrete elements. It is capable of a powerful effect upon its viewers.

We must compare occasions, therefore, not only according to the degree of discord and harmony they attain but also according to the force or strength of their beauty. This complicates the judgment of comparative values. An experience of great strength is certainly preferable to a trivial one even if it is considerably less harmonious. On the other hand, a slight gain in strength may not counterbalance a loss of harmony, and great strength accompanied by serious discord may be inferior to a simple and placid harmony.

Whitehead tells us that there are two aspects constitutive of the " strength " of beauty.[21] One is the breadth or complexity of the elements that are brought into unity. Whitehead calls this " massiveness." The other is " intensity proper," which is " comparative magnitude without reference to qualitative variety." [22] We must reckon, then, with more massive harmonies with lesser intensity and more intense harmonies with lesser massiveness. Neither factor in itself determines the strength of the beauty, and hence no single scale for the evaluation of beauty is possible.

This complexity in the process of evaluation does not mean that such evaluation is impossible. Many comparative evaluations present themselves as obvious and universally relevant. Furthermore, a single ideal hovers over all, in which the several factors relevant to evaluation are themselves harmonized. This is the ideal of maximum

[21] *AI* 325.   [22] *AI* 325.

strength of beauty. This maximum depends upon a harmonious balance of maximum massiveness and maximum intensity. On the other hand, the complexity of evaluation does point to the plurality of relevant ideals that may be legitimately espoused and to the inevitable conflict between those who cling to the simpler harmonies and those who would risk their sacrifice for the sake of greater massiveness. In such a conflict, there are no universal rights and wrongs.[23] Both are right in their ideals, and in our finitude we should not hope to escape from such tensions.

Even more important, there are many different forms of beauty of more or less equal strength. Each great civilization expresses some ideal of harmony which it succeeds in approximating to a considerable extent.[24] It may be possible to compare some civilizations according to the strength of the beauty attained, but on the whole we should simply recognize the plurality of achievement. Once the harmonious form has been attained and successfully repeated, the intensity of the beauty begins to wane unless some new ideal of harmony supervenes.[25] Change is required to sustain a maximum of beauty even if the new ideal is in itself no better than the old. Yet change must also entail disharmonies in transition. Again there are no simple answers.

Of the three traditional ultimate values, Whitehead has chosen beauty as the clue to what is finally worthwhile in itself. The presence of beauty constitutes an occasion of experience as valuable, quite apart from its relation to any future beyond itself. In other terminology, beauty is the only intrinsic value. However, Whitehead is also interested in goodness and truth. Goodness we will consider in the following section, where moral considerations are paramount, but truth must be treated here.

Truth is the conformity of appearance to reality.[26] Here again we come to that fundamental distinction in Whitehead between the two modes of perception. Appearance is

[23] *AI* 346.   [24] *AI* 357.   [25] *AI* 332.   [26] *AI* 309.

the world given to us in presentational immediacy. It is composed of the sensa we project upon our environment as if they occupied regions in the contemporary space about us. It includes language as well, both heard and seen. Reality is the total nexus of occasions constituting ourselves and the actual world that is causally efficacious for us. It is the source of all our knowledge of the contemporary regions and is presupposed in all presentational immediacy. It forms the background of all our conscious experience in which presentational immediacy provides the foreground.

A truth relation exists between appearance and reality when they have some characteristic in common. That means that when some quality given to us in presentational immediacy actually derives from the region with which it is associated, to that degree the appearance is true. For example, if I feel an ache in my foot, and there really are some cells in my foot the suffering of which is responsible for my feeling, then my feeling sustains to reality a relation of truth. If, on the other hand, the source of the ache is in fact at some other point of my body (as in the case when a leg has been amputated) then the truth relation does not obtain. Also, even if some damage to my foot is responsible for the ache, if the subjective experiences of the cells in my foot in fact bear no relation to the experience I feel as an ache, then there is no truth relation. Whitehead's judgment is that within the body there is considerable conformity of the percipient or dominant occasion to the feelings of the other actual occasions it prehends, but that when we go beyond the body, as in our visual experience of colors, any such element of conformity becomes much more doubtful.[27] There is some conformity of my experience of green to the experience in the eye, but there can be little assurance of any further conformity with the paint molecules or the occasions of experience in the blade of grass.[28]

[27] *PR* 182–183; *AI* 275, 378.
[28] See, however, the discussion of peace in Ch. VII, pp. 276–277.

In a broader sense, however, appearance can and usually does sustain a relation of truth to the world beyond the body. Appearance gives us individual things located in a certain geometric relation to our bodies. It peoples our world with individual entities. When our bodies are functioning healthily and no unusual medium intervenes (such as water or a mirror), appearance in this respect has a relation of truth to reality. These individuals turn out to be societies of actual occasions, usually corpuscular societies of special importance in relation to human purposes.

Truth also has special importance in relation to propositions. By a proposition Whitehead does not mean a sentence with a certain grammatical structure.[29] In his view, sentences are incurably vague, and the same sentence may express many different meanings according to who is speaking and the total situation in which he speaks.[30] Each of these meanings is a proposition. The proposition is a connection of some actual occasion or nexus of actual occasions with some ideal possibility for its realization. In the simplest case the idea of the possibility arises out of the experience of the nexus itself. In that case the proposition simply associates the nexus and the possibility it already realizes. For example, if my foot is aching, I may entertain the idea of my foot as aching. In Whitehead's terms I would be entertaining a proposition whether or not I verbalized it in a sentence.

Now I might entertain this proposition in a variety of ways. I might feel surprise or anger, for example. It might also be an occasion for making a judgment. Normally in this case my judgment would be simply that my foot is aching. However, I might be one who believes in the unreality of pain or that the feeling of pain is always purely mental. I might then judge that my foot does not ache.

Every proposition is either true or false. It is true if the actual occasion or nexus that is the logical subject of the proposition in fact sustains that relation to the eternal ob-

[29] *AI* 312.　　　　[30] *PR* 297; *Imm* 699–700.

ject that the proposition attributes to it. It is false if this relationship does not obtain. But Whitehead emphasizes that this property is by no means the major one.[31] Many propositions are entertained without reference to their truth or falsity. For example, the propositions expressed in the individual sentences of a novel do not cry out for judgment as to their truth or falsity. Likewise, when we consider redecorating a room we entertain the idea of a wall as being colored a particular shade of green without any interest in the fact that it is not now so colored. Whitehead tells us repeatedly that it is more important that a proposition be interesting than that it be true. There are innumerable true propositions that are so trivial as not to be worth entertaining. There are many false propositions that alter the course of history, sometimes for the better.

This same de-emphasis on the importance of truth can be applied to appearance in the form of sense experience. Appearance can be beautiful and thereby contribute to the beauty of occasions of experience quite apart from any truth relation to reality. The most valuable aspects of appearance may often have the least truth. Hence, we see that truth in both of these instances, the truth of propositions and the truth of sense experience, can be neutral with respect to value.

However, Whitehead does not leave the discussion here. Although truth has no intrinsic importance and can even be harmful on occasion, nevertheless truth usually contributes to beauty and apart from it beauty is incomplete and in danger of triviality.[32] The whole of the experience that requires harmonization includes reality as well as appearance. If the appearance alone is harmonized and the reality is excluded from important contribution, the beauty that can be attained is trivial. Experience in the mode of causal efficacy, the experience that relates us to the reality of other entities, contributes indispensably to the massive-

[31] *PR* 281; *AI* 313.   [32] *AI* 342–345.

ness of the total experience. But if this reality is to be harmonized with the appearance, there must be some inner unity between the two. Such a unity is truth.

So important is truth for the attainment and preservation of the higher forms of beauty that truth quite properly comes to be sought as an end in itself. Whitehead almost seems in the end to assign it an intrinsic value distinguishable from beauty,[33] but he can be consistently understood to mean that there is a certain element of harmony inherent in truth itself such that to some degree any experience has beauty when it has truth. Far more important, however, is the indirect contribution of truth to the attainment of all strength of beauty.

3. GOODNESS AS MORAL VALUE

Whitehead was far more interested in propositions about beauty than in propositions about goodness.[34] Nevertheless, he recognized the need for the latter as well. An understanding of the characteristics that make for intrinsic value is an absolute prerequisite for any judgment about the goodness of conduct, for right conduct must be directed toward the realization of high values. But an exhaustive understanding of beauty as intrinsic value still leaves many questions unsettled, and Whitehead's own account of beauty emphasizes this.

For example, we noted that the direct quest for the maximum of beauty immediately possible may lead to endless repetitions that lose their intensity. The very success of a culture in its quest for beauty leads eventually to its decay. The only hope is that it will be grasped by some new ideal of beauty that can spark new " adventure " toward new attainment.[35] In this situation the direct attainment of available beauty must be sacrificed for the

[33] *AI* 343.

[34] Whitehead stresses that "morals constitute only one aspect of The Good, an aspect often overstressed " (*MT* 104).

[35] *AL* 354, 357–361. See below, pp. 110–111, 217.

sake of a greater beauty to be attained in the future.[36]

But how much sacrifice of the present for the future is justified? Certainly it is not always best to sacrifice present enjoyment for a greater future enjoyment. This would be nonsensical, for it would postpone enjoyment forever.[37] We must find some balance between present enjoyment and a concern to contribute to the future. But further, we find that a part of our enjoyment of the present arises from our sense of its contribution to that future.[38]

This situation in which moral perplexity and reflection arises is rooted in fundamental metaphysical categories. Every occasion aims at intensity of feeling both in its own subjective immediacy and in the relevant occasions beyond itself.[39] This means that absolute self-interest is metaphysically excluded! Every occasion's self-actualization has a view to its impact upon future occasions and this sense of relevance for the future is essential to its satisfaction.

The ethical importance of this metaphysical analysis is well worth elaboration. Many thinkers have held that all our decisions are made in terms of what will satisfy our own desires or what we believe to be in our own interest. If we make a decision that seems to be beneficial to others and to entail some sacrifice of ourselves, we are told that this is because of our desire to enjoy the admiration of others or to enhance our own self-approval. According to this view, our subjective aim is always at our own beauty.

Proponents of this position, however, generally fail to consider the question of the relation of the present self to the future self. Is this absolutely and self-identically the same self? Then do we always give equal weight to our distant future experiences and to our present ones in terms

---

[36] *AI* 309. Whitehead writes that " the effect of the present on the future is the business of morals " (*AI* 346).

[37] *AI* 346.

[38] *AI* 346. Whitehead writes, " Wide purpose is in its own nature beautiful." (*AI* 342.)

[39] *PR* 41.

of this calculus of self-interest? It is fairly clear that we do not, since we seem, at times, to grasp an immediate opportunity for pleasure at the expense of recognized future disadvantages of considerable seriousness. Is it, then, the momentary self that seeks its own satisfaction without regard to consequences? But clearly, that is also false, since we frequently work for future gratification. The fact is that we sometimes seize opportunities for present gratification without counting the cost, and sometimes make great sacrifices for the future.

The self-interest theorist may agree that in fact we are not wholly consistent as to the degree to which we take our own future into account, but he will insist that we take no other future into account except as it may be instrumental to our own. My point here is that although it may be impossible strictly to disprove this doctrine, it can be stripped of all its apparent plausibility. Is it in fact the case that I may sacrifice my present interest, genuinely sacrifice it, for the sake of a future ten or twenty years from now, and that it is impossible that I sacrifice my interest, just as genuinely, for the sake of my child's happiness a moment hence? This would be understandable if I had total imaginative identification with that future self and none at all with my child, but this is not my experience. And Whitehead shows that, despite the importance of personal identity through long spans of time, the relationship of my present occasion of experience to future occasions of my experience is not entirely unlike its relation to future occasions of other persons such as my child. The self-interest theory of ethics fits neither the facts of experience nor the metaphysical view of Whitehead.

Whitehead stresses that every occasion aims at intensity of feeling not only for itself but for the *relevant* future. The whole question hinges on what is relevant. I have argued that to suppose all my own future experiences relevant and no other future experiences relevant is to be guilty of a highly nonempirical dogmatism. The factual situation seems to be that we differ widely as to what future appears relevant to us. In some moments we may actualize ourselves with reference only to a very limited future, quite possibly limited to future occasions of our own experience. At other times, we may reckon with a very extensive future involving many persons besides ourselves.

Whitehead suggests that morality always has to do with taking into account the larger rather than the more limited future.[40] The tendency of the moralist is always to insist upon the wider horizons where individuals tend to relapse into narrower ones. There is a real tension here, comparable in some respects to the tension between the achievement of a simple harmony immediately and the adventurous acceptance of disharmony now for stronger beauty later. However, we are now focusing attention upon the question of who shall enjoy the stronger beauty. Do we adventure only for our own sakes, for the sake of those closest to us, or can humanity as a whole enter into our vision? A typical passage from Whitehead will show how he deals with these questions.

" Morality of outlook is inseparably conjoined with generality of outlook. The antithesis between the general good and the individual interest can be abolished only when the individual is such that its interest is the general good, thus exemplifying the loss of the minor intensities in order to find them again with finer composition in a wider sweep of interest." [41]

This quotation is typical because it shows us Whitehead pointing to that ideal which transcends tensions otherwise irresolvable. Just as in the discussion of beauty we say that the tension between the ideals of perfect harmony and strength might war with one another except as they attain synthesis in the ideal, so here the aim at immediate intensity of feeling and the aim at intensity limitlessly beyond itself can attain synthesis only in an occasion with such concern for the general good that it finds its greatest

[40] *AI* 346, 371, 375–376.   [41] *PR* 23.

beauty in its enjoyment of its contribution to that good. At every point short of this ideal, there will be some inevitable tension between immediate enjoyment, a proximate future, and the vaster reaches of the future beyond our vivid imagination.

This tension, however, does not amount to a simple opposition. Only an occasion that enjoys considerable strength can make a valuable contribution to the future.[42] Further, the sense of making a contribution beyond itself belongs to the satisfaction of the occasion and adds to its strength of beauty.[43] The attempt to serve the future by negating the present is self-defeating, just as is the effort to ignore the future in order to achieve fuller beauty in the present.

The proper and necessary concern to encourage behavior in terms of the wider generality of outlook leads to the formulation of concrete principles of behavior in codes. These codes have great social importance, but unfortunately they are typically treated as if they possess authority beyond that of their utility.[44] They are presented as if in their detailed formulations they place an ethical demand upon all persons in all situations. For this reason, progress and enlightenment inevitably discredit them.

There are many appropriate ideals of beauty at which cultures may strive; hence, concrete codes of behavior designed to facilitate the attainment of such beauty vary widely.[45] Each has its value in its season, but no particular moral principles at this level of specificity can transcend the relativity of historical circumstance. Hence, morals as generally conceived are irremediably relative.[46]

At a much more abstract level, it is possible to formulate universal principles. Whitehead proposes two. " These are the principles of the generality of harmony, and of the importance of the individual." [47] Once again, even here, we find a tension, for Whitehead sees that the first leads to the impersonal pursuit of order and the second to the

[42] *AI* 377.   [44] *AI* 374.   [46] *MT* 20.
[43] *AI* 346.   [45] *AI* 374–377.   [47] *AI* 376.

love of individual persons. But again he has a solution in the ideal. " The antithesis is solved by rating types of order in relative importance according to their success in magnifying the individual actualities, that is to say, in promoting strength of experience." [48]

Here we have Whitehead's culminating suggestion for the evaluation of moral codes. That code is best which promotes that kind of order which promotes maximum attainment in the strength of beauty enjoyed by individuals. Presumably these individuals include subhuman individuals as well, but the overwhelmingly important individuals are human persons. Each man finds ideal intensity of experience for himself as he makes his aim the attainment of just such an order. Meanwhile, at the finite and imperfect level at which life is lived, tensions remain.

4. AN ETHICAL THEORY

I find Whitehead's discussion of value, including moral value, eminently satisfying. However, there is a range of ethical questions on which he throws only indirect light. In this section, therefore, I will present the outline of an ethical theory, formulated in terms that are harmonious with Whitehead's expressed views, reaching conclusions similar to his, but supplementing his work by treating questions neglected by him.

Whitehead's genuine concern for morality causes him to give attention to moral values and ultimate ideals. But human decision-making, despite its concern for such questions, must focus concretely on the choice between present alternatives in the particular moment. That this is so is sharply emphasized by Whitehead's philosophy in which all decision and all reality is focused in the individual occasion of experience,[49] but he does not approach ethical inquiry from the perspective of the individual faced by such choices and asking the ethical question: " What ought I to do? "

[48] *AI* 376. [49] *PR* 254.

In our day, reflection on this question has peculiar urgency because of the widespread charge that no answer to the question can have cognitive meaning. According to this view, the answer, " You ought so to act as to maximize strength of beauty," would be without cognitive import even if there were prior acceptance of Whitehead's theory of value. The question could still be asked, " Why should one seek to maximize such value, if at the moment he prefers to act in some other way? " Indeed, it is objected that the word " ought " can have only an expressive force such that sentences containing it in a prescriptive way are not statements at all.

I believe the noncognitivists are correct at this level. Distinctively ethical assertions do not directly communicate factual information, and where such communication is taken as the essential characteristic of statements, ethical assertions are not, as such, statements. This, however, in no way detracts from their importance or from their status as correct or incorrect. The threat to their seriousness arises only when the noncognitivist makes a further charge, namely, that ethical assertions are not uniquely warranted by statements. This would mean that, given any total state of affairs, mutually contradictory ethical assertions might have equal warrant. If that be so, ethical assertions must ultimately be arbitrary expressions of irrational feeling rather than the highly reflective and uniquely prescriptive assertions they claim to be.

Our first question is, then, whether there is or can be any particular kind of factual statement that tends uniquely to warrant ethical assertions. Light will be thrown upon this question if we consider what the word " ought " expresses. For this purpose we turn to Whitehead.

The word " ought " seems to express a sense of obligation. In Whiteheadian terms a sense of obligation must be a subjective form. A subjective form always clothes the prehension of some entity. In this case the entity must be some imagined conduct or act. If I feel that I ought to do something, that means that my sense of obligation attaches to my idea of myself as performing that act. This " idea " is in Whitehead's terminology a proposition.[50] The prehension of this kind of proposition is an " imaginative feeling." [51] The sense of obligation is the subjective form of an imaginative feeling of a proposition of which one's future self is the logical subject and a possible mode of behavior is the predicate.

That this subjective form of imaginative feelings occurs in most normal adults in our culture is not widely disputed. There can certainly be meaningful discourse about it. I may affirm that I entertain a particular imaginative proposition with the subjective form of obligation. This would itself be a statement, that is, the affirmation of a proposition, and it would be either true or false. If the truth of this statement warrants the further assertion, " I ought to actualize that proposition," then we have found the solution of the problem. Ethical assertions would be uniquely warranted by factual statements about the subjective form of the prehensions of imaginative propositions.

But this is not the case. It is not self-evident that the fact that my sense of obligation is the subjective form of the feeling of a proposition warrants the assertion that I ought to actualize that proposition. On the contrary, I may decide that the reason I feel I ought to act in that way is that I was conditioned in childhood to have such feelings and that in fact quite a different kind of act is called for. For example, I may find that my feeling of obligation attaches to the maintenance of segregation because I was brought up to feel that way, and I may now believe that I ought to act contrary to that feeling.

We may note repeatedly in our own experience that with regard to many of our ethical feelings, intellectual understanding as to how we came to have them weakens their hold on us. We see, perhaps, that our society has conditioned us to view an act as abhorrent which we now

---

[50] See above, p. 106.   [51] *PR* 399 ff.

realize need not appear objectionable at all. The feeling does not disappear at once. We continue to find that our sense of obligation tends to attach to the avoidance of this kind of act, but the attachment weakens, and we regard it as objectively erroneous because adventitious.

However, the fact that many of our moral feelings are weakened by increasing self-understanding does not prove that this is the case with all. There may be some, the strength of which is unaffected by critical analysis of their sources. If there are such, we speak of them as inescapable. If in any given situation there is some mode of behavior that I believe to be inescapably qualified, in my imaginative feeling of it, by the sense of obligation, then the judgment that I ought to act in the manner in question is undeniable. My judgment that I ought to act that way would be warranted by the correctness of my belief that the sense of obligation inescapably functions in the subjective form of that imaginative feeling. It is unwarranted if my sense of obligation actually attaches to that mode of behavior only adventitiously.

The decisive questions for personal ethics are, then, as follows. First, are there any possible modes of behavior the subjective form of the imaginative feeling of which inescapably includes the sense of obligation? Second, if so, what are they? If the answer to the first question is no, then we may say that no judgment of the form, " I ought to act in a certain way," is warranted. Insofar as men are persuaded that this is the case, we may safely predict that the sense of obligation will play a role of decreasing importance.

Before attempting to determine any point at which I personally find an inescapability of attachment of my sense of obligation to possible modes of behavior, we must recognize that most ethical assertions are more pretentious than those thus far discussed. Often I assert that everyone ought to act in a certain way, or simply that that way of acting is right without qualification. Indeed, my conviction that I ought to act in a certain way often seems dependent on my view that it is right without qualification. The fact that others seem sincerely to disagree with my judgment poses a problem for me.

If the assertion that a certain act is right, or that everyone ought to act in that way, is warranted with regard to any type of act, then clearly the assertion, " I ought to act in that way," is also warranted. However, the converse is not the case. Hence, we will begin by considering candidates for universal normative principles. Such principles are assertions about what is right for men generally. They are warranted by statements about the inescapable inclusion of the sense of obligation in the subjective forms of their imaginative feelings of certain possible modes of behavior.

When we pose the question in these terms, we find that among all those who have written on the subject of ethics, there seems to be agreement that in some sense men ought to be rational or reasonable. This agreement cannot be dismissed as the mere bias of philosophers for it is certainly reflected in common morality as well. Even the apparent exceptions, such as Nietzsche, are not really such, for despite the glorification of an immorality which, in some respects, is regarded as irrationality, his call for the superman is an appeal to true reason against the false reasoning of the philosophic schools and the churches. Kierkegaard and other religious thinkers may point to life that is beyond moral obligation, but they do not dispute the reality of moral obligation. Still more obviously, the noncognitivists who deny the meaningfulness of ethical assertions seem continuously to presuppose that we ought to be reasonable in our treatment of their suggestions. Whenever a person is fully convinced that his moral judgment is thoroughly reasonable, we may assume that he is unlikely to feel the need of further justification. Indeed, morality is virtually synonymous with rationality of action.

The question is whether any univocal meaning can be

assigned to " rational " or " reasonable " when applied to action. Clearly, it has meant many different things. For some, it has been identical with calculating prudence; for some, with calculating benevolence; for some, with un-calculating acceptance of intrinsically rational principles; for some, with a method of solving problems of conduct. All these positions and others have profound appeal which should not be minimized or ignored simply because of their apparent conflict.

The most elementary level of rationality in conduct seems to be suggested by the idea of prudence. If I am contemplating an immediately pleasant action which will have extremely deleterious results for me in the future, I feel that I ought not to perform that action. If I ask my-self whether, on fuller reflection about my reason for feel-ing this way, my sense of obligation may cease to attach itself to the nonperformance of the action in question, I incline strongly to the negative view, and I find it diffi-cult to believe that at this point other rational beings differ from me.

It may be objected that my sense of obligation has noth-ing to do with the matter. I deny this, but it is true that probably upon reflection I would *prefer* to avoid doing my future self harm, quite apart from my moral scruples. The sense of obligation is not *clearly* operative except when it *conflicts* with preference or is determined apart from it. But let us suppose that the appeal of the pleasure is very great indeed, that I *want* to shut my eyes to the consequences and plunge blindly in, that I do not *want* to reflect, since reflection might weaken desires that I do not want to have weakened. Surely temptation does present itself in that form not infrequently. In such circumstances, is it not clear that my sense of obligation continues to attach itself to the path that would be dictated by reflec-tion, whether or not its doing so determines the final de-cision? When I willfully refuse to reflect or to be influ-enced by the fruits of reflection, I am surely aware that

I do wrong, that is, my sense of obligation inescapably attaches to the course of action that I am not pursuing.

A second objection may be that there are persons who do not recognize any obligation to consider consequences. Some, of exceedingly low intellectual capacity, lack both adequate imagination with respect to the future and a clear sense of cause and effect. Others, of highest sophistication, reject all evaluation or determine to live only for the moment. To all such persons, future consequences appear irrelevant to present decision, and there is no purely ethical basis on which we can say they ought to consider them.

This objection would have force if we wished to affirm that everyone should consider a given range of consequences in reaching a decision, for the specification of that range would inevitably be arbitrary. However, this is not the present intention. We wish only to affirm that everyone ought to consider whatever seems to him to be relevant to his decision. In the extreme case in which nothing seems relevant, one is not required to consider anything. This objection, therefore, clarifies, but does not conflict with, the principle, which may now be formulated.

In reaching a decision, one ought to give full consideration to whatever available knowledge and experience appears to him to be relevant. This universal normative judgment is warranted by the following statement formulated in Whiteheadian terms. When one endeavors to reach a decision, the sense of obligation is inescapably included in the subjective form of the imaginative feeling of oneself giving full consideration to whatever knowledge and experience appear relevant. Negatively, the principle means that one should never willfully exclude consideration of available knowledge or experience that he sees as relevant.

The application of this principle is extremely flexible, depending upon all sorts of opinions about the world, man, and God. If one believes, for example, that an ever-watchful God severely punishes violation of laws he has arbitrarily proclaimed, one may avoid many actions that others would regard as harmless or even morally desirable. In addition, the application of the principle depends upon personal temperament. A warmhearted, tender nature will consider consequences to others, whether man or beast, far more fully than a person whose sympathies are extremely limited. Thus, both intellectual and emotional development will affect the application of this principle. Moral growth is understandable even at this level, therefore, not only in terms of improving obedience to the principle but also in terms of superior maturity in its application.

However, it seems that moral growth or maturity also tends to introduce a new principle. I have argued that the principle stated above is universal, recognizing its irrelevance to those who regard no knowledge or experience as relevant to reaching decisions. From this point on, however, a selective process must be acknowledged to be at work. These more advanced principles are probably incipiently present from an early stage in development, but it may be that ordinary social life can exist in which they are not clearly operative. Yet there does seem to be some ability to recognize their legitimacy when they are propounded to those at lower levels of development, and once they have been understood and appropriated, the process can be reversed only by a tour de force.

The first important jump is to the view that relevant data should be considered *impartially* or *disinterestedly*. The difference between this and the first principle is greater than might at first appear. The first principle asserted only that consequences should be considered. Presumably they are considered in the light of existing interests. If I hate a person and further knowledge gained about him is not likely to change my attitude toward him, the first principle provides no ground for avoiding his injury so long as it will not adversely affect other interests of mine. I am here taking myself as the point from which everything is to be viewed. Bad consequences to those toward whom I am indifferent remain irrelevant to me.

Now, however, I am asserting as a second-level ethical principle that there is a higher point of view than my own, and that when I have reached a certain level of development, I inescapably recognize it as more " rational " and therefore also more moral. I recognize that I ought to consider consequences to others in the same way as I consider consequences to myself.

The third level in the hierarchy of moral principles is also the last. In a sense, it completes our circle and opens again the question of what ought we to do. The first two principles only specify that we ought to use our reason in certain ways in arriving at a decision. The third tells us that having used our reason comprehensively and disinterestedly, we still must not fall back upon our preference, but must act according to our duty. What we finally *ought* to do on full disinterested consideration is not necessarily what we will *in fact* do. It is finally what full disinterested consideration leads us to recognize that we *ought* to do.

The third principle may be stated as follows: Every morally developed person ought always to act as he inescapably sees he ought to act on full disinterested consideration of all available knowledge and experience which appear to him to be relevant. This normative judgment is warranted by the following statement: In a morally developed person, the sense of obligation is inescapably included in the subjective form of the imaginative feeling of himself acting as he inescapably sees he ought to act on full disinterested consideration of all available knowledge and experience which appear to him to be relevant.

It cannot be emphasized too strongly that despite the apparent redundancy or circularity of this formulation, a new element of utmost importance is here introduced. Previously, we have only noted, first, that willful refusal to consider matters recognized as relevant to a decision is inescapably felt as wrong, and, second, that at a more advanced level of moral development, the refusal to acknowledge any higher point of view from which to consider such matters is felt as wrong. But if one does consider all these matters, then what? Then one acts as such consideration leads him to desire to act. This may be quite differently from the way he would have acted if he had remained willfully ignorant. But is it possible still to raise the question of moral rightness?

My desire to injure another person may be overcome by considering impartially his interests as well as mine. But it may not. Having thought quite disinterestedly about all that is involved, I may yet decide to hurt him. Clearly, there is a separate question involved when we say, " Ought I to hurt the person? " Hence, clearly it is possible to ask the question, " To what formal principles of action does our sense of obligation inescapably attach when we think disinterestedly, except, reflexively, to disinterested thinking? "

Once the principle of disinterestedness is accepted, this extension is not likely to meet much resistance. It is fairly obvious that although disinterestedness of thought is morally important, it should lead to disinterestedness of act. Hence, we must again ask the question " To what principle of action does our sense of obligation attach on full disinterested consideration of all relevant factors? " I believe there are two answers.

First, the sense of obligation is brought by full disinterested consideration of all relevant factors to support that action which will increase intrinsic value. We will assume here the understanding of intrinsic value as strength of beauty developed above.[52] We can now define intrinsic value as that which is, in fact, preferred on full disinterested consideration, thus providing a clearer basis for evaluation of the theory of value there developed.

But second, the sense of obligation is influenced by factors other than the anticipated consequences of the action.

[52] See above, sec. 2.

It is affected by appropriateness to the past as well as by future results. For example, the sense of obligation does not unquestioningly attach to the breaking of a solemn promise simply because the results of breaking the promise would appear to be slightly better than the results of keeping it. On the contrary, our prior acts place us in a position of responsibility, a position in which others have rightful claims upon us. Whatever acts we have given others the right to expect of us, we are under some obligation to carry out.

It seems impossible to subsume either of these answers under the other. Yet in view of the tensions between them, some resolution is required. In seeking such a resolution, we may turn for help to the ethics of Kant. He introduces the principle of disinterestedness at still another point which is important for our analysis of ethics. He says that we should so act that we can will that the maxim by which we act become a universal rule. That is, we should not make an exception in our case to a rule we want others to follow.

Kant tries to argue that our inability to will the universality of a maxim is formal, that is, dependent upon some logical self-contradiction. However, this is not necessarily implied by the principle itself. We may be unable to will that this maxim be followed by all because such action would lead to consequences we cannot approve. Thus, we are told that even if the particular consequences likely to follow from our act (let us say, breaking a promise) are consequences that we disinterestedly prefer, we must consider also what the consequences would be if everyone broke promises whenever they judged the consequences preferable. This would give us pause, for such behavior would disrupt the fabric of society.

Kant's application of his principle was so extreme that he has had few followers. He interprets the maxim of acts in such a general way as to prohibit many that seem quite justifiable to ordinary moral consciousness. For example, he forbids lying even under the most extreme circumstances because we cannot will that everyone lie when it is to his advantage to do so. But can we not will that everyone lie when lying would protect the lives of innocent friends from an insane criminal? Surely nothing in the categorical imperative as such forbids this.

Chiefly the categorical imperative in Kant's examples forbids action directed toward one's own advantage over against obedience to principles. Our first rule above already rejected purely selfish action. Action ought to be directed according to its contribution toward the greatest good. We have turned to Kant because our ethic of consequences did not seem to account for some of our inescapable moral judgments. Hence, we may interpret Kant's principle quite differently. The point is that we may judge according to it whether we ought to achieve a better consequence by breaking a promise, by asking whether we would regard it as desirable that regularly when the scales are balanced in a certain way all persons should break a promise of a certain solemnity in order to achieve an advantage of a certain magnitude. Clearly in this way of viewing the situation, the promise-breaking must weigh much more heavily than in a pure ethic of consequences, for the ideal to which I look forward will not include easy promise-breaking as a part. Yet it will not preclude promise-breaking if the advantage is quite great, for example, if a child's life is at stake. Indeed, I believe that this principle will explain the characteristic judgments of the morally sensitive person.

The final ethical principle may then be formulated as follows: An ethically developed man ought to act in that way in which he would will, on full consideration of all relevant factors, that all men should act, given just these relevant factors. Once again we can see that this principle is warranted by the factual statement that in ethically developed men the sense of obligation is inescapably included in the subjective form of the imaginative feeling of that mode of behavior.

By a circuitous route we have returned to a point very close to that to which a consideration of Whitehead's discussion of moral values also brought us. There we concluded that " that [moral] code is best which promotes that kind of order which promotes maximum attainment in the strength of beauty enjoyed by individuals." [53] Conformity to that moral code and obedience to the ethical principle at which the analysis in this section arrives should coincide.

5. DUTY, LOVE, AND THE INITIAL AIM

Probably one reason Whitehead did not carry out the kind of analysis I have offered in the preceding section is that he felt some distaste for the overrigorous pursuit of righteousness. There is a profound paradox in man's ethical experience. Man ought always to do the right. Yet the life lived in the constant effort to achieve this ideal, even to the extent of its success, ends in failure. It is right to live in terms of that kind of order the generalization of which will produce the greatest strength of beauty in individual lives. Yet the strenuous effort to live in just that way leads to a certain rigidity, insensitivity, and pride that militate against the achievement of beauty both in oneself and in others. We can never rightly reject the ethical principle of disinterestedness in reflection and action, for it is the very essence of rightness of conduct. Yet we must look for some way of transcending it, or of including it in a higher synthesis.

In this connection Whitehead points us to love, which is, he says, " a little oblivious to morals." Unlike morality, " it does not look to the future; for it finds its own reward in the immediate present." [54] Beyond suggestive hints such as this, Whitehead does not elaborate the fascinating and difficult question of the relation of love and ethics. We must pursue the discussion a little further, guided only

[53] See above, p. 113. [54] *PR* 521.

indirectly by his statements.

Love and ethics are in real tension with each other, but they cannot be regarded as contradictory. Love is of utmost importance for ethics. Only as there is love of one's own future self and love also for other persons, and finally, for humanity as a whole, can there be any meaning to the ethical imperatives. Yet the ethical imperatives always transcend the actual love felt, demanding a recognition of the appropriateness of love, and hence, of action appropriate to love, far beyond the existing capacities of personal and imaginative concern. To reject ethics in the name of love, meaning by that, love actualized and not love owed, will in almost every case narrow the horizons of action and dismiss from relevance the enemy, the stranger, and even the long-absent friend.

Furthermore, love is unjust. We love, and always will love, some more than others. We constantly, and rightly, must check our love in the interest of fairness. If love as normal human concern dominates our lives, all too often it will be ourselves who are its object, and the long and tortuous process, whereby ethical thought and feeling have led us beyond preoccupation with ourselves, may be undone.

Furthermore, many of the decisions we make in life, and must make, are far too impersonal to be facilitated or motivated by love. Whitehead points out that the beauty of the idealism of the New Testament ethic depended in part upon the fact that those who affirmed it originally had no responsibility for the stability and preservation of the society to which they belonged. They could propound demands expressive of pure love and even in some measure embody them, whereas if the responsible leaders of that society had followed them, all order would have collapsed.[55]

We cannot solve the tensions between righteousness and love simply by subordinating the former to the latter. But at the same time, we cannot solve them by subordinating love to righteousness. We cannot advance beauty in the

[55] *AI* 19–21.

world by loving only when we ought to love and because we ought to do so. Perhaps we can increase love by dutifully nurturing it, but the finest flowering of love depends upon spontaneity as well. We do not want people to love us only out of a sense of duty.

Without the spontaneity of love, beauty loses its strength. We can become brittle, resentful of the spontaneities of others, self-righteous. We can become incapable of genuinely contributing to the beauty of other lives, no matter how hard and dutifully we try. We will be compelled by our very sense of duty to seek to cultivate the spontaneity our dutifulness has caused to wither.

Duty and love, then, require each other and yet exist in tension with each other. In this respect, they are like the aim at immediate intensity and at intensities beyond oneself, or like the achievement of a simpler harmony and the adventure toward another ideal. We cannot do without either, yet they seem constantly to threaten each other. As in the other cases, I suggest that Whitehead would have us accept this situation as that in which we must live while viewing an ideal beyond us in which the tensions are resolved. That ideal must be a limitless love for man as man, or even for life as life, personalized to every individual, yet impartial among all. In such a love, duty would be fulfilled.

There is another direction in which Whiteheadian philosophy allows us to look for the resolution of the tension between duty and love. Freedom, we have noted, lies in the individual occasion's modification of its own subjective aim.[56] All the discussion of value, duty, and love as directive of human behavior must finally focus on how we can and should reflectively modify our aims or purposes. As conscious persons we can alter the balance between the aim at immediate intensity and the aim at the relevant future; we can broaden or narrow that future; we can introduce principles and codes of conduct to which we commit ourselves.

[56] See above, p. 96.

Much of this discussion has been taken from Whitehead, and I believe that none of it is contradictory to his intention. Yet Whitehead might tell us that we try too hard, that we are too insistent on lifting our purposes into consciousness and examining them, that such tensions as those between love and duty reflect the frustrations of a life that strives for too much autonomy. This is a speculation, but it is a speculation justified and required by Whitehead's metaphysics.

The subjective aim originates at the outset of each new occasion. Indeed, it determines the perspective from which that occasion will prehend the past. In this originative stage it is called the initial aim. In this form the aim is given to the occasion, it is not created or chosen by it. The initial aim of subsequent occasions in the living person will be affected in part by the way in which earlier occasions have modified their aims, but it includes also an element of autonomy.

The initial aim is always the aim at that ideal harmony possible for that occasion.[57] It is an aim at a balance between the intensity of that occasion's experience and its contribution beyond itself. When we are dealing with occasions in societies, such as a vegetable, it is clear that the aim is far more directed to the health of the society as a whole than to any immediate realization of intensity in the individual occasion. Occasions in " empty space " may have little aim beyond their own trivial enjoyment. In both these occasions, the capacity for modification of the aim by the decision of the occasion in question, though real, would be negligible.

In the human occasion the range of freedom is far greater. Also the balance between immediate intensity and the effect upon the future must be far more flexible. Yet according to the metaphysical principle, every human occasion is initiated by an aim at that harmony that is the ideal possibility for that occasion. Sometimes the situation

[57] *PR* 128, 381.

may be such that the best possibility is still evil.[58] But there can be no better choice.

If this is so, then there must be open to man an attitude quite different from the drive for rational self-determination which we have been considering so far. There must also be open to man a way of life in which each moment is taken as it comes, in terms of the new possibilities it affords, and in which something given to man, something over which he has no control, is trusted for guidance in the realization of these possibilities. Now immediate enjoyment, now sacrifice for the future; now duty, now love; such alternations might characterize roughly the quality of self-actualization in successive moments. But the tensions between these alternatives might be resolved at a level beyond man's power of decision.

In other words, there may, after all, be some reason to trust conscience, intuition, or instinct. Each of these terms has its dangerous connotations. We know that interiorized parental commands or fear of consequences may be called conscience. Ideas may be intuited as true, purely on the basis of the pleasure they provide or their satisfaction of some compulsive need. Instinct may be the wisdom of the body rather than of the soul. Even in these senses conscience, intuition, and instinct often prove good guides, but these should not be confused with the initial aim. The initial aim is not received from society or other persons, from one's own past or from the body. It is that new thing which in conjunction with the whole force of the past initiates the process in which a new occasion comes to be. Since we are speaking of a new occasion of human experience, the initial aim is proper to that. It determines fundamentally the direction in which that occasion of human experience will actualize itself. And within that direction it constitutes an urge toward the highest available ideal.[59]

[58] PR 373.
[59] For much fuller discussion of the initial aim, see below, pp. 151 ff.

One could draw from this doctrine the conclusion that man should adopt in his volitional life a maximally passive attitude. Since the initial aim is at the best possible fulfillment beyond man's powers to understand, and since man's exercise of freedom seems only to lead to a deviation away from this ideal possibility, there is some prima facie support for this view. However, it does not express Whitehead's own attitude toward life, and it does not follow from more careful reflection on the metaphysical situation.

The initial aim is always at some intensity of feeling. The higher intensities of feeling require consciousness. Beyond consciousness there is self-awareness, and with self-awareness there comes the awareness of freedom. The movement of man in this direction, long before he could exercise control over his own development, is the effect of the initial aim of his own occasion of experience combined with those in all the occasions making up his body. In a still wider context, we see that it has taken billions of years for this kind of consciousness to come into existence.

If this is so, then the initial aim must often be at that kind of self-actualization which accepts responsibility for itself and for its world. The exercise of those dimensions of freedom at which the initial aim aims cannot be contrary to that aim. The greatest intensity of experience may often be dependent upon the greatest efforts at self-modification.

But the fact that we may be called to such heroic self-determination in some occasions of our life does not mean that we may not at other times be called to a more relaxed acceptance of circumstances as they develop or to a spontaneous love arising quite unforeseen and beyond the bounds of duty. Perhaps it is possible to achieve such sensitivity, unconscious though it must certainly be, that we can hear and heed these changing dictates by which the direction of our lives is given to us.

6. PEACE

Just as within the context of Whitehead's philosophy one can and must go beyond righteousness as the ultimate norm for conduct, so also one can and must go beyond beauty and strength of beauty as the ultimate value. On this subject Whitehead himself leads the way and we will only follow. The supreme value that transcends beauty without setting it aside, he calls " peace." [60] Inevitably in his discussion of peace he points beyond the readily conceptualizable and gropes to express dimmer but more powerful feelings and needs of the human soul. For this reason, here more than elsewhere, I urge the reader to turn to Whitehead's own formulation.[61]

Whitehead gives no single clear definition of peace. Instead, by describing it in many ways, he tries to evoke in the reader the sense of that to which he refers. Peace is " that Harmony of Harmonies which calms destructive turbulence and completes civilization." " It is a positive feeling which crowns the ' life and motion ' of the soul." It " carries with it a surpassing of personality." " It is primarily a trust in the efficacy of Beauty." [62]

Perhaps we can best grasp what Whitehead is saying if we ask ourselves what need we have to go beyond beauty. In answering this question, I will not follow Whitehead closely, but I believe that I will be expressing at least one side of his concern and sensitivity.

The problem with beauty is that it fades. Consider the most intense of harmonious experiences. It occurs, and it passes. To some degree it can be remembered and memory gives poignant pleasure. But in time it will be beyond any conscious recall. Yet such moments are the supreme goal of life; there can be nothing beyond them, more valuable or more ultimate.

In this situation the quest for beauty and its preservation must be intense. Beauty must be achieved again and

[60] *AI* 367.   [61] *AI* Ch. XX.   [62] *AI* 367.

again. Otherwise, its past achievement is worthless. A certain ruthlessness seems to become inevitable, a need for experience after experience, each of which in turn passes into oblivion. Perhaps a certain cynicism may arise, the sense that, after all, such achievements are not worth the effort. Since beauty and discord alike fade away, it does not seem to matter which occurs. One may alternate between a harsh quest for more and better beauty and a resigned indifference leading to nihilism.

If beauty is to be sought without ruthlessness, and if it is to be enjoyed without the poignant doubt of its worth, there must be an intuition that the worth of beauty exceeds its momentary enjoyment, that its attainment is self-justifying beyond the ability of reason to grasp its value.[63] But this must mean that our private experience has value beyond itself and beyond our subsequent memories of it, that it contributes something to the whole of things, that it participates in some wider totality and shares in some larger harmony.

Whitehead's deepest sensitivity here is that purely personal enjoyment, his own or someone else's, closed in upon itself, cannot satisfy the ultimate hungers of the human soul. The value one seeks must finally be more than the passing sum of human attainments. Otherwise, the restlessness of the soul is not quenched. Peace is the sense that indeed there are aims in the universe beyond our own and that our aims can be harmonious with them and contribute to them. It is the sense that what we attain is taken up into that larger whole and preserved in harmony with all the other achievements of value.

"The experience of Peace," Whitehead tells us, "is largely beyond the control of purpose. It comes as a gift. The deliberate aim at Peace very easily passes into its bastard substitute, Anaesthesia." [64] The aim at peace leads to anaesthesia, because it leads to the curtailing of experience in the avoidance of disruption. But peace is not at all a limitation but rather an openness of experience. In-

[63] *AI* 367–368.   [64] *AI* 368.

terest is "transferred to coordinations wider than personality" and thereby " self " is lost.[65]

The truth of what is known in the gift of peace cannot be proved. Philosophy in general must limit itself to an account of what is given in ordinary human experience. There is no logical process by which we can move from this common experience to the demonstration of the ultimate harmony of the universe. But there are exceptional experiences which stand out from ordinary experience.[66] From these experiences arise those direct intuitions which give us peace.

Here, we are on the threshold of religion, or more accurately, well across the threshold. The discussion of peace cannot finally be separated from the discussion of God, and that discussion I have systematically omitted from these chapters on man. We can note here, however, that what is altogether beyond evidence from ordinary modes of experience is not the reality of God in general but that particular mode of relatedness to him which gives rise to peace. Peace is not a function of particular cognitive beliefs more or less intensely held; it is a direct apprehension of one's relatedness with that factor in the universe which is divine. It is for this reason, and not because of a general introduction of the doctrine of God, that Whitehead appeals in these passages to the special and privileged experience.

It is time now to turn directly to a consideration of Whitehead's doctrine of God. It arises out of philosophical necessity and is only slightly affected, as in the discussion of peace, by special religious insight or need. Hence, in the subsequent chapters it will be discussed chiefly in philosophical terms, that is, in terms of what is given to us in ordinary experience and its rational interpretation. Only afterward [67] will we return to the discussion of religious experience to see what light the understanding of

---

[65] *AI* 368.
[66] *AI* 379. See also *RM* 29–32; *PR* 521.
[67] See below, Ch. VI, sec. 2.

man and God throws upon the religiously important relations between them. In these discussions it will become clearer what Whitehead means by peace and especially what metaphysical beliefs support it and are in turn sustained by it.[68]

[68] See below, pp. 221 ff.

IV

Whitehead's Doctrine of God

1. "SCIENCE AND THE MODERN WORLD"

Nathaniel Lawrence [1] and William Hammerschmidt [2] agree in distinguishing three periods in Whitehead's philosophical development, dated according to the publication of his books. In the early period, down to 1922, Whitehead was preoccupied with mathematics, logic, and philosophy of science. The only published indications of a wider humanistic interest in this period are a few essays on education. Even these tend to emphasize the role of mathematics and science. In the philosophy of nature developed in the closing years of this period, Whitehead attempted systematically to exclude the knower from nature and to show that nature can be coherently understood without reference to any contribution on the part of the perceiver. The ultimate philosophical problem of the relation of the knower to the world of nature, he says, is left undetermined by his philosophy of nature. [3] Nevertheless, his work of that period left many readers with the impression that nature and its structures are ontologically autonomous and also that the knower may be understood as a part of nature.

In the transitional period from 1925 through 1927

[1] Lawrence, *Whitehead's Philosophical Development,* p. xix.
[2] Hammerschmidt, *Whitehead's Philosophy of Time,* p. 7.
[3] *PNK* vii.

Whitehead was working toward a comprehensive vision. He introduced the knower into the world of nature.[4] The knower, the percipient event, provides the clue to nature in general. The result is a position quite different from both the idealism and the naturalism current at that time, or indeed at any time. This new vision, of idealistic naturalism or naturalistic idealism, is given its full exposition in the final period.

In the transitional period, Whitehead published three major books. They are *Science and the Modern World, Religion in the Making,* and *Symbolism, Its Meaning and Effect.* The two most important works of the final period are *Process and Reality* and *Adventures of Ideas.* Of these five books, by far the most significant for the study of his doctrine of God are *Science and the Modern World, Religion in the Making,* and *Process and Reality.* Although they were all published within the period 1925 to 1929, still there are significant developments in the thought expressed, and these have special importance with respect to the doctrine of God. In this chapter, I propose to summarize Whitehead's thought about God as it develops in these three books.

Science and the Modern World is based largely on the Lowell Institute Lectures delivered in February, 1925.[5] In these lectures as delivered, there was little to suggest that Whitehead was on the verge of devoting serious attention to the development of a doctrine of God. There were historical references to ideas of God and one passage dealing with the appeal to God on the part of thinkers who required him for the solution of the problem of the order of nature. Of this appeal he was very critical. " My point is that any summary conclusion jumping from our conviction of the existence of such an order of nature to the easy

---

[4] I have called attention to Whitehead's lack of terminological consistency on this point. See above, pp. 60–61. However, there is no substantive problem.

[5] *SMW* x.

assumption that there is an ultimate reality which, in some unexplained way, is to be appealed to for the removal of the perplexity, constitutes the great refusal of rationality to assert its rights." [6] By itself this suggests a highly negative attitude toward the project of introducing God as an explanatory principle into philosophy. However, in the light of his later work, the slight qualification he makes here is highly significant. " In a sense all explanation must end in an ultimate arbitrariness. My demand is, that the ultimate arbitrariness of matter of fact from which our formulation starts should disclose the same general principles of reality, which we dimly discern as stretching away into regions beyond our explicit powers of discernment." [7]

One other passage in the lectures points more positively toward his later doctrine of God, although in it the word " God " does not occur. " The underlying activity, as conceived apart from the fact of realisation, has three types of envisagement. These are: first, the envisagement of eternal objects; secondly, the envisagement of possibilities of value in respect to the synthesis of eternal objects; and lastly, the envisagement of the actual matter of fact which must enter into the total situation which is achievable by the addition of the future. But in abstraction from actuality, the eternal activity is divorced from value." [8]

This passage is difficult to interpret in its context because of the obscurity of the notion of envisagement. The substantial activity here called the underlying and eternal activity Whitehead associates with Spinoza's " one infinite substance," [9] and value he identifies with the occurrence of actuality for itself as opposed to its effects on others.[10] The passage seems to say that the ultimate metaphysical reality that underlies and expresses itself in every concrete occurrence of actuality or value " envisages " possibilities both in pure abstraction and in their relevance for actual entities, as well as " envisaging " the actual entities them-

6 *SMW* 134–135.   8 *SMW* 154–155.   10 *SMW* 136.
7 *SMW* 135.   9 *SMW* 181, 255.

selves. Perhaps " envisaging " means no more than taking account of. Certainly the anthropomorphic connotation is not intended, since value or actuality is specifically denied to the envisager.

Before Whitehead wrote the preface to the book in June of the same year, he had written the chapters on " Abstraction " and " God " that constitute his first systematic excursion into what he understood as metaphysics. Metaphysics he defined as " a dispassionate consideration of the nature of things, antecedently to any special investigation into their details." [11] In the chapter on " Abstraction," Whitehead analyzes the way in which eternal objects are together with each other quite apart from their involvement in events. He affirms that they have both an individual essence and a relational essence.[12] The individual essence is simply what that possibility for actualization is in itself, in abstraction from its relations with all other possibilities. The relational essence is the necessary interconnectedness that all eternal objects have with each other. By virtue of the relational essence of every eternal object, each actual entity in which an eternal object is ingredient is also related to all the other eternal objects. But in terms of their individual essences only a selection of eternal objects ingresses into each actual occasion.

The general realm of eternal objects expresses innumerable possibilities for actualization that are incompatible with our present world order. Whitehead writes: " The spatio-temporal relationship, in terms of which the actual course of events is to be expressed, is nothing else than a selective limitation within the general systematic relationships among eternal objects. By ' limitation,' as applied to the spatio-temporal continuum, I mean those matter-of-fact determinations — such as the three dimensions of space, and the four dimensions of the spatio-temporal continuum — which are inherent in the actual course of

[11] *SMW* 227.   [12] *SMW* 229–230.

events, but which present themselves as arbitrary in respect to a more abstract possibility. The consideration of these general limitations at the base of actual things, as distinct from the limitations peculiar to each actual occasion will be more fully resumed in the chapter on ' God.' " [13] This is the first explicit indication in Whitehead's writings that there is a place for " God " in his system.

The chapter on God begins by noting that Aristotle, the greatest of metaphysicians, introduced God into his system without reference to any religious influences.[14] Whitehead also intends in this chapter to be moved only by metaphysical considerations. To this end, he reviews the metaphysical situation to which the discussion of abstraction, along with the book as a whole, has led him. For this purpose he adopts a terminology borrowed from the philosophy of Spinoza.

First, Whitehead agrees with Spinoza that there is some one ultimate reality actualizing itself in all the entities we can know or think. In this sense there is substance. But in Whitehead's view this substance is not a static entity undergoing change. It is, rather, itself the active ongoingness of things. To suggest both his agreement and disagreement with Spinoza in his ultimate monism, Whitehead affirms substantial activity as the ultimate reality at the base of things.[15] What this means is that the occurrence of events, the sheer fact that something happens, is not itself accidental and is not subject to explanation by anything beyond itself.

Substantial activity, as such, is totally formless and neutral with respect to form. Yet it cannot occur except in some definite way. The analysis of the world in the preceding chapters of *Science and the Modern World* has showed that all definite entities can be analyzed into actual entities and eternal objects. This means that substantial activity necessarily adopts these forms which are then de-

---

[13] *SMW* 232.   [14] *SMW* 249.   [15] *SMW* 254–255.

clared, in accordance with Spinozistic terminology, to be its attributes. *In concreto,* substantial activity is given only in actual entities which are called its modes.[16]

Whitehead now confronts another problem. Both substantial activity and the realm of pure possibility are entirely neutral with respect to what kinds of actual entities shall occur: for example, as to the number of dimensions they shall have. Yet with vast regularity myriads of actual entities are actualized in terms of a four-dimensional space-time continuum. How is it to be explained that what is entirely indeterminate in terms of the metaphysical principles thus far recognized is in fact, in the world we know, quite determinate? Whitehead is convinced that honesty requires us to posit an additional metaphysical principle which functions to provide the requisite determination. This metaphysical principle he calls the principle of determination,[17] of concretion,[18] or of limitation,[19] and he regards this principle as a third attribute of substantial activity alongside eternal objects and actual entities.[20]

But the question of the number of dimensions is only illustrative of a larger issue.[21] Whitehead's explanation in *Science and the Modern World* of the respects in which the principle of limitation limits the actual entities and of how this limitation is effected is extremely brief. Partly as a result of this brevity I find myself unsure on a number of points as to how it is to be understood. For this reason, I quote the decisive passage in full before attempting any exegesis, so that the reader may check my suggestions against Whitehead's statements.

" In its nature each mode is limited, so as not to be other modes. But, beyond these limitations of particulars, the general modal individualisation is limited in two ways: In the first place it is an actual course of events, which might be otherwise so far as concerns eternal possibility, but *is* that course. This limitation takes three forms, (i) the spe-

---

[16] *SMW* 255. [18] *SMW* 250. [20] *SMW* 255–257.
[17] *SMW* 257. [19] *SMW* 256. [21] *SMW* 256–257.

cial logical relations which all events must conform to, (ii) the selection of relationships to which the events do conform, and (iii) the particularity which infects the course even within those general relationships of logic and causation. Thus this first limitation is a limitation of antecedent selection. So far as the general metaphysical situation is concerned, there might have been an indiscriminate modal pluralism apart from logical or other limitation. But there could not then have been these modes, for each mode represents a synthesis of actualities which are limited to conform to a standard. We here come to the second way of limitation. Restriction is the price of value. There cannot be value without antecedent standards of value, to discriminate the acceptance or rejection of what is before the envisaging mode of activity. Thus there is an antecedent limitation among values, introducing contraries, grades, and oppositions." [22]

My difficulty with this passage is that I am not clear how sharply to distinguish the limitations that are required for the process as such from the limitations required for the emergence of values. In the light of other writings, it is difficult to see these as clearly distinct. Further, it is difficult to know whether all the three forms of limitation taken as needed for the process to occur are equally dependent on the principle of limitation. In the light of other writings, the influence of past occasions and the self-determination of the new occasion seem to contribute much of the limitation referred to under (ii) and (iii).

However, much is clear that is only reinforced by later writings. An actual entity cannot come into being apart from antecedent limitations. The actual entity cannot settle for itself the logical or cosmological relations to which it will conform. If this is not predetermined for it, it can have no basis for entering into those relations with the past apart from which it cannot occur at all. Further, in view of the fact that we now recognize every type of order

[22] *SMW* 255–256.

as contingent, we must assign the occurrence of one type of order rather than another, not to the metaphysical situation as such, but to a decision which, from the metaphysical standpoint, is arbitrary.[23] Here again the example of the number of dimensions will suffice to clarify the meaning. This decision cannot be a function of the substantial activity as such, of the eternal objects, or of the actual entities. Hence, we must posit the principle of limitation as an additional metaphysical factor.

It is also clear in this passage that Whitehead sees that such determination of the metaphysically indeterminate as is effected by individual actual entities must depend upon the aim at some value. The actual entity could make no selection of what to aim at if there were not some givenness about the value. This givenness presupposes some antecedent evaluation or ordering of values. For this ordering, likewise, the principle of limitation is required.

If Whitehead had left the situation at that point, it is doubtful that much controversy would have been raised. Some would have dismissed the whole discussion on the assumption that it is meaningless because it is metaphysical. But if we allow metaphysics at all, the introduction of a third attribute of the underlying substantial activity would have seemed a normal way to round out the system.

Whitehead, however, did not leave matters thus. He went on to call the principle of limitation or concretion "God," and to declare that, in fact, it has been the object of man's worship in all religions.[24] This means both that his argument for the existence of the third attribute of the substantial activity is an argument for the existence of God and that the God of religion is not the metaphysical ultimate or absolute, since he is only one of three attributes of the substantial activity. For the first half of this consequence of his doctrine, Whitehead has never been forgiven by those who believe that sophisticated thought has once

[23] *SMW* 257.   [24] *SMW* 257. Cf. *PR* 47.

and for all learned to do without God.[25] For the second half, he has earned the rejection of most theologians.[26]

From the perspective of traditional Western theism the identification of God with anything less than the ultimate appears paradoxical. If the principle of limitation is an attribute of substantial activity, then it would seem that substantial activity should be called God rather than one of its attributes. Whitehead invites comparison of the substantial activity with Spinoza's one infinite substance, and in Spinoza it is that substance which is called God — certainly not one of its attributes.

Whitehead's reason for rejecting this alternative is that he is convinced that the object of authentic religious concern is characterized more decisively by goodness than by metaphysical ultimacy. If he is regarded as " the foundation of the metaphysical situation with its ultimate activity, . . . there can be no alternative except to discern in Him the origin of all evil as well as of all good. . . . If He be conceived as the supreme ground for limitation, it stands in His very nature to divide the Good from the Evil." [27] It will be our special concern in studying the further development of Whitehead's doctrine of God to see how he conceives God's relation to the underlying activity.

2. " RELIGION IN THE MAKING "

Whitehead recognized, in *Science and the Modern World*, that metaphysics alone could not go " far towards the production of a God available for religious purposes." [28] Certainly this applies to his own doctrine as there developed. But Whitehead also indicated that a metaphysical doctrine is " a first step without which no evidence on

[25] Lawrence reports the reactions of Russell, Stebbing, and Murphy, pp. 282–283.

[26] William Temple, *Nature, Man, and God* (Macmillan and Co., Ltd., London, 1934), p. 260. See also, E. L. Mascall, *He Who Is* (Longmans, Green & Co., Inc., 1943), pp. 150–160.

[27] *SMW* 258.

[28] *SMW* 249.

a narrower experiential basis can be of much avail." [29] Now that he had himself taken the first step, he noted, "What further can be known about God must be sought in the region of particular experiences, and therefore rests on an empirical basis." [30] This conviction on his part led quite naturally to the investigation of religion. This investigation of the evidence from religion combined with further metaphysical reflection provided the material for Whitehead's second series of Lowell Institute Lectures, delivered the next year, and published as *Religion in the Making*.

A slight but significant shift takes place in Whitehead's understanding of the relation of religion and metaphysics between the two books. In *Science and the Modern World*, metaphysics was to complete its work and thereby provide a first step in the knowledge of God to which additions could be made from religious experience. In *Religion in the Making*, however, Whitehead proposes that religion "contributes its own independent evidence which metaphysics must take account of in framing its description." [31] This change may be largely verbal, since metaphysics may here be conceived more broadly to include the whole of speculative philosophy,[32] but the emphasis is more on reciprocity and less on the dependence of religious knowledge on prior philosophical doctrine.

Nevertheless, most of what Whitehead tells us about God in *Religion in the Making* is primarily based on the further development of his philosophical thought. He does not import into his philosophy any doctrines that have emerged into dominance in particular religious traditions. For example, he devotes considerable attention to rejecting the view that religious experience provides a basis for affirming that God is personal.[33] He does affirm that re-

[29] *SMW* 250.
[30] *SMW* 257.
[31] *RM* 79.
[32] See the definition of metaphysics in the footnote, *RM* 84.
[33] *RM* 62–66.

ligion yields evidence " in favor of the concept of a rightness in things, partially conformed to and partially disregarded." [34] Religion also contributes " the recognition
that our existence is more than a succession of bare facts.
We live in a common world of mutual adjustment, of intelligible relations, of valuations, of zest after purposes, of
joy and grief, of interest concentrated on self, of interest
directed beyond self, of short-time and long-time failures
or successes, of different layers of feeling, of life-weariness
and of life-zest." [35] Whitehead proposes, then, that philosophy should take account of these dimensions of human
experience, but it does not appear that they should be par-
ticularly restrictive or prescriptive in the further development of the doctrine of God.

In the more purely philosophical sections of the book
Whitehead repeats, supplements, and alters the position he
stated in *Science and the Modern World*. The repetition
and supplementation is illustrated in the following passage: " The universe exhibits a creativity with infinite freedom, and a realm of forms with infinite possibilities;
but . . . this creativity and these forms are together im-
potent to achieve actuality apart from the completed ideal
harmony, which is God." [36] Fundamentally this is a simple
restatement of the argument in the earlier book. However,
at one point it suggests an element that was unspecified
there. God is a " completed ideal harmony." In other passages this is stated in a variety of ways. God is said to hold
" the ideal forms apart in equal, conceptual realization of
knowledge," — so that " as concepts, they are grasped together in the synthesis of omniscience." [37] God is a conceptual fusion of values, " embracing the concept of all
such possibilities graded in harmonious, relative subordi-
nation." [38] Thus, we find that the way in which God functions as the principle of limitation is by ordering the
infinite possibilities of the eternal objects according to prin-

[34] *RM* 66.   [36] *RM* 119–120.   [38] *RM* 157.
[35] *RM* 80.   [37] *RM* 153.

ciples of value. It is by the addition of this "ideal conceptual harmony"[39] to the other antecedent circumstances out of which a new entity arises that some measure of harmony and order is maintained in the universe. Otherwise there could be no actual world.[40] In these quotations we can see that the envisagement of the eternal objects, which was referred, in the first Lowell lectures, to the underlying substantial activity,[41] is here attributed to God. This envisagement is not something additional to his function as principle of limitation, but it explains how that principle operates.

In commenting earlier on the attribution of envisagement to the underlying activity, I noted that it could not be understood as having any of its usual anthropomorphic connotations. Since the underlying activity was regarded as not being actual, it was hard to understand what might be meant by its function of envisaging. Even if in the earlier book the envisaging had been attributed to God, the situation would not have been changed, since Whitehead wrote in *Science and the Modern World* that " God is not concrete "[42] and that certainly meant, not actual. However, in *Religion in the Making* a remarkable change has occurred without explanation. God is consistently referred to as an actual entity.[43] This is not a rejection of the view that he is the principle of concretion (or limitation) but the affirmation that it is an actual entity that performs the function of providing the limitations that make concretion possible. Hence, envisagement can be understood as a way in which an actual entity is conceptually related to ideal possibilities.

That God is an actual entity rather than a nonconcrete principle also allows for the attribution to him of many other characteristics which would have seemed out of place in the earlier book. Whitehead speaks of God as having

[39] *RM* 156.
[40] *RM* 104, 157.
[41] See above, p. 137.

[42] *SMW* 257.
[43] *RM* 90, 94, 98, 99, 152.

purpose,[44] knowledge,[45] vision,[46] wisdom,[47] consciousness,[48] and love.[49] This is remarkably personalistic language, and it is interesting to note that it all occurs in the more philosophical part of the book rather than where he is surveying the evidence of religious experience. There, as we noted, he insists that religious experience does not justify our speaking of God as person. He further criticizes the Semitic conception of God as personal creator of the world.[50] He even denies that religious experience provides adequate warrant for affirming the actuality of God, since " the Eastern Asiatic concept of an impersonal order to which the world conforms " is given equal status with other doctrines.[51] Apparently the basic reason for the change in tone and language is that the function of providing limitation to ensure order and value could be assigned only to an actual entity. Once God is regarded as an actual entity, the use of personalistic language follows naturally, for our basic clue to the nature of an actual entity is given in our own immediate human experience.[52]

God is, however, a very special type of actual entity. He is contrasted with all others by virtue of being " nontemporal." [53] " The definite determination which imposes ordered balance on the world requires an actual entity imposing its own unchanged consistency of character on every phase." [54] " He must include in himself a synthesis of the total universe. There is, therefore, in God's nature the aspect of the realm of forms as qualified by the world, and the aspect of the world as qualified by the forms. His completion, so that He is exempt from transition into something else, must mean that his nature remains self-consistent in relation to all change." [55]

[44] *RM* 100, 104, 158, 159.
[45] *RM* 154.
[46] *RM* 153.
[47] *RM* 160.
[48] *RM* 158.
[49] *RM* 158.
[50] *RM* 70–71.
[51] *RM* 68–69.
[52] See above, pp. 27–28.
[53] *RM* 90.
[54] *RM* 94.
[55] *RM* 98–99.

A problem arises when we press the nontemporality of God. Does God confront every new temporal entity with his ideal envisagement of value in just the same way? Would he confront them in the same way even in another cosmic epoch in which space-time were not a four-dimensional continuum but had three or five dimensions? If so, it is hard to see how, after all, he functions as the principle of limitation. That Whitehead seems to have recognized this is indicated by the following passage. Speaking of God, he writes:

" He is the binding element in the world. The consciousness which is individual in us, is universal in him: the love which is partial in us is all-embracing in him. Apart from him there could be no world, because there could be no adjustment of individuality. His purpose in the world is quality of attainment. His purpose is always embodied in the particular ideals relevant to the actual state of the world. Thus all attainment is immortal in that it fashions the actual ideals which are God in the world as it is now. Every act leaves the world with a deeper or a fainter impress of God. He then passes into his next relation to the world with enlarged, or diminished, presentation of ideal values." [56]

This passage also points to the final new element in the doctrine of God in this book. God is understood as being affected by the world. In an earlier quotation this relation was described as including " the aspect of the world as qualified by the forms." [57] The envisagement of the actual entities as well as of the eternal objects is now attributed to God rather than to the underlying substantial activity. There is interaction between God and the world. God makes possible order and value in the world, the world then acts upon God, and God's new relation to the world is affected. Thus, the general principle of the interaction of actual entities is applied to God who now appears as the supreme actual entity.

In *Science and the Modern World,* we encountered four

[56] *RM* 158–159.   [57] See above, p. 147.

metaphysical principles: the underlying substantial activity and its three attributes — eternal objects, actual entities, and the principle of limitation. In *Religion in the Making,* subtle but important changes have occurred in the understanding of these four elements in the philosophic system. First, the underlying substantial activity is now called creativity [58] and plays so minor a role in the analysis that it has barely been mentioned in the preceding account. This in itself might be a merely verbal change or a change of emphasis. But, in fact, it is much more than that. We are no longer invited to compare Whitehead's thought with that of Spinoza. We read no more of attributes and modes, and the tendency toward monism of the earlier book gives way to an emphatic pluralism of actual entities. Whereas substantial activity was that of which all the other three were attributes, creativity is accorded no such favored place. Complete interdependence of the four principles is stressed rather than the primacy of any one.[59] Second, since God is now conceived as an actual entity, we might consider the four metaphysical principles as reduced to three: creativity, eternal objects, and actual entities including God as a special case. If we do so, however, we have to remember that there is a major philosophical difference between God and the temporal actual entities.

After *Religion in the Making,* nothing really new is added to the doctrine of God. He is an actual entity who envisages and orders the realm of eternal possibilities. He adds himself to the world as the vision of ideal possibility, from which every new occasion takes its rise, thereby ensuring a measure of order and value in a situation that could otherwise be only chaotic and indeed could achieve no actuality at all. The world, in its turn, reacts upon him so as to affect the way in which he, in his turn, acts upon it. All the ingredients are here. But many questions remain unanswered. What finally is the relation of God to creativity? How does God make available to each occasion its appropriate ideal? What status have the eternal objects in

[58] *RM* 90.   [59] *RM* 90–93, 156–157.

relation to God's envisagement? How does the world in its turn act upon him? How can this be harmonized with the doctrine that God is nontemporal? These and other questions we can take with us to the greatest of Whitehead's philosophical writings, *Process and Reality.*

3. "PROCESS AND REALITY"

In 1927 and 1928, Whitehead gave the Gifford Lectures. This provided the occasion for what proved to be by far his most sustained analysis of philosophical questions. The focus of the Gifford Lectureship on natural theology rendered fully appropriate an expansion and enrichment of his previous work on the idea of God, although this remained a very small part of the total task he set himself. These lectures in expanded form were published in 1929 as *Process and Reality.*

In *Science and the Modern World,* we noted how Whitehead first criticized the introduction of God into philosophical systems and then himself introduced him. There was no strict contradiction. What Whitehead objected to there and again in later writings was not the introduction of God as an explanatory factor as such, but the failure to explain how God performs the requisite function.[60] Yet Whitehead's own treatment there is highly vulnerable to that criticism, and *Religion in the Making* does not entirely escape the same objection. In *Process and Reality,* the way God functions as the principle of limitation is extensively articulated for the first time.

Consider the situation as Whitehead sees it. The actual occasions of experience exist for a moment and then perish. As they perish, they obligate their successors to take some account of them. Then there are the unchanging possibilities for realization, the pure possibilities that Whitehead calls eternal objects. Finally, there is recognized as the underlying metaphysical principle of the universe the ultimate activity, the sheer ongoingness of na-

[60] *PR* 78, 219, 289; *FR* 24; *AI* 171.

ture, which Whitehead now calls creativity. No one of these factors singly and no combination of them can explain the concrete particularity of what in fact becomes. Unless we affirm that this concrete particularity is an illusion, we must acknowledge that another factor is working.[61]

From the richer analysis of *Process and Reality*, we may propose that the new occasions provide the principle of their own limitation and definiteness.[62] It is the nature of each actual occasion to have a subjective aim at a determinate satisfaction. It prehends both the eternal objects and the temporal entities in its past in terms of this aim, and in successive phases of its own becoming it fashions a new creative synthesis which is itself.

The question must now be pressed a step further. How does the new subjective aim occur? Can the occasion for whose definiteness it is responsible be viewed as producing this aim out of nothing? Even if that could be meaningfully affirmed, we would still have to reckon with the randomness of its choice. Any occasion might select any aim and it might select any locus or standpoint in the extensive continuum. Order could only be sheer chance. But, in fact, the actual occasions that constitute our bodies are constantly aiming at satisfactions directed to the healthy functioning of our bodies as a whole. Some limitation is imposed upon the selection of aim by actual occasions.

The self-determination of just what an occasion shall aim to become operates within limits set for it in its initial phase. The initial phase of the subjective aim of an occasion Whitehead often calls simply the initial aim.[63] This aim is given to the occasion to determine its limits by the principle of limitation which transcends every temporal occasion and which Whitehead calls God. By analyzing the initial aim, first in terms of how it functions in the becoming occasion and then in terms of how it is derived from God, we will be able to understand much more clearly

[61] *SMW* 256–257.   [62] *PR* 75, 343, 390.   [63] See above, p. 96.

how God works in the world.

In ordinary language when we speak of man's aim in life or in a particular act, we sometimes mean a pure possibility he strives to actualize. For example, an artist may have as his aim a certain type of beauty. At other times we mean by the man's aim the *actualization* of a possibility. In our example this would mean the actualization of that type of beauty in a painting or piece of sculpture. At still other times, we mean by a man's aim the act of aiming, which would be the artist's purposeful desire to achieve the goal in question. Usually we intend all three of these meanings and have no need to discriminate them, since in fact they cannot be separated in the moment in which the aim (in any of these senses) is effective.

The same ambiguity can be found in Whitehead's usage. He writes of the initial aim, sometimes with the eternal object as such primarily in view, sometimes with a focus upon the satisfaction aimed at, and sometimes as the act of aiming at the actualization of the possibility in that satisfaction. Again, no serious confusion need result, for the eternal object can constitute the aim only when an occasion is actively aiming at its realization; the satisfaction aimed at is always the actualization of some determinate possibility (eternal object) ; and the act of aiming is always directed toward such an actualization. The focus of attention in these pages will be upon the act of aiming itself.

In the first place, the initial aim so understood determines what locus or standpoint will be occupied by each occasion.[64] This, in turn, determines just what occasions will constitute the past of the new occasion.[65] Although these features of the functioning of the initial aim are not stressed by Whitehead, they have considerable systematic importance for understanding the relation of God to the occurrence of new occasions. Hence, some explanation is necessary even at the price of a short excursus.

The spatiotemporal continuum is, in fact, always ac-

[64] *PR* 195, 434.   [65] *PR* 435–436.

tualized in a particular way. That is, every actual entity occupies a quite definite region which is its standpoint. But when we turn from the settled past to the future, we find that the continuum as such tells no tales as to how it shall be atomized.[66] The actual standpoints to be realized may be large or small and may have a variety of shapes. Any given region may be divided in an infinite number of ways, just as there is no limit to the number of ways in which a sheet of paper can be divided by lines drawn upon it.

If we ask how this infinitely divisible continuum comes to be divided precisely as it does so that there is a plenum of occasions, we cannot answer in terms of the efficacy of the past. Occasions now perished cannot settle just what regions shall become the standpoints of their successors. Further, one cannot appeal here to the self-determination of the occasion. The occasion that determines itself does so in terms of a perspective which is already settled for it. This settlement is given in the initial aim of the new occasion.[67]

It is important to emphasize that the determination of the exact locus and extent of each occasion affects not only its internal development but also its relations with other occasions. Specifically, it determines exactly which of these occasions will be contiguous to it and, of these, which will be contemporary and which past. Thus, by determining the standpoint of each occasion, God determines also just what other occasions it will prehend.[68]

In the second place, the initial aim also determines at what kind of satisfaction the occasion will initially aim and thereby influences, without determining, the satisfaction

[66] *PR* 104–105.

[67] *PR* 104, 195, 434.

[68] *PR* 435–436. This passage is exceedingly confusing, since it seems to attribute this determination to the self-determination of the occasion. But when read in conjunction with p. 434, this interpretation is excluded.

actually attained. What kind of satisfaction the initial aim is directed toward is determined by the relevant possibility for its actualization, as established by its past, that will give it the greatest intensity of feeling and also contribute maximally to the future of the nexus of which it is a part.

Whitehead writes of the initial aim both that it is always at the best possible actualization, given that situation,[69] and that it includes indeterminations awaiting determination by the occasion itself in subsequent phases of its inner development.[70] These statements appear to be in some tension with each other. If the initial aim is at the best possibility, must it not be quite specific and must not its development in subsequent phases be a deviation away from this specific ideal? On the other hand, if the initial aim is indeterminate, how can it be directed toward the ideal?

The solution is found in Whitehead's idea of graded relevance.[71] Some particular possibility must be ideal, given the situation. But closely related to this possibility are others, appropriate to the situation although deviating from the ideal. The initial aim thus involves the envisagement of a set of related and relevant possibilities from among which the final satisfaction of the occasion will in fact be chosen. These are all bounded by the definite limits required for the maintenance of minimal order. Yet they allow for so large a measure of self-determination that higher levels of order are subject to destruction by occasions that reject the ideal possibilities they confront in favor of others of lesser value. Whitehead shows here the sensitive balance between the freedom and the determinism of the cosmos, and how order is sustained and enhanced while constantly threatened by the possibility of decay.

The initial aim of each occasion is derived from God.[72] It is in this way that God plays his exceedingly important role as the principle of limitation. At this point, we shall

---

[69] PR 134–135, 195, 373.
[70] PR 74, 342–343, 375.
[71] PR 248. See also PR 315, 425, 522.
[72] PR 104, 343, 373, 527.

turn our attention from the question of how the initial aim functions within the actual occasion to the question of how God functions in providing the initial aim to each occasion.

Already in the earlier books it is clear that God functions as principle of limitation by ordering the eternal objects. If these existed simply as an indifferent multiplicity, there would be no basis for selection, hence no limits, no definiteness, no order. God provides limits by ordering this indefinite multiplicity. But this account remains vague and leaves many questions unanswered. In *Process and Reality,* the account is carried much farther, although substantial uncertainties remain.

Whitehead gives us two principles on the basis of which any further speculation must move. First, he tells us that God's ordering of the eternal objects is primordial, and that in a sense which clearly means eternally unchanging.[73] Indeed, this timeless envisagement of possibilities constitutes God's primordial nature. Second, the ordering is such as to specify the initial aim for each new occasion.[74] These principles appear at first to be in some tension with each other. If there is some one eternal ordering of possibilities, it would seem that there is only one mode of order possible for the universe. But Whitehead writes of other cosmic epochs in which completely different modes of order will prevail.[75] Also, it is extremely difficult to see how one unchanging order can provide a specific and novel aim to every new occasion.

The solution seems to be that the eternal ordering of the eternal objects is not one simple order but an indefinite variety of orders.[76] God's ordering of possibilities is such that every possible state of the actual world is already envisioned as possible and every possible development from

---

[73] *PR* 46, 523–524.

[74] *PR* 74, 343, 373, 527.

[75] *PR* 139, 148, 171.

[76] I propose this as a solution to the problem Christian solves by denying any eternal ordering. See Christian, pp. 271–277.

that actual state of the world is already envisioned and appraised. Thus, the one primordial ordering of eternal objects is relevant to every actuality with perfect specificity.[77] God's ordering of the eternal objects has particularized efficacy that takes account of every detail of the actual situation, but this does not mean that God successively produces a new ordering as each new occasion arises.

The question remains as to how a particular eternal object or set of eternal objects becomes effective in a novel occasion as that at whose realization it aims. We see that God's primordial nature so orders the eternal objects that one such possibility is indeed from eternity identified as the ideal given that situation. But how does the actual occasion become privy to that fact? Whitehead tells us little more than that the initial aim is derived from God. However, a further explanation is suggested. In its less debatable aspects it will be introduced here. A fuller account of my own attempt to understand this problem in Whiteheadian terms is reserved for the next chapter.[78]

Whitehead speaks of God as having, like all actual entities, an aim at intensity of feeling.[79] In terms of the developed value theory of *Adventures of Ideas,* we may say his aim is at strength of beauty.[80] This aim is primordial and unchanging, and it determines the primordial ordering of eternal objects. But if this eternal ordering is to have specified efficacy for each new occasion, then the general aim by which it is determined must be specified to each occasion. That is, God must entertain for each new occasion the aim for its ideal satisfaction. Such an aim is the feeling of a proposition of which the novel occasion is the logical subject and the appropriate eternal object is the predicate. The subjective form of the propositional feeling is appetition, that is, the desire for its realization.

If God entertains such a propositional feeling, we may conjecture that the new occasion prehends God in terms of this propositional feeling about itself and does so with a

77 Cf. PR 134.   79 PR 160–161.
78 See below, pp. 179–185.   80 See above, Ch. III, sec. 2.

subjective form of appetition conformal to that of God.[81] If so, the initial phase of the subjective aim is also the feeling of a proposition of which the occasion itself is the logical subject and the appropriate eternal object the predicate. The subjective form of this propositional feeling, like that of God from which it is derived, is appetition.[82]

In the preceding paragraphs I have gone a little beyond the confines of description of Whitehead's account in *Process and Reality* in the direction of systematization. Such systematization involves interpretation, and one interpretation can always be countered by another. What is clearly stated by Whitehead is that the initial aim is derived from God's ordering of the eternal objects and that this aim limits the range within which the occasion can find its satisfaction. We have seen in the preceding chapter that this limitation does not constitute a strict determination.[83] Each occasion has a final voice in its determination. But it is by this initial aim that the general order of the universe is sustained, and likewise all the more special societies that constitute our world.

In the formulation of the problem of limitation we followed *Science and the Modern World* in speaking of four ultimates: actual entities, eternal objects, substantial activity, and God. In *Religion in the Making*, temporal occasions and God were identified as both being actual entities sharing a common ontological status. In explanation of this shift from treating God as a " principle " to treating him as an actual entity, I noted that Whitehead must have recognized that only something actual could perform the role of the principle of limitation. The underlying assumption is made clear in *Process and Reality*, where it is called the ontological principle. This principle states " that every condition to which the process of becoming conforms in any particular instance, has its reason *either* in the charac-

---

[81] *PR* 37.

[82] For further development of this interpretation, see below, Ch. V, sec. 1.

[83] See above, pp. 95–97.

ter of some actual entity in the actual world of that concrescence, *or* in the character of the subject which is in process of concrescence." [84] This means that apart from actual entities there can be nothing that is effective, nothing that acts or has an influence.[85] Since God must be effective, otherwise he could not be the principle of limitation, he must be an actual entity.

In *Process and Reality,* however, it becomes clear that the ontological principle also affects the status of the eternal objects.[86] They too must be effective. Indeed, the principle of limitation operates only by their graded effectiveness for new occasions. If they were not the reason for anything, there would have been no cause to introduce them into the system at all. But certainly eternal objects are not actual entities. They were distinguished from actual entities by their indifference to actualization, by their ability to be actualized indefinitely without in any way being modified in the process. They do not come to be and perish; they remain eternally what they are.

If eternal objects are effective in the becoming of actual occasions, it must be by virtue of some agency beyond themselves. That agency can only be God. It now becomes clear that God's envisagement of the eternal objects is necessary, not only to secure definiteness of outcome in nature but to secure any agency whatsoever for them. Eternal objects can affect the course of events only through their envisagement by God. Thus God is not only the principle of limitation but the principle of potentiality as well. Apart from their envisagement by God, Whitehead writes, eternal objects are a bare multiplicity " indistinguishable from nonentity." [87]

---

[84] *PR* 36.

[85] *PR* 254.

[86] *PR* 73.

[87] *PR* 392. Note also *PR* 46: " Apart from God, eternal objects unrealized in the actual world would be relatively non-existent for the concrescence in question."

This doctrine of God's envisagement of the eternal objects as the basis of their effective relevance to the world may seem strange to nominalistic ears. A further discussion of the problem to which this doctrine is an answer may help.

Whitehead defines an eternal object as " any entity whose conceptual recognition does not involve a necessary reference to any definite actual entities of the temporal world." [88] By this definition there can be little doubt that there are eternal objects. We do think of colors, shapes, and even qualities of feeling, not only as qualifications of particular actual entities but also apart from such qualification. We may think about the relation of two colors, for example, or of a color and a quality of feeling without any reference to particular actualizations. Still more obviously, we can think about geometrical shapes and arithmetic relations without any such reference. Whitehead as a mathematician was especially conscious of the very important role played by thought of this kind, but even common speech bears ample witness to the fact that ideas need not have concrete reference.

Now the question arises, When we think about eternal objects, what is happening? Is something objective to ourselves present to our minds? If so, what is it? The common answer is that these are *mere* abstractions. But that is to beg the question. What are abstractions? Are they anything at all? If they are simply nothing, then it would be impossible to think about them, hence they must be something. Perhaps they are subjective ideas and exist only in the subject entertaining them. The problem with this solution is that when I think of triangularity I do not seem to be thinking of my idea of triangularity but of a structure the properties of which may far exceed my knowledge. Whitehead agrees with Plato that these forms are objective to thought and determinative of it rather than produced by the thinking process.

[88] *PR* 70.

On the other hand, Whitehead disagrees with the tendency in Plato to assign privileged ontological status to these abstractions.[89] They exist objective to us and are effective upon us, but it is only as they are actualized in our experience that they achieve full actuality. Apart from this, they are only potentials.

Now Whitehead confronts the problem as to where such potentiality can be.[90] That it exists is empirically proven by its effectiveness in experience. But how can what is merely potential have an effect upon what is actual? If it is totally separated from actuality, it cannot have any effective status. Only what is actual can act. This is where Whitehead's nominalism triumphs. Abstractions can't *do* anything. Yet the eternal objects *do* something. Hence they must participate in some way in actuality. But their effectiveness in the temporal world is not dependent on their prior actualization there. If it were, there could never be any novelty of any kind. Hence the only possible answer is that the eternal objects participate in God's actuality. In Whitehead's terms, they are " envisaged " by him.[91]

The general doctrine of God developed in *Process and Reality* was implicit in *Religion in the Making,* but at two points substantive changes have occurred. First, whereas in *Religion in the Making,* Whitehead specifically stated that God's relation to the eternal objects is not different from that of the other actual entities,[92] in *Process and Reality,* Whitehead shows that the eternal objects constitute a realm only by virtue of God's envisagement of them. God's relation to the eternal objects is prior to and presupposed by that of all other entities.

Second, the ordering of the eternal objects in relation to the new occasion is seen as essential not only for their aim at a value compatible with the order of the universe but also for all realization of novelty.[93] It is only by virtue of God's ordering of the eternal objects that one conceptual

[89] *Imm* 687.   [91] *PR* 50.   [93] *PR* 377, 382, 529.
[90] *PR* 73.   [92] *RM* 157.

feeling, conformal to that of a past temporal actual occasion, can give rise to a new conceptual feeling of an eternal object not present in the prehended occasion. Apart from God, there could be no novelty in the world. Whitehead says that this is a secular function of God, not relevant to religious experience.[94] In any case, it constitutes a further argument for the necessity of God's existence.

The discussion has thus far focused upon what Whitehead calls the primordial nature of God. This is God as the principle of limitation and the organ of novelty who achieves these ends by his ordered envisagement of the realm of eternal objects. This is the only way God was conceived in *Science and the Modern World.* It is the primary emphasis in *Religion in the Making* and in the first 522 pages of *Process and Reality.*[95] However, in *Religion in the Making* and in scattered passages in *Process and Reality* there is another theme. Alongside the description of God as the primordial actual entity are passages about the effect of the temporal occasions upon God. For example, in *Religion in the Making,* Whitehead described God as " the ideal companion who transmutes what has been lost into a living fact within his own nature." [96] Now in the closing pages of *Process and Reality,* Whitehead returns to this theme of what he now calls the consequent nature of God.[97]

In the discussion of the primordial nature of God, even though Whitehead sees importance for religion, philosophical considerations alone are relevant. The survey of religious experience in *Religion in the Making* serves chiefly to reinforce the philosophical conclusions. In the discussion of the consequent nature, on the other hand, it is clear that philosophical and religious concerns are interrelated in Whitehead's presentation. Here, however, we will focus on the philosophical.

The consequent nature of God is God's physical pole, his prehension of the actual occasions constituting the tem-

---

[94] *PR* 315–316.   [95] *PR* 523.   [96] *RM* 154–155.   [97] *PR* 523–533.

poral world. Since these occasions come to be successively, there is a successiveness in the divine nature that suggests temporality. However, the perpetual perishing that constitutes the temporality of the world is absent to God. Hence, God in his consequent nature is called everlasting.[98]

God's prehension of the temporal occasions objectifies them with a completeness necessarily lacking in such prehensions within the temporal world. Furthermore, since there is no perishing in God, that completeness remains forever. This means that every achievement of value in the temporal world is preserved everlastingly in God's consequent nature. This sense of the preservation of values in God's memory was of great religious importance to Whitehead. Partly for this reason, some of his expressions of this preservation seem to suggest an element that the philosophical position in general does not clearly imply. That element is the living immediacy of the occasions as preserved in God.[99] The more normal assumption would be that just as in temporal experience only that which is past is prehended, so also in God's experience temporal occasions are prehended only as they perish. They could no longer enjoy subjective immediacy. It is reasonable to suppose that God's prehension would be far more inclusive of the elements in the satisfaction of the prehended occasions, but the subjective immediacy of the occasion is not one of those elements.

Perhaps Whitehead himself never meant that the occasions preserved in God retained their own immediacy.[100] The relevant passages can be read to mean that the values attained continue everlastingly to contribute to the living immediacy of God's experience. If he did mean to affirm that in God's consequent nature temporal occasions retain their own subjective immediacy, then considerable speculative development would be required to explain it. This

---

[98] PR 524–525.
[99] PR 524 f., 527, 530–532.
[100] Cf. Christian, pp. 340–342.

would involve making an exception in God's case from the general, but not categorial, principle that contemporaries do not prehend each other. It may be argued that if human occasions of experience prehend God, and they do, they must prehend him as a contemporary, since God as actual entity is contemporary with all other occasions. This might mean, then, that God also prehends temporal occasions in their contemporaneity, and therefore shares the immediacy of every becoming occasion. If so, then this immediacy would be retained forever in God's consequent nature.[101]

Whitehead does not quite say that God's prehension of the world includes the world completely. The general philosophical principle is that every becoming occasion objectifies every past occasion in some way. Hence, in its application to God this would mean that some aspect of every occasion is retained everlastingly in God. Of course, Whitehead means more than this. Even temporal occasions are able to reenact certain past occasions with some fullness. It is natural to assume that in God's case the limitations imposed by men's spatiotemporal perspectives disappear. But there remains even for God the necessity of harmonious integration of all the data in a unified satisfaction. Hence Whitehead writes, of the consequent nature of God, that " it is the judgment of a tenderness which loses nothing that can be saved." [102] It abstracts from the evil in the world while retaining the positive values contained even in experiences of evil.

Another important feature of God's consequent nature is that it is conscious.[103] Whitehead does not explain this, but from his general discussion of consciousness the reason can readily be learned. God in his primordial nature alone

[101] The change I propose in Ch. V, sec. 2, from thinking of God as an actual entity to thinking of him as a living person reduces the force of this speculation.
[102] PR 525.
[103] PR 524.

has no consciousness because this nature consists in purely conceptual feelings, and such feelings are never conscious.[104] Consciousness requires the interweaving of the physical feelings with conceptual feelings. This involves God's prehension of the world, his consequent nature.

A final feature of the consequent nature of God is barely treated in the last two paragraphs of the book. Like most of the rest of the ideas about God in *Process and Reality*, it was foreshadowed in *Religion in the Making*. It is demanded by the principle of universal relativity that just as God in his consequent nature prehends us, so also we prehend God's consequent nature. This prepares the way for Whitehead's final summary of the interactions between God and the world. " There are thus four creative phases in which the universe accomplishes its actuality. There is first the phase of conceptual origination, deficient in actuality, but infinite in its adjustment of valuation. Secondly, there is the temporal phase of physical origination, with its multiplicity of actualities. In this phase, full actuality is attained; but there is deficiency in the solidarity of individuals with each other. This phase derives its determinate conditions from the first phase. Thirdly, there is the phase of perfected actuality, in which the many are one everlastingly, without the qualification of any loss either of individual identity or of completeness of unity. In everlastingness, immediacy is reconciled with objective immortality. This phase derives the conditions of its being from the two antecedent phases. In the fourth phase, the creative action completes itself. For the perfected actuality passes back into the temporal world, and qualifies this world so that each temporal actuality includes it as an immediate fact of relevant experience." [105]

In this completed doctrine of God, Whitehead had come a long way from the first introduction of the principle of limitation as one of the three attributes of substantial activity. His warning in *Science and the Modern World* that

[104] *PR* 521.   [105] *PR* 532.

metaphysics could not go far toward presenting an idea of God available for religion is less obviously relevant to the later formulations of the philosophical doctrine. Nevertheless, Whitehead emphasizes what he sees as the great difference between his doctrine and traditional theological formulations. He especially repudiates the doctrines of God as the unmoved mover and as eminent reality.[106] He rejects the attribution to God of any characteristics that make him an exception to the scheme of categories by which all other actual entities are understood.[107] He insists that God and the world each presuppose and require the other, so that neither temporal nor ontological priority can be assigned to either.

The attack upon traditional Western theism is especially clear in Whitehead's famous antitheses:

" It is as true to say that God is permanent and the World fluent, as that the World is permanent and God is fluent.

" It is as true to say that God is one and the World many, as that the World is one and God many.

" It is as true to say that, in comparison with the World, God is actual eminently, as that, in comparison with God, the World is actual eminently.

" It is as true to say that the World is immanent in God, as that God is immanent in the World.

" It is as true to say that God transcends the World, as that the World transcends God.

" It is as true to say that God creates the World, as that the World creates God." [108]

Lest any reader should suppose that he finally abandoned his rationalism in his attempt to state the relations of God and the world, Whitehead states immediately preceding this passage that " in each antithesis there is a shift of meaning which converts the opposition into a contrast." [109] Furthermore, immediately after the passage, he proceeds to explain how the antitheses are to be understood in the

[106] *PR* 519.   [107] *PR* 521.   [108] *PR* 528.   [109] *PR* 528.

light of the differences between the two natures of God. The main point is to underscore the contrast of the implications of his philosophy with the traditional doctrines that have insisted only on the permanence, unity, eminent actuality, transcendence, and creative power of God. All of these he affirms, but only in polar tension with other factors usually negated of God.[110]

I have written, and Whitehead sometimes writes, as though there were no philosophical reason for affirming the consequent nature of God other than the demand of a coherent completion of the idea of God as actual entity. This is not quite true. There are two points in *Process and Reality* at which he seems to give independent philosophical arguments for the existence of the consequent nature of God. The two arguments are closely related in character, and both affirm the need that there be a perspective in which what is sheer multiplicity from any temporal point of view has unity. In the first instance, Whitehead is discussing the claim of his own thought to approximate to truth. What can this mean? We all sense that there is some structure to which our formulations more or less adequately approximate. But if we are trying to speak of reality as a whole, where is this structure? Whitehead answers that it can only be in the consequent nature of God. Otherwise we would have only a multiplicity of finite and distorting perspectives that could afford no standard.[111]

The second argument is more obscure. It runs like this. The initial data of a complex feeling constitute a single nexus that has a pattern. But this pattern is not prehended by the members of the nexus. Is the pattern then imposed upon the nexus by the prehending occasion? Whitehead thinks not. When we perceive a pattern, we perceive something that is given to us, not something we create. But if it

[110] The dipolar understanding of God has been brilliantly and thoroughly expounded by Hartshorne in such books as *Man's Vision of God, The Divine Relativity,* and *Philosophers Speak of God.*
[111] *PR* 18–19.

is given to us and is not in the data prehended, it can only be in the consequent nature of God.[112]

A third argument can be derived from Whitehead's thought by implication. The evidence for it is less clearly found in *Process and Reality* than in *Religion in the Making,* yet it seems to be present in the philosophy of Whitehead in such a way that this third argument is really more fundamental than the two just summarized. If God is understood to provide different initial aims to each occasion, and in each case just that aim that is ideally suited to it, then God seems, in the provision of the initial aim, to be taking account of the world in all its change. This effect of the world upon God is an essential part of the process whereby God functions as the principle of limitation.

Whatever weight we may attach to these arguments, Whitehead's own thought placed the burden of the argument for God's existence upon the necessity of a principle of limitation. Further, he associated this principle with the primordial nature of God. Hence in his presentation, the consequent nature of God appears more as a speculative extension of the doctrine than as an essential part. My own position on this point will be developed in the next chapter.[113]

Even where Whitehead has in view his doctrine of God as actual entity, including both a primordial and a consequent nature, there is occasional recurrence in *Process and Reality* of a note largely absent from *Religion in the Making.* There are several passages in which God seems once again, as in *Science and the Modern World,* to be definitely subordinated to creativity. For example, even in the last pages, from which much of this discussion of God is taken, he writes: " Neither God, nor the World, reaches static completion. Both are in the grip of the ultimate metaphysical ground, the creative advance into novelty." [114] Elsewhere in the book he writes of God as, like every actual entity, " a creature transcended by the creativity which it

112 *PR* 352–353.   113 Ch. V, sec. 1.   114 *PR* 529.

qualifies," [115] and even as the " primordial, non-temporal accident " of creativity.[116] Just what Whitehead is to be understood as meaning by this language, and more important, what his systematic position requires that these expressions mean, we will consider later.[117] Here they are reported for purposes of providing, somewhat comprehensively, the evidence the book gives as to his sensitivity and intention. Clearly he retained throughout his life the sense that the ultimate fact is the process itself of which God, the eternal objects, and the temporal occasions are all explanatory.[118]

4. THE CHARACTER OF THE ARGUMENT

This concludes the survey of Whitehead's statements about God. How are we to evaluate what has been done?

[115] *PR* 135. See also, *PR* 46.

[116] *PR* 11.

[117] See below, Ch. V, sec. 5.

[118] Of the later writings, only *Adventures of Ideas* is worth noting with regard to its treatment of the doctrine of God. Even here there is relatively little explicit discussion. A glance at the index indicates only one occurrence of the term " God," and that one is a historical reference! And although there are indeed a number of other occurrences of the word, its relative rarity does suggest the change. However, a reading of the book quickly alters the picture. Whitehead has chosen to couch his whole philosophical discussion in the book in Platonic terms and to adopt " Eros " as the term for the primordial nature of God. Eros is the power in the universe urging toward the realization of ideals, and as such it plays a major role in *Adventures of Ideas.*

The consequent nature of God, here as everywhere, receives less attention. Nevertheless, it is not omitted. There is a reference to " the everlasting nature of God " that " may establish with the soul a peculiarly intense relationship of mutual immanence " (*AI* 267). Then there is the chapter on " Peace," concluding the book and speaking sometimes explicitly, more often implicitly, of God and of man's apprehension of him. Here the consequent nature appears as the " Unity of Adventure " (*AI* 381). In many ways, *Adventures of Ideas* is Whitehead's most religious book.

Whitehead's last book, *Modes of Thought,* and his late lecture, " Immortality," provide evidence that there was no significant alteration of the major doctrines of *Process and Reality.*

Has Whitehead "proved" the existence of God? Does his description of God's nature follow in every detail from the argument for his existence? Have we here an inescapable truth that every honest mind must now accept whether or not it wishes to believe in God, and whether its own religious intuitions conform to this doctrine or militate against it? Obviously the answer to these questions is no. Nothing is proved in this sense. But in that case, what value has the discussion? Have we done nothing more than consider the private, and fundamentally arbitrary, opinions of one man?

Whitehead points out that every proof depends for its force upon the self-evidence of its premises.[119] There are no simply obvious premises on the basis of which one can construct an argument for the existence of God. If there were, the argument itself would hardly be needed. The primary task of philosophy is to arrive at an adequate and immediately persuasive description explanatory of the world we actually know. Once this description is accepted, certain conclusions will follow, but the real problem is to arrive at the adequate description.

Whitehead's argument for the existence of God, insofar as there is an argument at all, is primarily the traditional one from the order of the universe to a ground of order. It is an argument that has taken many forms in the history of thought. Sometimes a particular formulation has received such heavy emphasis that when that formulation was shown inadequate, the argument itself was supposed disproved. To many, it has seemed an unedifying sight that those who defend theism on cosmological grounds have time after time given up their arguments only to come back with new ones which in turn are later surrendered. If there is truly a proof of the existence of God, why should it not be offered once for all in an irrefutable form? Does not the constant effort to find an adequate argument indicate that those who seek it are attempting to rationalize and justify beliefs that have no rational justification? Many

[119] *MT* 66–67.

honest and sensitive persons have been led by such questions to refuse all further attention to cosmological and teleological arguments for God's existence.

I propose, in agreement with Whitehead, I believe, an alternative interpretation of this situation. There is a deep human intuition that the order of the world requires for its explanation some principle of order that cannot entirely be attributed to the entities that constitute the world. To many people, this intuition amounts to a virtual certitude. It seems incredible to them, for example, that the marvelous, intricate, and dynamic adjustments constantly made by the cells in the human body, apart from which human life is impossible, are somehow self-explanatory. They seem surely to depend upon a wisdom that cannot be attributed to the cells themselves.

But how can such conviction be expressed in an argument that will have philosophic force or carry conviction to those who see no need to appeal to a higher wisdom? The answer depends entirely upon how the science of that time — science in the broadest sense — understands the cell and its functioning. If, for example, nature is seen as a great machine made up of lesser machines ultimately composed of particles of matter in law-abiding motion, then the cell also will be understood as being a law-abiding machine. In that case, the marvelous fact that these little machines are productive of human life will be seen as pointing to the wisdom of the one who imposed upon little particles of matter so wonderful a system of laws. The argument will be the old one from the watch to an intelligent maker.

The argument is not a proof, if by a proof we mean the movement from inescapable premises by logically necessary steps to a conclusion. The argument depends entirely upon two premises neither of which is indisputable: first, that the universe and all its parts are really machine-like in character; second, that machine-like things are possible only as the expression of intelligent workmanship. Either premise may be denied. Yet if the fundamental description is accepted, the conclusion has nearly the force of self-evidence.

Unfortunately, some defenders of theism in the eighteenth century wedded themselves to this view of the complex machine and its maker and associated it with the view that such special forms of the machine as the human body came into existence fully formed in an aboriginal creation. Hence the argument was peculiarly vulnerable to the new understanding of the evolutionary processes in nature which came to dominance in the nineteenth century. Random variation and the survival of the fittest appeared to provide explanations of the emergence of new forms, including the human, on principles that removed the need for an intelligent creator and lawgiver. The scientific theory was itself attacked by religious thinkers in order to preserve the force of the old argument! Such strategy could only result in thoroughly discrediting the argument, and even the doctrine it was intended to support.

But the new understanding of nature did not, any better than the old, explain the order of nature. The emergence of the living from the inorganic may be viewed as a random variation, but it certainly has nothing to do with the survival of the fittest. A stone is far more capable of survival than a plant or animal, and on the whole the lower forms of life are more readily adapted to survival than are the higher. Some other force seems to be at work in nature besides random variation and the survival of the fittest — some appetition toward more complex forms of order more difficult to sustain but more valuable in their results.

Furthermore, the understanding of all life in terms of evolution implies that the previous understanding of the inorganic was in error. From the *simply* material, the wholly inert, the totally passive lumps of the earlier theory, it is incredible that random variation could produce life and mind. But if the image of the purely material machine is set aside, the problem of explaining the orderliness of things reappears with intensified force.

My point is that the problem of order must recur, however we understand the nature of the world. The order is indisputably there, whether or not there may also be disorder. The order may be understood either as entirely imposed or as arising out of the nature of things themselves. Whitehead believes that elements of both are essential to an adequate analysis.[120] But however it is viewed, there will always remain an inexplicable factor so long as we consider only the temporal entities themselves.

We can, of course, refuse to ask those questions which lead to this final conclusion. We can limit our questions to those which fall fully within the scope of the particular sciences each of which so circumscribes its work that questions of such ultimacy cannot arise. We can declare all other questions meaningless on the grounds that they cannot be settled by empirical evidence. But if we do ask these questions, we will be led to answer in terms of some source of order that transcends the objects of scientific investigation, whether it be beyond or within the ordered world.

I am asserting this dogmatically. The evidence can only be the several attempts to formulate a comprehensive explanation. These must vary according to the description of the structures of the world in which they find their premises. No one argument formulated from any set of premises can constitute a proof of the existence of God in the usual sense. Each only displays how a more or less adequate account of the order of the world points to some principle of order.

The strength and importance of Whitehead's argument for the existence of God, therefore, does not lie in some new and more penetrating structure of the argument. The argument is little more than a pointing to the need of a principle of limitation. The importance lies in the unusual thoroughness and adequacy of the description of the world from which the argument begins. If one is persuaded that

[120] *AI* 146–147.

Whitehead's account is indeed the most penetrating that now exists, that it does justice to the complexity of the phenomena of science and of history alike, then the fact that it too leads, almost in spite of the author's apparent intention, to a doctrine of God as the source and ground of order is an important further confirmation of the inescapability for speculative reason of some kind of belief in God.

More important than the mere fact that Whitehead too could not understand the world apart from God, is the particular form that his doctrine of God takes. This, of course, is a function of the categories in which the description of the world is developed. If the world is viewed as a complex machine, then the correlative doctrine of God is likely to be that of a creator who stands outside of his creation. But if the world is viewed in organic terms, then the principle of life, order, and growth must be immanent to the organisms. That there *is* something which we may properly call God is sufficiently indicated by the kind of order that is visible to all. But what that " something " is, where it is, how it functions, these questions can be reflectively considered only in the light of the categories in terms of which the world is understood.

In *Science and the Modern World,* Whitehead told us little except that there must be some principle of limitation that makes for the realization of value. But in *Religion in the Making* and *Process and Reality* he worked through the questions of what such a principle must be in itself and how it must function. It must be an actual entity that brings the realm of possibility into effective and limiting relation to the becoming occasions of the world. It can do this only if it functions at the outset of every new occasion to give it an aim toward that kind of self-actualization which is compatible with the larger orders of nature. Here is the essence of his philosophical doctrine of God.

But there is more that can be suggested as the reasonable and probable implication of what has been worked out with some rigor. If God is an actual entity, then it is appropriate to attribute to him the structures characteristic of other actual entities. To refuse to do this would require far more justification than to carry through the application to God of the categories. Whitehead insists that " God is not to be treated as an exception to all metaphysical principles, invoked to save their collapse. He is their chief exemplification." [121] Hence, we must attribute to God not only the conceptual ordering of the eternal objects by virtue of which he lures the occasions of the world toward order and value; we must attribute to him as to all other actual entities physical feelings as well. Whitehead's own explanation of what he is doing here and what philosophical status is to be attributed to it is a model of care and honesty.

" We must investigate dispassionately what the metaphysical principles, here developed, require on these points, as to the nature of God. There is nothing here in the nature of proof. There is merely the confrontation of the theoretic system with a certain rendering of the facts. But the unsystematized report upon the facts is itself highly controversial, and the system is confessedly inadequate. The deductions from it in this particular sphere of thought cannot be looked upon as more than suggestions as to how the problem is transformed in the light of that system." [122] It is shortly after this passage that Whitehead introduces his major discussion of the consequent nature of God.

There is another factor involved, in Whitehead's view, in the philosophical development of a doctrine of God. Scattered widely throughout the history of mankind there have been " somewhat exceptional elements in our conscious experience . . . which may roughly be classed together as religious and moral intuitions." [123] The adequacy of a philosophical scheme must be tested against these intuitions just as much as against the findings of the natural sciences. And just as clues to the ultimate nature of things

[121] PR 521.   [122] PR 521.   [123] PR 521.

that arise in the sciences must be taken with great seriousness by the philosopher, so must the clues that emerge in
moral and religious intuition. Hence, the suggestions that
arise from the application of the general scheme of thought
to this special question of the nature of God may be weakened or may gain cogency according to the reading of these
great intuitions of the race by which men live. Whitehead
believes, of course, that his own speculative suggestions are
appropriate to these intuitions, as well as conformal with
what his scheme demands. To him, the ability of his philosophy to do justice both to science and religion must be its
supreme test of relevance.[124] In Chapter VI, we will consider whether his philosophic doctrine can illumine aspects
of religious experience in relation to which he did not
himself test it.[125]

[124] *PR* 23. [125] See below, Ch. VI, sec. 2.

V

A Whiteheadian Doctrine of God

1. GOD AS ACTUAL ENTITY

In most of this book I have identified myself fully with the position I have expounded on Whitehead's authority. Even in the preceding chapter, where I focused upon the development of his views, I largely identified myself with my presentation of his thought in *Process and Reality*. Whitehead's philosophical reasons for affirming God and his attempt to show that God is not an exception to all the categories appear to me philosophically responsible and even necessary. Nevertheless, at several points questions occur that Whitehead seems to answer in ways which create more problems than would some alternative answer. Whitehead has succeeded in interpreting God in such a way that, with very minor exceptions, he exemplifies the categories necessary to all actual occasions.[1] However there are other features characteristic of all actual occasions but not included among the strictly necessary categories. Whitehead's philosophy would be more coherent if he had interpreted God as conforming to these features of actual occasions as well.

In this chapter, I undertake to develop a doctrine of God more coherent with Whitehead's general cosmology and metaphysics than are some aspects of his own doctrine. This project presupposes that there are elements of inco-

[1] Christian, Ch. 15.

herence in Whitehead's doctrine of God. This incoherence does not amount in most cases to strict inconsistency. But Whitehead holds before philosophers an aim at something more than mere logical consistency. Consistency is only freedom from contradiction.[2] Undoubtedly Whitehead's writings also include points of self-contradiction, but these are minor and easily remedied. The further criticism of a philosophy as incoherent has to do with its " arbitrary disconnection of first principles." [3] To the extent that the four ultimate elements of his system (actual occasions, God, eternal objects, and creativity) are arbitrarily disconnected, to that extent some measure of incoherence remains in Whitehead's own philosophy. It is my intention to show both that Whitehead moved far toward overcoming such incoherence and also that one can go, and therefore should go, farther yet.

Lest this appear unduly pretentious, a few further words of justification are in order. In the preceding chapter it was shown that when Whitehead first introduced God as a systematic element into his philosophy, he made no attempt to assimilate this principle to any other category.[4] God was to be viewed as a unique attribute of the substantial activity alongside of eternal objects and actual occasions. Further, there is direct continuity between what is said of God in *Science and the Modern World* and what is said of the primordial nature of God in *Process and Reality*.[5] In the latter book it is explicitly recognized that the primordial nature of God is an abstraction from God as actual entity,[6] yet most of the references to God in that book are references to this abstraction. When in the end Whitehead discusses more fully the consequent nature, he tells us that, unlike the primordial nature, this is fully actual.[7] Yet he

[2] *PR* 5.

[3] *PR* 9.

[4] See above, pp. 140 ff.

[5] Whitehead equates the primordial nature of God with the principle of concretion. (*PR* 373–374, 523.)

[6] *PR* 50.

cannot strictly mean this, for again and again he tells us that actual entities are the only finally concrete individual things.[8] He means to say that God is concrete by virtue of his consequent nature, and even that is not precise. Unless God is much more of an exception than Whitehead intends, God is concrete by virtue of being an actual entity, and being an actual entity involves both the primordial and the consequent natures. The reason Whitehead introduces concreteness with the consequent nature is that at this point he takes for granted the primordial nature and that the consequent nature is its complement, whereas when he previously discussed the primordial nature, the consequent nature was not in view.

The objection to Whitehead's formulation, then, is that too often he deals with the two natures as though they were genuinely separable. Further, he frequently writes as though God were simply the addition of these two natures. Thus God's primordial nature performs certain functions and his consequent nature others. But according to Whitehead's own understanding, this cannot be the precise and adequate formulation. Actual entities are unities composed of a synthesis of their mental and physical poles, but they are not exhaustively analyzable into these two poles. In such analysis we would omit precisely the subjective unity, the concrete satisfaction, the power of decision and self-creation. It is always the actual entity that acts, not one of its poles as such, although in many of its functions one pole or another may be primarily relevant. Whitehead must certainly have meant to say this also about God, but his separate and contrasting treatment of the two natures is misleading — indeed, I believe that he was himself misled into exaggerating their separability.

That Whitehead wrote much of the time, even in *Proc-*

---

[7] *PR* 524.

[8] For Whitehead's acknowledgment of the misleading character of his language on this subject, see Appendix B in Johnson, *Whitehead's Theory of Reality,* esp. pp. 214, 218.

ess and Reality, without holding clearly in view his own doctrine of God as an actual entity, is illustrated by the extraordinary treatment of the category of reversion, the category that explains the emergence of novelty in the actual occasion. It has to do with the way in which the prehension of an eternal object derived from objectification of an antecedent occasion gives rise to the prehension of a related but novel eternal object. In the initial statement of the categories, this prehension is understood as a new conceptual feeling.[9] However, in the course of his fuller exposition in the second part of the book, Whitehead realizes that the prehension of the novel eternal object must be an objectification of that possibility as envisioned in God, hence a hybrid prehension of God. At this point he states that " by the recognition of God's characterization of the creative act, a more complete rational explanation is attained. The category of reversion is then abolished; and Hume's principle of the derivation of conceptual experience from physical experience remains without any exception." [10] To carry through the process of rethinking the account of actual occasions and eternal objects in the light of the full doctrine of God will be in line with the direction in which Whitehead's own thought was moving at this point and will also alter in subtle, but at times important, ways the precise form of the doctrine of God.

My aim at each point is to achieve " a more complete rational explanation " in just the sense meant by Whitehead in the preceding quotation. This is the same goal as that of achieving greater coherence of first principles. The attempt is to explain the way in which God is related to actual occasions, eternal objects, and creativity, in such a way that at no point do we attribute to him a mode of being or relation inexplicable in terms of the principles operative elsewhere in the system.

This program may well begin with reference to the perplexing problem as to how the eternally unchanging primordial nature of God can provide different initial aims to every occasion.[11] That each occasion has its unique, appropriate aim given to it, Whitehead is clear. God's aim at universal intensity of satisfaction determines a specific aim at the appropriate satisfaction of each individual occasion. But it is very difficult to imagine how these individual aims can be wholly timeless and yet become relevantly effective at particular moments of time.

In the preceding chapter we saw that the initial aim can be conceived as a feeling of a proposition clothed with the subjective form of desire for its actualization.[12] A proposition is a togetherness of some actual entity or nexus of actual entities with some eternal object. For example, "The stone is gray," is a sentence that expresses a proposition of which the subject is a nexus of molecular actual occasions and the predicate is the eternal object gray. Many propositions are felt without being expressed in language. The initial aim would almost always be the feeling of an unexpressed proposition. In this case, the subject of the proposition would be the occasion itself, and the predicate would be that form of actualization which is ideal in that situation.

In temporal occasions the initial aim is always an aim at some intensity of feeling both in the occasion itself and in its relevant future.[13] We have seen that the relations of an individual's own future and those of others introduce tensions that are highly relevant to man's ethical thinking.[14] In God, however, there are no such tensions because the ideal strength of beauty for himself and for the world coincide.[15] Hence, we may simplify and say that God's aim is at ideal strength of beauty and that this aim is eternally

[11] See the discussion on this point above, pp. 155 ff.

[12] See above, pp. 156–157.

[13] PR 41.

[14] See above, pp. 110 ff.

[15] In PR Whitehead uses "intensity" to refer somewhat loosely to what is analyzed in AI as strength of beauty. See PR 134–135, 160–161, 373, 381.

unchanging. On the other hand, even in God there must be tensions between immediate and more remote realizations of intensity.

Assume a similar situation in man, although I have denied in Chapter III the likelihood of the occurrence in a man of what would be for him a rigid selfishness. The man aims at the realization of some ideal satisfaction in the present occasion and in his future occasions. His subjective aim in the strictest sense is a propositional feeling about himself in that immediate moment of becoming, but this aim is determined in part by propositional feelings about future occasions of his own experience. He aims at actualizing himself in the present in such a way that these future occasions will have the possibility of enjoying some measure of beauty. Instrumental to this goal must be the behavior of occasions of experience other than his own, for example, occasions in his body and in other persons. He must entertain propositional feelings about them also. There will be a large complex of such propositional feelings, entertained with an appetite for their becoming true, synthesized in the one propositional feeling of his own satisfaction. He aims at so actualizing himself that other occasions will actualize themselves as he desires. His aim at ideal satisfaction for himself will be unchanging, but it will take a different form according to every change in his situation.

In God's case there is nothing selfish about the constant aim at his own ideal satisfaction, since this may equally well be described as an aim at universal satisfaction. But in other respects there is no reason not to see the situation as analogous. Certainly God's aim is unchangingly directed to an ideal strength of beauty. In this unchanging form it must be indifferent to how this beauty is attained.[16] But if God's aim at beauty explains the limitation by which individual occasions achieve definiteness, then in its continual adaptation to changing circumstances it must involve

[16] *PR* 160–161.

propositional feelings of each of the becoming occasions as realizing some peculiar satisfaction. God's subjective aim will then be so to actualize himself in each moment that the propositional feeling he entertains with respect to each new occasion will have maximum chance of realization.[17] Every occasion then prehends God's prehension of this ideal for it, and to some degree the subjective form of its prehension conforms to that of God. That means that the temporal occasion shares God's appetition for the realization of that possibility in that occasion. Thus, God's ideal for the occasion becomes the occasion's ideal for itself, the initial phase of its subjective aim.

If the dynamic of the relation between God and man can be understood in this way, it is analogous to the dynamic of the relation between at least some temporal occasions and some occasions in their future. For example, the human actual occasion frequently so actualizes itself as to aim at influencing other occasions in the body. This may be a matter of raising the hand or swallowing food, or it may be far more complex. In general, the body is highly responsive to this influence, although not absolutely so. One may also attempt to actualize himself so as to influence future occasions of his own experience, as when he determines not to forget an appointment or to resist a particular temptation in the future. These decisions also have some real influence on the future, although still less perfectly so. Finally, one attempts by his self-actualization to influence future occasions in other persons, with some, although much less, success.

A new occasion, then, may feel past occasions in the temporal world in terms of their aim for it, and it will be affected to some degree in the formation of its subjective aim by these feelings. If this is so, then Whitehead's sharp distinction within the initial phase of an occasion between the initial aim and the initial data may be modified. The new

[17] This is at least a possible interpretation of Whitehead's statements. (PR 134, 343; AI 357.)

occasion prehends all the entities in its past. These entities include God. All the entities will be positively felt in some way, some by simple physical feelings, others by hybrid physical feelings. These hybrid physical feelings will include feelings of propositional feelings about the new occasion, and these in turn will include propositional feelings whose subjective forms include desire for realization. In its prehension of these propositional feelings, the subjective form of the new occasion will at least partly conform to that of the past occasions it prehends. Hence, its aim for itself will always partly conform to the aim that past entities have entertained for it. Among the entities so felt, God will always be by far the most important one and, in some respects, prior to all the others.[18] The subjective aim of the new occasion will be some synthesis and adaptation of these aims for it, which it also feels conformally.

It would be possible to support this analysis in some detail by citation of passages from Whitehead that point in this direction. However, I resist this temptation. The analysis as a whole is not found in this form in his writings, and it deviates from the apparent implications of some of his statements in at least two ways. First, it rejects the association of God's aim exclusively with the primordial nature, understood as God's purely conceptual and unchanging envisagement of eternal objects; this rejection is required if we deny that God's immutable aim alone adequately explains how God functions concretely for the determination of the events in the world. Second, it interprets the subjective aim of the actual occasion as arising more impartially out of hybrid feelings of aims (propositional feelings whose subjective form involves appetition) entertained for the new occasion by its predecessors. In other words, it denies that the initial phase of the subjective aim need be derived exclusively from God.

[18] Probably the function of determining the locus and extension of the new standpoint must be assigned exclusively to God. See above, p. 153.

In *Process and Reality,* much more sharply than in *Religion in the Making,* Whitehead treats the causal efficacy of the consequent nature of God for the world quite separately from that of the primordial nature.[19] I believe that this is a mistake. If God is an actual entity, God will be prehended by each new occasion. We will assume that God's aim for it, a propositional feeling for which the new occasion is the logical subject and some complex eternal object the predicate, will in every case be prehended and play a decisive role in the determination of the subjective aim of the occasion. But the occasion's feeling of this propositional feeling in God need not exhaust the objectification of God in the new occasion.

In my feeling of my immediate past I may feel conformally the intention of that immediate past that in this moment I shall carry out some project. But my feeling of that past also feels many other aspects of that past, perhaps its discomfort or its hope for some more distant future. Similarly, there is no reason to suppose that the prehension of God's aim for the occasion will exhaust the prehension of God in that occasion. Hence, Whitehead was right to insist that in addition to deriving the initial aim from God, men also prehend God in some other way.[20] But just as he was wrong to identify the derivation of the initial aim wholly with the primordial nature, so also he is wrong to identify the other prehensions of God solely with the consequent nature if this is simply identified with God's physical prehensions of the world. Whitehead's own writings about the consequent nature seem to attribute to it a synthesis of the physical prehensions with the conceptual ones.[21] If so, there need be no quarrel — only an insistence that there can be no sharp distinction between the reception of the initial aim and the other prehensions of God.

According to my view, the actual occasion is initiated by a prehension of all the entities in its past, always including God. Some of these entities, always including God, have specific aims for this new occasion to realize. The subjective aim of the new occasion must be formed by some synthesis or adaptation of these aims for which it is itself finally responsible. In addition, the past entities, including God, will be objectified by other eternal objects. What these other eternal objects will be, complex or simple, is determined partly by the past entities and partly by the new subjective aim.

2. GOD AND TIME

Whitehead's discussion of the relation of God to time, like much of what he says about God, is primarily focused on the primordial nature of God. For this reason, the emphasis is on the nontemporality, primordiality, and eternity of God. God's envisagement of pure possibility is beyond the influence of events. When Whitehead does discuss the consequent nature of God, he necessarily introduces some kind of process into God, for the consequent nature is affected by what occurs in the world. Whitehead never tries to solve this problem by denying the reality of the temporality of the world. On the contrary, he accepts the doctrine that there is real becoming in God. Still, he refuses to say that God is temporal.[22] How is this possible?

Whitehead distinguishes between two types of process. "Time," he reserves for physical time, the transition from one actual occasion to another.[23] It is an abstraction from that process. This means that time is not, as in the Newtonian scheme, there prior to actual occurrences. Nor is it, as in the Kantian scheme, a way in which the mind necessarily orders the phenomenal flux. What is given ultimately are actual occasions with real internal relations to past occasions. Time is an important aspect of these relations.

From the point of view of physical time the actual occasions are temporally atomic. That is, they are indivisible

---

[22] Note the partial exception in *AI* 267.
[23] Cf. *PR* 107, 196, 442–444.

into earlier and later portions, but they are not, like points, indivisible because unextended. Each actual entity has temporal extension, but the temporal extension happens all at once as an indivisible unit.[24]

However, one can analyze the process of becoming of the actual occasion, and indeed, Whitehead develops an extremely elaborate analysis.[25] Each occasion begins with an initial phase constituted by its initial data and its initial aim. It ends in its satisfaction through which it becomes a datum for further occasions. Between the indeterminateness with which it begins and the determinateness with which it ends, each occasion passes through a succession of phases in which complex syntheses of data replace the mere data.

There is, clearly, some continuity between the physical time derived from transition from one occasion to another and the process internal to the becoming occasion. In terms of physical time the occasion must be said to become all at once, yet it is eminently clear that some phases of the becoming presuppose others; [26] and Whitehead does not hesitate to use such temporal terms as earlier and later.[27]

The complexities of the relation between time as an aspect of the succession of occasions and the process internal to occasions need not be resolved here, since the basic principles necessary for understanding God's relation to time have already been noted. However, some further effort to explain Whitehead's meaning will not be amiss.

Physical time is observed or measured time. Observation and measurement presuppose objective occurrences. The absolute unit of objective occurrences is the becoming of an occasion of experience. This occasion is related to other occasions only at its initiation (as prehender) and at its consummation (as datum for prehension). Hence, in principle, its own inner process of becoming is irrelevant to its observable relations. For every perspective other than its

24 PR 434.   26 PR 225, 234.
25 PR, Part III.   27 E.g., PR 132, 337.

own, the occasion either is not at all or is completed. One cannot observe, from without, an occasion in the process of becoming. From the perspective of the becoming occasion, of course, the situation is different. It does experience itself as a process of becoming, and indeed only as such.

We are now prepared to ask how Whitehead relates God to time. We have already noted that his most frequent formulations seem to deny temporality to God altogether. God is the nontemporal actual entity. However, in the brief treatment of God as consequent as well as primordial in the concluding pages of *Process and Reality,* Whitehead introduces a threefold distinction.

Actual entities other than God are temporal. This means that they perish as soon as they have become. For Whitehead, " time " is physical time, and it is " perpetual perishing." The primordial nature of God is eternal. This means that it is wholly unaffected by time or by process in any other sense. The primordial nature of God affects the world but is unaffected by it. For it, before and after are strictly irrelevant categories.

The consequent nature of God is " everlasting." [28] This means that it involves a creative advance, just as time does, but that the earlier elements are not lost as new ones are added. Whatever enters into the consequent nature of God remains there forever, but new elements are constantly added. Viewed from the vantage point of Whitehead's conclusion and the recognition that God is an actual entity in which the two natures are abstract parts, we must say that God as a whole is everlasting, but that he envisages all possibility eternally.

It is then quite clear that the description of God as nontemporal does not mean that there is no process in God. Before and after are relevant terms for describing this process. There is God before he has prehended a given human occasion and God after he has prehended that occasion. Time and history are real for him as well as for tem-

[28] *PR* 524 ff.

poral occasions. God's being as affected by temporal events also, in turn, affects subsequent temporal events.[29]

The easiest way to understand this would be to regard God, like human persons, as a living person.[30] A living person is a succession of moments of experience with special continuity.[31] At any given moment I am just one of those occasions, but when I remember my past and anticipate my future, I see myself as the total society or sequence of such occasions. God, then, at any moment would be an actual entity, but viewed retrospectively and prospectively he would be an infinite succession of divine occasions of experience. It is clear that Whitehead himself thought of God as *an* actual entity rather than as a living person. The thesis I wish to develop is that, despite this fact, the doctrines he formulated about God compel us to assimilate God more closely to the conception of a living person than to that of *an* actual entity.

The argument begins with the fact that Whitehead recognizes process in the consequent nature of God. Such process must be conceived either as the kind of process that occurs between occasions or as that kind which occurs within an occasion. Whitehead's position that God is *an* actual entity requires the latter doctrine. But the chief distinction between internal process and physical time is that the process occurring within an occasion has no efficacy for other occasions except indirectly through the satisfaction in which it eventuates. If the process in God's consequent nature is thought of in these terms, it cannot affect the events in the world. Yet Whitehead explicitly affirms just such an influence. Furthermore, if in the light of the discussion in the preceding section, we recognize the indissoluble unity of the primordial and consequent natures of God even in God's function as principle of limitation, then

[29] *PR* 532.

[30] See above, p. 50. Hartshorne prefers this doctrine (e.g., Kline, p. 23).

[31] See the discussion of personal identity above, Ch. II, sec. 4.

we must acknowledge that what is involved is not only the special case of the causal efficacy of God's consequent nature, but also the basic efficacy of God in the provision of the initial aim for each occasion. God's causal efficacy for the world is like the efficacy of completed occasions for subsequent occasions and not like that of phases of the becoming of a single occasion for its successors.

It may be objected that it is my development of Whitehead's thought in the preceding section that is in trouble here rather than Whitehead's usual formulations. If only the primordial nature of God were causally efficacious for the world, and if it were indifferent to time, then the problem would not arise. But if, as I hold, God can function as principle of limitation only by entertaining a specific aim for each becoming occasion, that aim must take account of the actual situation in the world. In that case, the problem does arise. Furthermore, since Whitehead unquestionably affirms the causal efficacy of the consequent nature of God, the problem also occurs for his explicit formulation. We must either reject this doctrine of the causal efficacy of the consequent nature and also affirm that an entirely static God can have particularity of efficacy for each occasion, or else we must recognize that the phases in the concrescence of God are in important respects more analogous to temporal occasions than to phases in the becoming of a single occasion.

The same problem may be posed in terms of God's satisfaction. In all other entities satisfaction is not attained except as the completion of the entity. If God is a single entity who will never be completed, then on this analogy, he can never know satisfaction. It would be odd that God should eternally aim at a goal that is in principle unreachable, and Whitehead explicitly refers to God's satisfaction as something real.[32] Apparently, satisfactions are related to the successive phases in God's becoming as they are related to temporal actual occasions, and not as they are related

[32] *PR* 48, 135.

to successive phases of the becoming of such occasions.

In at least these two respects Whitehead's account of God is more like an account of a living person than of an actual entity. Yet Whitehead never suggests this position. Are there any systematic reasons for affirming that God is *an* actual entity rather than a living person? First, it is clear that as long as the primordial nature is chiefly in view, God would be thought of as a singular entity. If this were the only reason, we could easily set it aside. But we have seen that even when the consequent nature is in view, Whitehead avoids speaking of God as temporal. Unless we speak of him as temporal, we cannot speak of him as a living person, for the living person is defined by a temporal relationship among actual occasions.

There are two closely related characteristics of living persons that Whitehead wishes to deny with respect to God. They are, first, lack of complete self-identity through time and, second, loss of what is past. God must, without qualification, be self-identically himself, and in him there must be no loss. Whether or not these are strictly philosophical requirements of his system, they are powerful intuitions one must hesitate to set aside.

In my earlier discussion of the personal identity of living persons, I suggested that such identity is attained to the degree that there are immediate prehensions by each new occasion in the person of the occasions constituting the past of that person.[33] I recognized there that this did not entirely solve the problem since there would also be prehensions of the temporally noncontiguous experiences of other persons that would complicate the picture. In God's case, however, prehensions of all earlier entities would not be something other than his prehension of his own past, since they would all be included in his consequent nature. Therefore, his unity must be complete. Similarly, loss in the temporal world is the result of the very fragmentary way in which past occasions are reenacted in the present.

[33] See above, pp. 77–78.

The vast majority of such prehensions are unconscious, and even in the unconscious we assume that the past is only fragmentarily effective. At any rate, the unconscious memory of a conscious experience loses a very important part of the remembered experience. In God we may suppose that no such loss occurs. He vividly and consciously remembers in every new occasion all the occasions of the past. His experience grows by addition to the past, but loses nothing.

One may still object that the concrete individuality of the past in its own subjective immediacy is lost. That is true. But if the same living person now enjoys a new experience that includes everything in the old and more, this loss seems to be no loss of value. While we humans are alive, the passing of time entails loss in two ways. First, the beauty of most past occasions seems to be gone beyond recall. Second, we move on toward the time when as living persons we will be no more.[34] This means that all the beauty we have known will have only the most trivial value for the future.[35] It also means that the compensation of novel experiences is nearing its end. But the passage of time in God would entail none of this loss.

The final objection to identifying God as a living person is that the envisagement of the eternal objects is a primordial and unchanging act and not an endless succession of acts. There is a certain plausibility to this argument, yet it is essentially arbitrary. When I gaze at an aesthetic object for one minute, I might well describe this as a single act. Yet Whitehead speculates that as many as six hundred acts may have taken place. Insofar as what is enacted in each successive act is the same, we may well conceive it as a sin-

[34] I am assuming here that we are not destined to live again beyond death. If we believe that we are, the sense of loss is greatly mitigated. For my discussion of this possibility, see Ch. II, sec. 3.

[35] I am omitting from consideration here the preservation of these values in God, so important to Whitehead at just this point. See below, pp. 219–220.

gle act. In our continually fluctuating experience no such absolute identity obtains from moment to moment, but in God's one unfettered envisagement of all possibilities, the absolute identity from moment to moment means that in our normal language it is a single unchanging and eternal act.

Specific problems remain, but for the most part they are already raised by Whitehead's formulation and should not be regarded as peculiar difficulties of this interpretation. For example, we may ask how many occasions of experience would occur for God in a second.[36] The answer is that it must be a very large number, incredibly large to our limited imaginations. The number of successive electronic occasions in a second staggers the imagination. God's self-actualizations must be at least equally numerous if he is to function separately in relation to each individual in this series. Since electronic occasions are presumably not in phase with each other or with other types of actual occasions, still further complications are involved. Obviously, this is altogether unimaginable, but since all the dimensions of our world revealed to us by physical science are also quite beyond imagination, in this sense, we should not be surprised that this is true of God.

My conclusion, then, is that the chief reasons for insisting that God is *an* actual entity can be satisfied by the view that he is a living person, that this view makes the doctrine of God more coherent, and that no serious new difficulties are raised.

3. GOD AND SPACE

It is possible in Whitehead to consider time in some abstraction from space without serious distortion. Successiveness is a relation not dependent upon spatial dimensions for its intelligibility. I understand Whitehead to say that

[36] Hartshorne asks this question of Whitehead with respect to the phases of becoming in God and suggests a similar answer. "Whitehead's Idea of God," Schilpp, pp. 545–546.

time, in the sense of successiveness, is metaphysically necessary whereas space, or at least anything like what we mean
by space, is not. There might be one dimension or a hundred in some other cosmic epoch. Since God would remain
unalterably God in any cosmic epoch, his relation to space
must be more accidental than his relation to time. Nevertheless, space, or rather space-time, is a real and important
factor in the only world we know, and we may legitimately
inquire how God is related to space-time. Since in this section we will not be focusing upon successiveness, we will
for convenience often speak simply of space.

Every occasion of experience actualizes a spatiotemporal
region that then constitutes its standpoint. In this connection we must note that what is fundamentally given is not
space but actual entities. Space is affirmed only because the
way in which actual entities prehend each other has a
dimension that produces in us the experience of spatial
extension. This idea allows us to say further that although
real space is constructed by the actualization of just those
occasions that do become, space could have been divided
up in other ways, indeed, in an infinity of other ways.
Thus, we may treat the space occupied by occasions in abstraction from the occasions that occupy it, and consider its
properties — properties which then also characterize whatever occasions, in fact, occur in our spatial cosmic epoch.

Space and time conjointly constitute the extensive continuum in our cosmic epoch. Every occasion occupies as its
standpoint some region within this extensive continuum.
In an epoch lacking spatiality, this region would be temporal only, but in ours, again, it is spatiotemporal. Now
the question is whether the fact that in our epoch occasions
occupy spatiotemporal regions means that God also occupies a spatiotemporal region. There seem logically to be
only three possible answers. Either God occupies some particular region, or his mode of being is irrelevant to regions,
or he occupies the entire continuum.

The first of these alternatives may be rather readily dismissed on philosophical grounds. Since God's functions as philosophically identified are related with equal immediacy to every occasion, any special spatial location is impossible. The choice between the remaining alternatives is far more difficult. Since God's own being is independent of spatiality, it is clear that there is an important sense in which God transcends space. But that does not settle the question as to whether in a spatial epoch he is characterized by spatiality.

To deal with this problem in the face of Whitehead's silence, we must begin with the relevant principles that he does provide us. God does prehend every spatiotemporal actual occasion and he is prehended by it, both in his primordial nature and in his consequent nature. Furthermore, these prehensions in both directions are unmediated.

Normally we think of unmediated prehensions as prehensions of occasions immediately contiguous in the spatiotemporal continuum. This suggests the doctrine of God's omnispatiality. Indeed, if contiguity were essential to unmediated prehensions, it would be necessary to posit God's omnipresence throughout space. However, even apart from consideration of God, we have seen that Whitehead qualifies this principle. He holds that in our cosmic epoch, prehension of the physical poles of other occasions seems to be dependent on contiguity, but that prehensions of the mental poles of other occasions may not be dependent on contiguity.[37] By this principle we could explain our prehension of God's primordial nature and God's prehension of our mental poles quite apart from any spatial relations. Further, since no metaphysical problem is involved in affirming that physical experience may also be prehended apart from contiguity, the doctrine of the radical nonspatiality of God is compatible with all the functions attributed to God by Whitehead. Indeed, since his thinking about God was largely formed with the primordial nature

[37] *SMW* 216; *PR* 469; *AI* 318.

in view, it is probable that nonspatiality was assumed by him.

If the nonspatiality and omnispatiality of God are both equally allowed by Whitehead's metaphysics, we can choose between them only on the basis of coherence. My own judgment is that that doctrine of God is always to be preferred which, other things being equal, interprets his relations with the world more, rather than less, like the way we interpret the relations of other entities. If we adopt this principle, there is prima facie support for the doctrine that God, like all actual occasions, has a standpoint. Since that standpoint could not be such as to favor one part of the universe against others, it must be all-inclusive.

The only serious philosophical objection to this doctrine arises from the rejection of the possibility that actual standpoints can include the regions that comprise other actual standpoints. This problem was considered in some detail in Chapter II,[38] and the arguments in favor of the affirmation of such regional inclusion of standpoints will here be only summarized. The argument is that whereas Whitehead neither affirmed this relation nor developed its implications, it does seem to be implied by the most natural reading of some of his cosmological assertions. It is compatible with his metaphysical doctrines and his understanding of the relation of space-time to actual occasions. Further, it is compatible with the doctrine that contemporaries do not prehend each other, since each of the entities participating in this special regional relationship would still prehend the other only when that other entity had passed into objective immortality. Finally, the doctrine that the regions that constitute the standpoint of actual occasions of human experience include those of subhuman occasions in the brain has several specific advantages.[39]

If we can think of the spatiotemporal regions of the occasion of the human person as including the spatiotem-

[38] See above, pp. 82–91.   [39] See above, pp. 83–85.

poral regions of numerous occasions in the brain, then we may think analogously of the region of God as including the regions comprising the standpoints of all the contemporary occasions in the world. If we follow the argument of the previous section, there would be some difference, for whereas the occasions of human experience have considerable temporal breadth in relation to the electronic occurrences in the brain, we have seen that the occasions of God's experience must be extremely thin in their temporal extension. The regions of other occasions would be included, not in that of a single occasion of the divine experience, but in the regions of a succession of such experiences.

Once again we have a choice of treating God as an exception or of speculating that he is more like other actual entities. If God occupies no region, yet is related to all equally, it is *as if* he were regionally contiguous with all regions. Whitehead may deny this and intend that, unlike all other actual entities, God's immediate physical prehensions of other entities do not involve him in having a regional standpoint. Since regional standpoints are not introduced into the categorial scheme, no self-contradiction is entailed. However, if God is related to every occasion as if he were physically present, it seems more natural and coherent to affirm that he *is* physically present. That could only mean that his region includes all other contemporary regions.

4. GOD AND THE ETERNAL OBJECTS

In *Religion in the Making*, we read that " the forms (i.e., eternal objects) belong no more to God than to any one occasion." [40] God is seen as envisaging all the eternal objects as well as all actual occasions, but Whitehead does not see this envisagement as fundamentally different in kind from that possible to other occasions. No problem of coherence arises.

[40] *RM* 157.

Further reflection led Whitehead, in *Process and Reality*, to make a more radical differentiation between the way in which God prehends the eternal objects and the way actual occasions prehend them. According to the ontological principle he affirmed: "Everything must be somewhere; and here ' somewhere ' means ' some actual entity.' Accordingly the general potentiality of the universe must be somewhere; since it retains its proximate relevance to actual entities for which it is unrealized. . . . This ' somewhere ' is the non-temporal actual entity. Thus ' proximate relevance ' means ' relevance as in the primordial mind of God.'

" It is a contradiction in terms to assume that some explanatory fact can float into the actual world out of non-entity. Nonentity is nothingness. Every explanatory fact refers to the decision and to the efficacity of an actual thing. The notion of ' subsistence ' is merely the notion of how eternal objects can be components of the primordial nature of God." [41]

This passage seems virtually to deny the eternal objects any status apart from God's envisagement of them. On the other hand, Whitehead is very clear that God does not create the eternal objects; [42] they *are* for him eternally. Still, Whitehead seems to assign to God a relation to eternal objects wholly different from that possible to any other entity. That is, does not God have an unmediated relation, whereas all other entities have only a mediated relation? If so, is there not again a danger of a final incoherence? Have we not introduced God to solve a problem without providing any clue whatever as to how it is done? This seems to be parallel to the weaknesses that Whitehead points out in other philosophers.[43]

It may not be necessary, however, to understand Whitehead in this sense. What the ontological principle demands is that no agency be attributed to eternal objects in themselves. It does not forbid that they be classified as one of

[41] *PR* 73.   [42] *PR* 392.   [43] *PR* 78, 219, 289; *FR* 24; *AI* 171.

the categories of existence.[44] Nor does it demand that their sheer existence be regarded as dependent upon God. Let us take as our point of departure the formulation of the ontological principle to the effect that " every explanatory fact refers to the decision and to the efficacity of an actual thing." On the basis of this formulation I suggest that the relation between God and the eternal objects can be restored to the situation we found in *Religion in the Making*, namely, that it belongs to no totally different mode from that of other actual entities to the eternal objects.

The apparent incoherence with respect to eternal objects arises at two points. First, it seems that God renders eternal objects effective for actual occasions in a way *radically* different from that in which temporal occasions make them effective for each other. Second, God seems to envisage eternal objects in a way for which the conceptual prehensions of actual occasions provide no analogy. It is my contention that the first of these areas of incoherence can be rather easily resolved into coherence if the conclusions of preceding sections of this chapter [45] are accepted, but that much greater difficulty attaches to the second. We will treat the problems in that order.

Whitehead appeals to the principle of universal relativity to argue that there are physical prehensions of the world by God and of God by the world. He has in mind the consequent nature of God, but I have argued that God as actual entity is involved. When we recognize the indissoluble unity of the mental and physical poles in God as in other actual entities, we have no difficulty in seeing that even when the mental pole of God is primarily involved, God as actual entity is involved. Whitehead's recognition of this led him to note that some of the feelings he usually called conceptual prehensions (prehensions of

[44] They are so classified, *PR* 32. However, Christian correctly calls attention to Whitehead's wavering on this point. See Christian, pp. 265–266.

[45] See especially sec. 1.

eternal objects) are really hybrid prehensions (objectifications of an actual entity by an eternal object derived from its mental pole) .[46] In this way Whitehead moves in the direction of assimilating the relation of actual occasions to God to the relation of actual entities to each other. This is a step toward coherence.

However, two points remain at which God seems to function in presenting eternal objects to actual occasions in a way *radically* different from that in which they present eternal objects to each other. These two points are the provision of the initial aim and the provision of relevant novel possibilities. The analysis of the becoming actual occasion in which these occur should be briefly reviewed.

Every occasion of experience arises in an initial phase in which there are initial data and the initial phase of the subjective aim. The initial data are all the actual occasions in the past of the becoming occasion. The initial aim is the desire for the achievement of a definite value allowed and made possible by the initial data. In accordance with the initial aim, the initial data are severally objectified by the new occasion in terms of eternal objects realized by them. The new occasion then reenacts these eternal objects as now constitutive of its own subjective immediacy.[47] But in addition to this reenactment of what is given in the initial data, there is also a " secondary origination of conceptual feeling with data which are partially identical with, and partially diverse from, the eternal objects " derived from the initial data.[48] Here novelty enters the new occasion. In subsequent phases of the becoming of the occasion, complex syntheses of conceptual and physical prehensions occur, but these are not our concern at this point.

In Whitehead's presentation God seems to be the sole ground of (1) the initial aim and (2) the relevant novel eternal objects. In section 1 above, it has already been argued that, without detracting from God's supreme and

[46] *PR* 343, 377.   [47] *PR* 39–40.   [48] *PR* 40.

decisive role, we can think of past actual occasions as also contributing to the formation of the initial aim.[49] That argument will not here be repeated. If it is accepted, then there is no incoherence at this point. Here we must consider whether in the origination of novelty, also, God's role can be coherently explained.

Whitehead already goes far toward a coherent explanation. He holds that God so orders the realm of otherwise merely disjunctive eternal objects that the prehension of one eternal object suggests that of another. The prehension of the novel eternal object is in fact a hybrid prehension of God.[50]

However, it is impossible to rest with Whitehead's brief and almost incidental statements on this point, for they raise additional problems to which he did not address himself. Let us consider in somewhat more detail the apparent meaning of his position.

A past actual occasion is objectified by eternal object X. This eternal object is then reenacted in the new occasion by a conceptual prehension of X. In addition, eternal object Y is also enacted in the new occasion. This means that God has been objectified by Y. Presumably the objectification of God by Y was triggered by the prehension of X derived from the past actual occasion. The dynamic by which this triggering occurs is not explained. Perhaps the objectification of a past occasion by X leads to the objectification also of God by X and this in turn leads to the objectification of God by Y because of the close association of X and Y in God. Already this seems somewhat farfetched.

In addition, it introduces two further problems. Whereas in relation to other actual occasions their causal efficacy for the new occasion functions only in the initial phase, this interpretation of the rise of novelty requires that God's causal efficacy function also in subsequent phases since " conceptual reversion " occurs after the in-

[49] See above, pp. 182–183.　　　[50] PR 377.

itial phase of the occasion.[51] Second, if the prehension of the novel eternal object is, in fact, a hybrid prehension of God, then the new occasion should deal with it as it does with other hybrid prehensions. This would mean that it not only would reenact the eternal object in its own subjective immediacy but also that there might again be " secondary origination of conceptual feeling" introducing new novelty. This would lead to a regress that is clearly vicious and completely unintended by Whitehead.

A much simpler theory, more coherent both in itself and with Whitehead's general position, is as follows. According to this theory, there is just one hybrid prehension of God, the prehension that includes the feeling of God's aim for the new occasion. This aim includes not only the ideal for the occasion but alternative modes of self-actualization in their graded relevance to the ideal.[52] It certainly includes God's conceptual feeling of eternal objects X and Y together with his feeling of relevance of Y to X. Hence no new hybrid prehension of God is required in subsequent phases. Although the new actual occasion may not actualize itself according to God's ideal aim for it, it will not include any possibility not provided as having some relevance for it in the initial hybrid prehension of God.

This interpretation also allows us to see that the difference between God's function in providing novelty and that of past occasions, although great, need not be total. Some ordering of eternal objects is possible also in temporal occasions and in principle may have some effectiveness for future occasions. The difference, the vast difference, is that God envisages and orders *all* eternal objects, whereas temporal occasions can order only an infinitesimal selection of eternal objects. But this kind of difference threatens no incoherence.

I assume, therefore, that the explanation of the deriva-

[51] *PR* 378.
[52] That this is Whitehead's intention is indicated in *PR* 74, 75, 342, 343.

tion from God of the initial aim and of novelty, need not attribute to God's causal efficacy for temporal occasions a function *radically* different from that exemplified in the interrelationships of other actual entities. If this is correct, there is no danger of incoherence, a danger that arises whenever an inexplicable mode of functioning is attributed to God. However, the second major problem noted above remains unsolved. Is God's envisagement of eternal objects totally discontinuous with the conceptual prehensions of temporal occasions?

The problem may be explained as follows. According to the ontological principle, eternal objects cannot be effective for actual occasions except by the decision of some actual entity. That seems to mean that the conceptual feelings of an actual entity always derive from its physical and hybrid feelings. An eternal object not given for the new actual occasion in some other actual entity cannot enter the new occasion. But in the case of God we seem to confront a total exception. Here all eternal objects are effective without the mediation of any other actual entity.

Either the ontological principle is simply inapplicable to the relation of eternal objects to God (in which case incoherence threatens) or the decision to which the effectiveness of eternal objects for God is to be attributed is God's primordial decision. If we adopt the latter position, as I believe we should, then we must ask whether in the case of temporal occasions as well the ontological principle allows that their own decisions can be explanatory of conceptual prehensions not derived from physical prehensions.

The question is not really whether such decisions occur or even whether there are actually any occasions capable of making such decisions. The question is whether in principle the kind of decision by which eternal objects become relevant for God is categorically impossible for all other actual entities. I see no reason to insist upon this absolute difference, and could even suggest that at the highest levels of their intellectual functioning human occasions *may* be able to conceive possibilities directly. Such a claim would supplement rather than contradict Whitehead's analysis of novelty in actual occasions as arising from hybrid prehensions of God. He focuses on the emergence of novelty as it precedes and is presupposed by all conscious reflection and decision, whereas I am speaking of new possibilities introduced by highly reflective consciousness.[53] However, I do not wish to press any claim beyond this: Whitehead should not preclude *in principle* the possibility that a temporal occasion may have toward some eternal object the kind of relation God has toward all.

If we may modify Whitehead's apparent position to this extent, then we can affirm with *Religion in the Making* that in principle " the forms belong no more to God than to any one occasion." The apparent incoherence introduced into Whitehead's thought by the application of the ontological principle to the role of the eternal objects can be removed.

5. GOD AND CREATIVITY

In Whitehead's analysis, God's role in creation centers in the provision to each actual occasion of its initial aim.[54] This role is of such importance that Whitehead on occasion acknowledges that God may properly be conceived in his philosophy as the creator of all temporal entities.[55] Yet, more frequently, he opposes the various connotations of

[53] Whitehead thought that " in our highest mentality " we may have clues to the kind of order that will be dominant in a future cosmic epoch (*ESP* 90). This indirectly suggests some openness to my speculation.

[54] In section 1 above, I have argued that past temporal occasions may also contribute to the formation of the initial aim. Some support for this is found in Whitehead's emphasis on the creative role of all actual entities (*PR* 130) and in the doctrine that an enduring object " tends to prolong itself " (*PR* 88). But the decisiveness of the role of God remains unquestioned.

[55] *PR* 343.

the term "creator," as applied to God,[56] and prefers to speak of God and the temporal world as jointly qualifying or conditioning creativity,[57] which then seems to play the ultimate role in creation.[58] In this section I will attempt to clarify both the role in creation attributed to God by Whitehead and the relation of God to creativity. The process of clarification will lead to the attribution to God of a more decisive role in creation than Whitehead himself intended.

The contribution to an occasion of its initial aim is not simply one among several equally important contributions to its actuality and nature. The initial aim is in reality the initiating principle in the occasion. Whitehead says that along with the initial data it constitutes the initial phase of the occasion. In some of his statements he seems to imply a general equality of functioning between the initial aim and other elements in the initial phase. But in fact in his detailed analyses no such equality obtains.[59]

In the first place, the initial aim determines the standpoint that the occasion will occupy, its locus and extent in the extensive continuum. This, in turn, determines what occasions will be in its past, in its present, and its future. That means that the initial aim determines which occasions will constitute the past and therefore, the initial data of the new occasion.[60]

In the second place, the initial data are not a part of the becoming occasion in the same sense as the initial aim. The initial data are the occasions in the past of the becoming occasion as they were in themselves in their own subjective immediacy. They are appropriated by the be-

---

[56] He especially resists any appeal to the will of God because of its suggestion of arbitrariness. (*PR* 344; *AI* 215.) See also *RM* 69–70; *PR* 519–520, 526.

[57] *PR* 30, 47, 130, 134, 135, 344, 374.

[58] Both God and the world "are in the grip of the ultimate metaphysical ground, the creative advance into novelty" (*PR* 529).

[59] *PR* 343.

[60] *PR* 104. For exposition of this, see above, Ch. IV, sec. 3.

coming occasion as it objectifies them. But how it objectifies them is determined by the initial aim.[61]

For these reasons we may properly think of the initial aim as the originating element in each new occasion. Since Whitehead regards God as the sole ground of the initial aim, he systematically attributes to God the all-decisive role in the creation of each new occasion, although he draws back from so strong a formulation.

However that may be, Whitehead does restrict the creative role of God in such a way that his sole responsibility for what happens is effectively and properly denied. First, the initial aim is the aim that is ideal for that occasion *given its situation*.[62] It is not God's ideal for the situation in some abstract sense. It is the adaptation of God's purposes to the actual world. Second, the initial aim does not determine the outcome, although it profoundly influences it. In subsequent phases the occasion adjusts its aim and makes its own decision as to the outcome it will elicit from the situation given to it. The actual occasion is its own creator, *causa sui*, Whitehead likes to say.[63] In the third place, God does not create the eternal objects. He presupposes them just as they, for their efficacy in the world, presuppose him.[64] In the fourth place, Whitehead envisions no beginning of the world, hence no first temporal creation out of nothing.[65] In every moment there is given to God a world that has in part determined its own form and that is free to reject in part the new possibilities of ideal realization he offers it. This is certainly a different understanding of God as creator from that which has been cus-

---

[61] *PR* 342, 420. Cf. Sherburne, p. 48.

[62] *PR* 373. Whitehead strongly opposes the Leibnizian doctrine that this is the best of all possible worlds. (*PR* 74.)

[63] E.g., *PR* 131, 228, 338, 339.

[64] *PR* 392.

[65] *PR* 521. Cf. Leclerc, pp. 194–195. I am not sure that the *possibility* " that creativity originally had only a single instantiation " is strictly ruled out by Whitehead's metaphysics, but I am not interested in arguing this question here.

tomary in many Christian circles, but it is nevertheless a doctrine of God as creator.

The problem on which I wish now to focus is that of the relation of God as creator to creativity. There are passages in which the dominant role in creation is apparently assigned to creativity, such as where God is spoken of as the accident or creature of creativity.[66] This seems to suggest that even if God creates individual occasions, God himself created by creativity. However, this is a misunderstanding. The way in which Whitehead conceives of creativity as related to God is not analogous to the relation of God to temporal occasions. To make this clear we may have recourse to Aristotle's terminology of the four causes, of which Whitehead also makes use.[67]

According to the ontological principle, only actual entities can have efficient or final causality for other actual entities.[68] God as an actual entity does have such efficacy for other entities, but creativity is not an actual entity and hence, cannot function as an efficient (or final) cause of anything. Therefore, if we mean by creator an efficient (or final) cause, creativity is not a creator, certainly not the creator of God. Similarly, creativity is incapable of functioning as the formal cause of any actual entity, since it is totally neutral as to form.

Whitehead explicitly explains that creativity is in his system what prime matter is in Aristotle, namely, the material cause.[69] This suggests, correctly, that the problem of a doctrine of creation in Whitehead is much like that in a philosophy based on Aristotle: the role of the creator is to provide form for a reality given to him. The creator does not create the reality as such. It is my thesis, however, that the role of the creator in Whitehead must be more

[66] PR 11, 135.
[67] PR 129, 320, 423. See also notes 68 and 69 below.
[68] PR 36-37.
[69] PR 46-47. Elsewhere he identifies the Category of the Ultimate, which includes "many" and "one" along with "creativity," as Aristotle's "primary substance" (PR 32).

drastic than in Aristotle, more drastic also than Whitehead recognized. To support this thesis, a brief consideration of the role of prime matter in Aristotle and of creativity in Whitehead is required.

The philosophical problem in Aristotle may be explicated by reference to the distinction between *what* things are and *that* things are. When Aristotle is explaining *what* things are, he never refers to prime matter. Since it is subject to any form whatsoever, it cannot explain the particular form of anything. However, if one asks why it is that there is anything at all, the answer must be that prime matter is eternal and demands some form.

Thinkers divide on the question as to whether that is an adequate answer. First, is it intelligible? It is at least sufficiently suggestive that one who thinks in terms of matter can have some dim intuition as to what is meant. One can see that the same matter takes different forms, as in ice, water, and steam, and that that which takes these several forms must have much less definite form than any of these individual forms of it. This suggests a relatively formless state of matter. If that which can be ice, water, and steam differs from that which can be wood or paper, this must be because it has some difference of form, however primitive. In that case, some still less definitely formed matter must be subject to alteration between these forms, since rain appears to be part of what enters into the formation of trees. At the end of such a hierarchy of less-formed matter we can posit prime matter, enduring unchanged through all the forms imposed upon it. This matter neither increases nor decreases, it is in no way affected by time, hence it must be conceived as eternal. Let us assume that this is intelligible, at least given the science of Aristotle's day or perhaps any science down into the nineteenth century.

Second, if it is intelligible, does it answer the question? Prime matter does not explain why there is prime matter. Only if one first posits prime matter can one explain why there will always be material things. But this may mean only that the question is meaningless. The question " Why? " in this case cannot be asking for a material or a formal cause, since that would be ridiculous. Prime matter is its own material cause and it has no form. It must be asking either for an efficient cause or for a final cause. The final cause of prime matter might be said to be the forms that can be actualized, but this is of doubtful meaning. And prime matter requires an efficient cause only if it came into being at some point in time or if it lacks in itself the power to sustain its own being.

Christian Aristotelians have developed the idea that prime matter and all the entities composed of it cannot be conceived as having in themselves the power to exist. They depend for their existence on a power beyond themselves. This power, or its ground, must be a necessary existent, or a being such that its essence involves its existence. Prime matter cannot be a necessary existent since it can be conceived as not existing. Hence, the necessarily existent is the efficient cause of the being of everything that is. It explains *that* there are things as well as what they are. It can then be assimilated to Aristotle's God who thus becomes both the efficient and the final cause of the world. Once this is done, there is no philosophical objection to asserting a temporal beginning of the creation, or perhaps better, a beginning of time itself.

This argument may be rejected on the grounds that there is no reason to go beyond the beginning of things to a ground of their being. Certainly Aristotle never intended to raise the question as to why there is anything at all. He asked only for an explanation of what in fact is. Many moderns sympathize with Aristotle at this point and refuse to accept the more ultimate question as an appropriate topic for inquiry. The being of things in their eyes simply is; it does not point beyond itself to a ground.

This rejection of the radical question as to why there is anything at all is also characteristic of Whitehead. Sometimes it almost sounds as if " creativity " is intended as an answer to that question,[70] but it can be so even less than Aristotle's prime matter. We must ask to what " creativity " refers and whether in the context of Whitehead's thought it is an intelligible concept.

Creativity, for Whitehead, does not " exist." This is clear in that it cannot be understood in terms of any of his categories of existence.[71] Creativity is specifically described as one of the ultimate notions that along with " many " and " one " are " involved in the meaning of the synonymous terms ' thing,' ' being,' ' entity.' " [72] We cannot think of an entity except as a unit of self-creativity in which the many factors of the universe become one individual thing which then becomes a part of the many for creative synthesis into a new one.

These " notions " are not treated by Whitehead as eternal objects [73] because, unlike eternal objects generally, they are necessarily referent to everything that is. The eternal objects express pure possibilities. These notions express absolute necessities. Hence, they jointly constitute

[70] For example, he speaks of " the creativity whereby there is a becoming of entities superseding the one in question " (PR 129).

[71] The categories of existence are listed in PR on pp. 32–33.

[72] PR 31.

[73] Johnson interpreted creativity as an eternal object in pages submitted to Whitehead, and Whitehead did not challenge this. If we follow Johnson here, the thesis that I am arguing, namely, that creativity cannot answer the question why occasions occur, is self-evidently established. See Johnson, Appendix B, p. 221. But creativity should not be understood as an eternal object. Eternal objects are forms or formal causes, and creativity is not. An eternal object is " neutral as to the fact of its physical ingression in any particular actual entity of the temporal world " (PR 70), but there can be no actual entity apart from creativity. There is a sense in which " creativity," like any other idea whatsoever, is an eternal object. That is, I can think about Whitehead's idea of creativity, and when I do so, I am thinking of an eternal object. Similarly, " actual entity " and " prehension " are eternal objects when thought of as ideas. But the entities to which Whitehead intends to refer us when he uses these terms are not eternal objects.

the " Category of the Ultimate and are presupposed in all the more special categories." [74]

Focusing now specifically upon creativity, we see that it is that apart from which nothing can be. It is not in the usual sense an abstraction,[75] for whatever *is* is a unit of creativity. Creativity is the actuality of every actual entity. We may think of all the forms embodied in each instance of creativity as abstractable from it, since creativity might equally have taken any other form so far as its being creativity is concerned. But it is confusing to speak of creativity as being itself an abstraction from its expressions, since it is that in virtue of which they have concreteness. Nevertheless, creativity as such is not concrete or actual.

Once again, as with Aristotle's prime matter, we may say that this is fundamentally intelligible. Whitehead knows that he can only point and hope that we will intuitively grasp that at which he points. But this is the method of philosophy everywhere. It must appeal to intuition.[76] The next question is as to whether this intelligible idea can answer the question as to why there is anything at all. Despite Whitehead's own failure to raise this question in its radical form, I now propose to give it serious consideration.

My contention is that " creativity " cannot go even so far in the direction of an answer as did " prime matter." Once we have intuited the idea of prime matter we see that from the Aristotelian perspective there must be something eternally unchanging at the base of the flux of things. But creativity is another word for the change itself. Whitehead constantly denies that there is any underlying substance which is the subject of change. Does the notion of change, or becoming, or process include in it some sense

[74] *PR* 31.

[75] At times Whitehead makes statements that seem to imply that creativity is an abstraction (e.g., *PR* 30), but in the absence of explicit statements to this effect, these passages should not be pressed.

[76] Indeed, all language requires an imaginative leap for its understanding. (*PR* 20.)

that this changing must have gone on forever and must continue to do so? On the contrary, it seems just as possible that it will simply stop, that there will be then just nothing. There is a radical and evident contingency about the existence of new units of creativity (actual entities) that is not characteristic of new forms of prime matter.

Whitehead, of course, was convinced that the process is everlasting. Creativity will always take new forms, but it will always continue to be unchangingly creative. My point is only that the notion of creativity in itself provides no grounds for this faith. Hence, as an answer to the question of why there is and continues to be anything at all, creativity cannot play in Whitehead's philosophy quite the role prime matter plays in Aristotle. In Whitehead every actual occasion is a novel addition to the universe, not only a new form of the same eternal stuff. Creativity is inescapably an aspect of every such entity, but it cannot be the answer to the question as to why that entity, or any entity, occurs. The question is why new processes of creativity keep occurring, and the answer to this cannot be simply because there was creativity in the preceding occasions and that there is creativity again in the new ones. If occasions ceased to occur, then there would be no creativity. Creativity can explain only ex post facto.

Creativity as the material cause of actual entities, then, explains in Whitehead's philosophy neither what they are nor that they are. If the question as to why things are at all is raised in the Whiteheadian context, the answer must be in terms of the decisions of actual entities. We have already seen that the decisive element in the initiation of each actual occasion is the granting to that occasion of an initial aim. Since Whitehead attributes this function to God, it seems that, to a greater degree than Whitehead intended, God must be conceived as being the reason that entities occur at all as well as determining the limits within which they can achieve their own forms. God's role in creation is more radical and fundamental than Whitehead's own language usually suggests.

If this is the " correct " Whiteheadian position, in what sense can we understand those passages that seem to subordinate God to creativity? Fundamentally they mean that God also is an instance of creativity. For God to be at all is for him to be a unit of creativity. In this respect his relation to creativity is just the same as that of all actual occasions. Creativity does not explain why they occur or what form they take, but if they occur at all and regardless of what form they take, each will be an instance of creativity, a fresh unity formed as a new togetherness of the antecedent many and offering itself as a member of the multiplicity of which any subsequent occasion must take account.

Like the Christian Aristotelians, I have stressed God's responsibility for the being as well as the form of actual entities. It may be wise to stress also the points of difference between the Whiteheadian doctrine developed here and this Aristotelian one. I am not claiming for God either eminent reality or necessary existence in contrast to contingent existence. Since God does exist, and since he aims at the maximum strength of beauty, he will continue to exist everlastingly. The necessity of his everlasting existence stems from his aim at such existence combined with his power to effect it. But I am more interested in God's power to cause actual occasions to occur than in the " necessity " of his existence. It is no objection to my mind that if that which has the power to give existence requires also that it receive existence, then we are involved in an infinite regress. I assume that we are indeed involved in an endless regress. Each divine occasion (if, as I hold, God is better conceived as a living person rather than a single actual entity [77]) must receive its being from its predecessors, and I can image no beginning of such a series. It is true that I also cannot imagine an infinity, but this problem obtains in any philosophy which supposes that something, whether God, prime matter, or creativity, has existed without a be-

[77] See above, sec. 2.

ginning. It is no special problem here.

In concluding this argument for God as the cause of the being as well as of the form of actual occasions, I want to suggest that Whitehead's thought moved in the *direction* I have developed. When the metaphysical questions were raised in *Science and the Modern World,* they were answered in terms of substantial activity and its three attributes. Comparison with Spinoza was specifically invited. Substantial activity seems to be thought of as an explanation of the universe in a way that would participate in efficiency as well as in passive materiality, but in fact the Aristotelian categories of causality do not apply to Spinoza's vision of infinite substance. In *Religion in the Making,* we saw that two of the attributes, God and temporal occasions, were grouped together as actual entities, leaving only substantial activity and its two attributes of eternal objects and actual entities. But beyond this, it is significant that the analogy to Spinoza disappears [78] and with it the term " substantial activity." In its place is creativity, which is ranked with actual entities and eternal objects coequally as an ultimate principle.[79]

In *Process and Reality,* there was introduced the ontological principle that denies efficacy to whatever is not an individual actual entity. The eternal objects were shown to depend for their efficacy upon God's envisagement. Creativity is interpreted as an " ultimate notion." Nevertheless, the connotations associated with substantial activity in the earlier work still find expression in a number of passages. These passages can be interpreted in terms of the doctrine that creativity is an ultimate notion of that apart from which no actual entity can occur; but when they are interpreted in this way, their force is altered, and one sus-

[78] Cf. *PR* 125.

[79] Indeed, creativity is subordinated to actual entities in their self-constitution as, e.g., in the following passage: " But there are not two actual entities, the creativity and the creature. There is only one entity which is the self-creating creature " (*RM* 102) .

pects that Whitehead meant more than this. My own conclusion is that although Whitehead was compelled by the development of his thought to recognize that creativity is not an agent [80] or explanation of the ongoingness of things, nevertheless, his feeling for its role continued to be greater than his definitions allowed. My suggestion is that if we adhere to the definitions and principles formulated with maximum care, we will be left with the question as to what causes new occasions to come into being when old ones have perished, and that when that question is clearly understood, the only adequate answer is God. This doctrine increases the coherence of Whitehead's total position.

In section 1 of this chapter, I introduced a qualification with respect to God's sole agency in the provision of the initial aim. I there argued that past occasions with aims for the new occasion might also contribute to this initial aim. In that way the role of creator may be understood as shared between God and past occasions along with the self-creation of the new occasion. Nevertheless, the radical decisiveness of God's role cannot be denied. In the absence of any aim for the new occasion on the part of past temporal occasions, God's aim is quite sufficient, whereas apart from God's efficacy the past must be helpless to procure a future.

If now we combine this conclusion of section 1 with the discussion of creation in this section, we may say in summary that God always (and some temporal occasions sometimes) is the reason *that* each new occasion becomes. God, past occasions, and the new occasion are conjointly the reason for *what* it becomes. Whatever it becomes, it will always, necessarily, be a new embodiment of creativity.

[80] *PR* 339.

VI

Religion

1. WHITEHEAD'S RELIGION

Some years ago a well-known book was written on the question of "the religious availability of Whitehead's God." [1] The conclusion reached in that book was decidedly negative. Some of Whitehead's other interpreters have agreed that his God and the God of religion, at least the God of Western piety, are different. This is certainly true if the God of Western piety is narrowly defined in terms of one or another of the more common images. Whitehead vehemently rejected the notion of a transcendent creator God who by an act of the will called all things into being out of nothing and continues to govern omnipotently from outside his creation. [2] Supernaturalist piety, in many of its connotations, is ruled out. But from the very first introduction of thought about God into his system of philosophical ideas, Whitehead affirmed that that of which he wrote was that which had inspired the worship of the ages. [3]

In Whitehead's view, not all of God's functions in relation to the world have relevance to this evocation of the religious response. He wrote also of the secular function of God, and he affirmed that the tendency to neglect this dimension of God's work in the world has been damaging for both philosophy and theology. [4] But in his view it is

[1] Ely.
[2] *RM* 69–70; *PR* 519–520.

[3] *SMW* 257, 275–276.
[4] *PR* 315–316.

the God of religious faith who also performs these secular functions.

Whitehead believed that the phenomenology of religion is to be explained by reference to man's apprehension of that reality which he discussed in philosophical terms. His account of religion is to be found primarily in *Religion in the Making,* although there are important discussions also in *Science and the Modern World* and *Adventures of Ideas.* For his work on religion Whitehead depended heavily on secondary sources, and his familiarity with these was limited. Despite these limitations, his work contains some illuminating insights. His comments on the great importance of ardent rationalism for the health of religion [5] are especially valuable. Nevertheless, the greatest value of these discussions is the light they throw upon his philosophy and upon the general way in which he understood philosophy to be related to religion.

Of greater interest is the relation of Whitehead's philosophical treatment of God to his own religious response. Here we have the most reliable starting point for considering how what he calls God is religiously relevant, for here he is contributing at firsthand to our understanding of religion in the modern world. The major elements of his own religious response can be summed up under five headings: worship, adventure, meaning, companionship, and peace. What can be said on each of these points is intimately interconnected with what is said on the others, but for purposes of our consideration separate treatment will be helpful.

Religion is not a means to any end beyond itself. Only in its decadence can it be supported on the ground that it contributes to the good of society. " Conduct is a by-product of religion — an inevitable by-product, but not the main point." [6] Religion is a vision of that " whose possession is the final good, and yet is beyond all reach," [7] and the reaction to this vision is worship.[8] One does not wor-

[5] *RM* 64, 85–86.   [7] *SMW* 275.
[6] *SMW* 274.   [8] *SMW* 275.

ship in order to achieve some good. One worships because that which he dimly apprehends evokes worship. Worship, in turn, strengthens and communicates the vision. But " the worship of God is not a rule of safety — it is an adventure of the spirit, a flight after the unattainable. The death of religion comes with the repression of the high hope of adventure." [9]

Unlike " worship," " adventure " is a term that is given a somewhat technical meaning in Whitehead's discussion of values. In this connection it has been treated briefly in Chapter III.[10] It may be explained here in connection with the problem there discussed as the relation between present attainment of some perfection of beauty and the partial sacrifice of such attainment for the sake of the future. If a culture has achieved some high form of beauty, it can continue to reproduce that achievement. Such reproductions have real value, but they begin to grow stale. There is a loss of zest and intensity. The culture begins to decline.

The alternative to such a decline is the occurrence of some new ideal of perfection as yet unrealized and not subject to immediate achievement. If this ideal seizes the imagination, it inspires new vigor of effort. This will entail a loss of harmony, a large element of present discord. Nevertheless, it is only thereby that new beauty with new strength can be attained. This quest for beauty not yet realized and perhaps only dimly imagined is the adventure with which Whitehead is concerned.

The relation between adventure and God can easily be shown. In every occasion God is the lure toward its ideal realization. This lure is toward a good partly to be realized in the immediate satisfaction and partly realizable only in the future. Whatever value might be realized in the immediate present and proximate future, God envisions possibilities of infinite variety in contrast to those presently attainable. He who is captured by the vision of some such possibility, and he alone, will respond to the call of adventure. Thus, God is the urge to adventure and the ground

[9] *SMW* 276.   [10] See above, pp. 108–109.

of the possibility of the response.

For the third aspect of Whitehead's religious response, I have used the term "meaning." Whitehead's general mood was one of quiet confidence. Life to him seemed worth living. But this confidence was not derived from any assurance about history or about nature. His own vision of all things was of their perpetual perishing. In this lies the ultimate evil in the world.[11] As we view the world, there is always loss as well as gain. The achievements of new civilizations are not primarily to be seen as better — they may well be inferior — but simply as different. This difference is important, even necessary, as we have seen above, but the constant superseding of old values by new ones that exclude them does not provide a basis for apprehending the meaning of life. Viewed only at this level, Whitehead wrote, " human life is a flash of occasional enjoyments lighting up a mass of pain and misery, a bagatelle of transient experience." [12]

In his own understanding, Whitehead's confidence was grounded in his vision of God. The vision of God does not assure the success of the good in the world.[13] Whitehead does not introduce God to guarantee an issue from the uncertainties of life different from that which empirical experience suggests. Our predictions as to the future of history and of nature must be made on the basis of our knowledge of these dimensions of reality, not in terms of a privileged belief about God. But the vision of God nevertheless guarantees the worthwhileness of present life whatever may be its temporal outcome.

[11] *PR* 517.

[12] *SMW* 275.

[13] There is a possible exception to this sweeping generalization. In connection with the phrase cited in the last paragraph, Whitehead bases a confidence in the future on his view that the religious vision itself, despite its frequent waning (as in recent centuries — *SMW* 269; *RM* 44) always " recurs with an added richness and purity of content " (*SMW* 275). This ground of confidence is not reiterated in later works.

In part it seems to be the sheer fact that there is a permanence " beyond, behind, and within, the passing flux of immediate things " that inspires the sense of the worth-whileness of these things themselves.[14] In part there is some sense that man's " true destiny as cocreator in the universe is his dignity and his grandeur." [15] But primarily Whitehead's treatment of this theme, that values are after all worth achieving despite their transience, is associated with his doctrine of the consequent nature of God.

In technical terms, the consequent nature of God is his physical pole or the totality of his prehensions of all other entities. In less technical terms this means God's knowledge and memory of the world. Yet this does not capture the full richness of Whitehead's intention. A prehension is a reenactment of that which is prehended; it means that what is experienced is taken up into the new experience. Thus, just as some fragments of the past are taken up vividly into our new human experiences, so all things in the world are taken up into God's experience. Whatever we do makes a difference to God. In that case, we cannot regard our slightest acts as finally unimportant. Further, what is taken up into God is not primarily our public behavior; it is our experience in the full intimacy of its subjective immediacy.[16] Our deepest thoughts and most private feelings matter, and they can matter to us because they matter to God.

Not only does God experience our experience and include it within his own, but also in him there is no transience or loss. The value that is attained is attained forever. In him, passage and change can mean only growth. Apart from God, time is perpetual perishing.[17] Because of him, the achievements of the world are cumulative. It is

---

[14] *SMW* 275.

[15] *Dial* 371.

[16] We have noted above, p. 162 that Whitehead may not have intended that the subjective immediacy itself is retained in God.

[17] *PR* 196.

this aspect of the vision of God which ultimately sustains us in the assurance that life is worth living and that our experience matters ultimately.

The fourth feature of Whitehead's apprehension of the religious meaning of the vision of God is companionship. This overlaps with what has just been said about the preservation of values in God, but it introduces a new note expressed in several moving passages. For example: " The depths of his existence lie beyond the vulgarities of praise or of power. He gives to suffering its swift insight into values which can issue from it. He is the ideal companion who transmutes what has been lost into a living fact within his own nature. He is the mirror which discloses to every creature its own greatness." [18] And again, " The image — and it is but an image — the image under which this operative growth of God's nature is best conceived, is that of a tender care that nothing be lost." [19]

In these passages we sense that Whitehead's doctrine of the consequent nature of God meant something more for him than the assurance that his life had meaning ultimately. It meant also that God cared as an ideal companion cares. Whitehead knew, of course, that this was anthropomorphic language and that terms like " companion " and " tender care " cannot be applied to God's relation to us without qualification. But this does not mean that this language about God is analogical in the Thomistic sense. On the contrary, the relation between God and man can be stated in univocal language. This was done in Chapters IV and V. But in the passages quoted above Whitehead states nontechnically, and therefore not altogether literally, the meaning of this relation to the human believer who experiences it. The language becomes richer in connotations, some of which must not be pressed, but it retains a basis in univocal predication.

There is a final factor in the relation of man to the consequent nature of God that further strengthens this sense

[18] RM 154–155.   [19] PR 525.

of the divine companionship. By reason of the relativity of all things, we know that we also prehend the consequent nature of God. In this fourth phase of the interrelations of God and man " the creative action completes itself. For the perfected actuality passes back into the temporal world, and qualifies this world so that each temporal actuality includes it as an immediate fact of relevant experience. For the kingdom of heaven is with us today. The action of the fourth phase is the love of God for the world. It is the particular providence for particular occasions. What is done in the world is transformed into a reality in heaven, and the reality in heaven passes back into the world. By reason of this reciprocal relation, the love in the world passes into the love in heaven, and floods back again into the world. In this sense, God is the great companion — the fellow-sufferer who understands." [20]

I have quoted this passage along with the others because the dull prose of my own writing may lead the reader to doubt the seriousness of Whitehead's religious intentions. Clearly, in passages like this, he means to wed the careful philosophical formulation of speculative doctrine with the rich warmth of his own emotional response. He believes in the wedding of the vividness of religious experience and the rigor of critical reason. Man's prehension of the physical pole of the divine actual entity is also his experience of " the fellow-sufferer who understands." And it is with this richer formulation that Whitehead closes his most technical philosophical treatise.

Adventures of Ideas also closes on a profoundly religious note. The concluding chapter is on " peace." I have dealt with peace before in Chapter III, and will not write at such length again. However, at that time I was attempting to explain Whitehead's theory of value without reference to God. Now we can see how peace depends upon, perhaps in a comprehensive sense is, the vision of God.

Thus far, in discussing the consequent nature of God, I

[20] *PR* 532.

have written as if God simply took up into himself the values of the world and preserved them. If that were so, God's consequent nature would include the evil in the world as well as the good. While we could take joy in contributing to his good, we must perforce find terror in our contribution to ultimate and undying evil. Such a vision would indeed give meaning to life, it would help to sustain adventure, but it would also lend anxiousness to human striving. It is Whitehead's belief that finally in God good and evil are not on the same plane. God weaves into his own nature all that is good, and what is evil in the world he transmutes into an enrichment of the total good. In this sense, in God the good triumphs.[21]

There is another factor, thus far inadequately indicated, that makes for peace. This is commitment to ideals beyond oneself such that one's own fate, perhaps even one's own contribution to the divine life, loses for oneself decisive significance. There can be a love of humanity in general that guides one's acts and determines one's feelings. This freedom from bondage to self-concern is a part of what Whitehead means by peace.[22] This too is a response to the vision of God.

But peace as the final inclusive response of man to the vision of God cannot be explained rationally or articulated in other terms. It refers to a state of serenity that is a gift. " The trust in the self-justification of Beauty introduces faith, where reason fails to reveal the details." [23] And this faith finally " comes as a gift." [24] It would not matter to Whitehead whether we said this gift of faith is the gift of God, or of life, or of nature, for it is in life and nature that God works. But we must recognize that the gift of faith comes " largely beyond the control of purpose." [25] The gift comes through the vision of " something which stands beyond, behind, and within the passing flux of immediate things; something which is real, and yet waiting

---

[21] *RM* 155; *PR* 525.　　[23] *AI* 367–368.　　[25] *AI* 368.

[22] *AI* 368.　　[24] *AI* 368.

to be realised; something which is a remote possibility, and yet the greatest of present facts; something that gives meaning to all that passes, and yet eludes apprehension; something whose possession is the final good, and yet is beyond all reach; something which is the ultimate ideal, and the hopeless quest." [26] That vision and the response to that vision is religion.

In all these ways the vision of God was for Whitehead the basis for all reality of meaning and all depth of feeling. Yet it would be very false to conclude that Whitehead was preoccupied with religion. He returns to it again and again, but the great body of his attention is focused on what we have learned to call penultimate questions. The vision of God is there in the background securing the importance of these questions. It is rarely itself at the center of the stage.

Whitehead's own spirit was urbane rather than intense. It would be false to say that he was not a deeply committed man, but for the most part he preferred the stance of the dispassionate observer. He stood aloof from all party spirit, especially in religion. In each religious movement he noted both strengths and weaknesses. One never senses that in any form of its expression can Whitehead find that with which he would identify himself finally. The one exception may be an element in Jesus' own ministry. Even here as historian he notes the peculiar conditions that made possible the emergence of a doctrine that is socially irresponsible.[27] Yet in that doctrine he sees a vision that is also very much his own. He writes, for example: " There is, however, in the Galilean origin of Christianity yet another suggestion which does not fit very well with any of the three main strands of thought. It does not emphasize the ruling Caesar, or the ruthless moralist, or the unmoved mover. It dwells upon the tender elements in the world, which slowly and in quietness operate by love; and it finds purpose in the present immediacy of a kingdom not of this

---

[26] SMW 275. [27] AI 19–21.

world. Love neither rules, nor is it unmoved; also it is a little oblivious as to morals. It does not look to the future; for it finds its own reward in the immediate present." [28] Whatever one may think of the historic accuracy of this portrayal of the message of Jesus, one can see that here was a figure by whom Whitehead was deeply moved.

Whitehead's vision begins with the world and moves out step by step toward its limits and beyond. Only as it is completed in that which is beyond itself, is its own importance and reality vindicated. Hence, in retrospect we can see that the whole enterprise of understanding and of life is suffused and sustained by the dim apprehension of the beyond. In this sense Whitehead's vision is religious through and through.

But there is another quite different way of responding to the vision at which Whitehead arrived. Rather than seek in it security of meaning for that which is immediately given in the world, one might reverse one's approach. He might begin with the vision of the whole and reevaluate the valuation of the parts in the light of that comprehensive vision. Jonathan Edwards, who well represents the alternative type of religious response to a philosophical vision, proclaimed as the essence of rational obligation that one should "consent to being." [29] By this he meant that one's attention and concern should be directed toward every entity in proportion to its being and excellence. The details of his exposition do not concern us here, but it will be found that they correspond closely with the theory of value and ethics developed in Whiteheadian terms in Chapter III. Despite the profound difference of spirit between Whitehead and Edwards, the similarity of their thought would make an exceedingly interesting study.

If we accept the view that consent to being is the ultimate principle by which life should be lived, and if we understand being and the distribution of being as White-

[28] *PR* 520–521.
[29] Jonathan Edwards, *Notes on the Mind,* Sec. 45.

head understands it, then a religious sensibility quite alien to that of Whitehead may result. In God all the being of the world is included and everlastingly preserved, and to it he adds the incomparable riches of his own vision. To consent to being must mean to love God wholly and ultimately, and that every act which follows from a motive in tension with the love of God is a violation of the final obligation imposed upon us by our rational power of self-transcendence. Of course, there can be in Whitehead's vision no antithesis between love of God and love of the temporal creatures. Love of God must express itself in love of the creature, for it is by contributing to the creature that we contribute to God.

My point in these brief comments is that a passionately theocentric faith may follow from the Whiteheadian vision just as appropriately as Whitehead's urbanely humanistic faith. Nothing in the cosmology itself determines such a question. The difference lies in the dimension of sensibility and especially religious sensibility. There are God-intoxicated men and there are others for whom the reality of God provides the context within which they can express their concern for their fellowmen. Somewhere between these two poles most religious men find themselves.

2. RELIGIOUS BELIEF AND RELIGIOUS EXPERIENCE

In the preceding section we have been considering Whitehead's own religious response to his philosophic vision. Undoubtedly there were elements in his religious experience that affected his philosophic doctrine. But our focus was upon his convictions and upon the way in which they gave meaning and peace to his life. In this section I propose to consider other ways in which Whitehead's philosophic vision, especially in the form in which I developed it in Chapter V, can evoke a religiously important response. I propose also, however, to consider what may be called more properly, religious experience, in the sense of conscious experience of God. Whitehead certainly allows for such experience, and his own vision may indeed have involved or been affected by experiential elements in this sense, but I will not try further to consider this question in terms of Whitehead's personal belief or experience. In this section I will treat religious belief and religious experience in abstraction from each other, how each may be understood from a Whiteheadian perspective, and how they should be conceived in their relations with each other.

In Chapter V it was argued at some length that God is the decisive factor in the creation of each new occasion.[30] *How* an occasion becomes is finally determined by its own decision, but *that* a new occasion occurs at all cannot be determined by itself. It may be that Whitehead intended to attribute the fact of its occurrence to creativity, but I have argued that his philosophic principles do not allow this. " Creativity " describes in the most comprehensive terms what occurs everywhere, even in God, but ultimately the creator of every occasion is God. God shares this role of creation with past temporal occasions, but in the end they in turn derive their being from beyond themselves. And in each moment the decisive factor is God. Whatever Whitehead's own intentions and preferences may have been, his thought systematically requires that we recognize God as the " ground of our being," as he upon whom we are dependent for our existence.

God's determination *that* an occasion occur does not determine precisely *how* it shall occur. On the other hand, it is far from irrelevant to *how* it shall occur. God offers to every occasion an ideal opportunity for its self-actualization or satisfaction. I have suggested that other past occasions likewise may communicate to the new occasion their aims for it, so that the initial aim of the occasion may already include some complexity. That satisfaction at which the occasion does in fact aim is some modification or specification of this initial aim that includes the ideal factor derived from God. The subjective form of the satisfaction

[30] See above, Ch. V, sec. 5.

of the occasion is affected by the relation of the satisfaction to the ideal aim given by God. The whole range of moral experience is an expression of man's relation to God.

That our environment provides an order that makes possible intensity and continuity of experience is also the work of God. God so adjusts the ideal aim of each occasion as to achieve relationships of social order and personal order. The gradually evolving order of the universe is his work, apart from which all higher phases of experience would be impossible.

We know God, then, as the ground of being, the ground of purpose, and the ground of order. Each of these dimensions of our total relationship to God is experiential in one sense, but not in the sense in which I am speaking of religious experience in this chapter. Our experience is deeply affected, indeed made possible, by these relationships with God. But we do not consciously experience God as we experience the results of his work. We do experience our existence as not of our own doing, as in this sense given. But in this we do not experience the giver. Our self-experience can be interpreted in terms of "thrownness" rather than as a gift of God.[31] We experience ourselves as having purposes and more vaguely as failing to be all that we could or should be. But we do not experience the giver of the purpose or the source of the norm of judgment. The experience allows itself to be interpreted simply in terms of an existential structure without reference to a ground. Likewise, we recognize an orderliness in the world as we experience it, but rather than attribute it to God, we may view it as grounded in nature itself or even in our experiencing processes.

Thus, the experience itself, in abstraction from all interpretation, is not a religious experience. However, experience does not factually occur in such abstraction.

[31] Martin Heidegger, *Being and Time,* trans. by John Macquarrie and Edward Robinson (Harper & Row, Publishers, Inc., 1962), pp. 223, 264, and *passim.*

Hence, for the man who lives by the theistic vision, in this case the Whiteheadian theistic vision, the experience of his being, his moral nature, and his orderly environment can be an experience of God in the secondary sense. The believer experiences his existence as a gift of God, his motives and acts in relation to God's purpose, and the totality of nature as God's ordered creation. From the point of view of the philosophical position developed in this book, the believer is philosophically correct.

If indeed the believer's interpretation is the correct one, then we may suppose that it is the more " natural " one. By a natural interpretation I mean one arising most spontaneously out of the experience itself, one least dependent on preformed intellectual convictions. A case could be made for this. Man does seem naturally religious, and this does mean among other things that he experiences life as in relation with suprahuman power. It does seem that a thorough secularization of interpretation depends upon a high degree of intellectual sophistication in which rational objections to religious belief play a large role.

However, we should not place too much weight upon this. Other explanations of man's natural religiousness are possible which contain no reference to the actuality of suprahuman powers. Furthermore, the monotheistic interpretation defended above has depended for its emergence either upon an inner purification of religion through the prophets or upon the rational philosophical development and critique of religion. For any full clarification, both are probably necessary. Hence, while preferring the view that the theistically interpreted experiences carry their warrant in themselves, that is, that the grounding in God is susceptible to some dim manifestation within these experiences, we must grant that the interpretive element is predominant.

Consciousness is a very special and limited feature of human experience. We have noted that consciousness presupposes experience and that most of our experience never attains consciousness. Hence, we should not suppose that the failure to experience God consciously means that we do not experience him at all, any more than the failure to experience consciously the innumerable events in our brain means that we are not, in fact, experiencing them. However, unlike man's relation to these latter events, some men do believe that they have special and vivid experiences of God, and I am here treating such experiences as religious experiences in the primary sense. Our question then is as to what aspects of our experience of God are most susceptible of becoming conscious as experiences of him. To approach an answer to this question, we must briefly survey the results of the analysis in Chapters IV and V as to the relevant respects in which man prehends God.

The primary factor in the relations between God and man treated thus far in this section has been God's provision to each occasion of its initial aim. Whitehead refers this function of God to the primordial nature. I have argued at some length that Whitehead has too sharply separated the two natures of God.[32] If we identify the primordial nature of God with his purely conceptual prehensions and the consequent nature with his purely physical prehensions, then much of the actuality of God can be assigned to neither nature. All the higher phases of experience, whether in man or God, involve the fusion of physical and conceptual prehensions in what Whitehead calls "impure prehensions."[33] All propositional feelings, for example, are impure prehensions, and I have argued that God entertains with respect to every new occasion an imaginative proposition of which the occasion is the logical subject, and an ideal possibility for its actualization — ideal given the condition of its world — is the logical predicate.[34] God's propositional feeling is clothed with the subjective form of desire that the proposition become true. If this be the correct interpretation of Whitehead, then the initial aim of the occasion, as the feeling of God's

[32] See above, Ch. V, sec. 1.   [33] *PR* 49.   [34] See above, pp. 181–182.

propositional feeling for it, is not a feeling of a pure conceptual feeling on God's part but a feeling of an impure prehension involving the interweaving of physical and conceptual prehensions. In the derivation of the initial aim from God, it is God as actual entity who is prehended, not simply the primordial nature.

Whitehead elsewhere discussed the prehension of the consequent nature of God as if that in its turn were quite separable from the prehension of the primordial nature. But this is equally misleading. There may, of course, be some prehension of God in terms of his purely physical feelings, but Whitehead's actual account of this prehension as " the love of God " flooding " back again into the world " [35] hardly suggests that only purely physical feelings are involved. I have proposed that we distinguish between our prehension of God's aim for us and our prehension of all other aspects of God rather than between prehensions of the primordial and of the consequent natures of God. All the important prehensions of God are hybrid prehensions, since they objectify him for the new occasion by eternal objects that occur in God's conceptual feelings. In this respect they are like a man's prehensions of past occasions in his own life history, especially the immediate past occasion of experience.

Hybrid prehensions differ greatly as to the extent to which they bring to focus in the new occasion the objectivity, otherness, or it-ness of the occasion prehended. In Whitehead's discussion of the prehension by the dominant occasion of the occasions in the body, he notes how many of the events, for example, in the central nervous system function only to communicate the feelings originating at the nerve endings.[36] These termini are objectified. I feel a toothache as an ache in my tooth, and I can be fully conscious both that I am in pain and that events in my tooth are being felt in my pain. If the transmission of the pain from my tooth to my brain is interrupted by novocaine,

[35] PR 532.　　　　[36] PR 184.

the cells in my tooth may continue to have the same feelings as before, but I as the dominant occasion in my body no longer reenact or objectify these feelings.

Consider as another example more nearly analogous to that of our prehensions of God, our prehensions of our own past occasions of experience. Specifically consider the prehension of the immediately preceding occasion of experience, perhaps a tenth of a second earlier. In this relation, much of what the present occasion includes in its consciousness is directly derived from what was consciously entertained in the predecessor occasion. Yet normally we do not consciously objectify that predecessor occasion. To do so at all requires a very unusual redirection of attention away from the worlds of sense experience and of reflection that usually absorb consciousness. Nevertheless, my consciousness of a certain purpose may be dimly qualified by the consciousness that my present entertainment of that purpose did not originate in the moment in question but derived from the preceding moment of experience. This sense of derivation from our own past as well as from our bodies and their environment has an important effect upon consciousness despite the fact that it is almost always at its periphery.

If Whitehead's philosophical analysis is correct, we, in fact, derive also from God. We should expect, therefore, that a dim sense of the derivation of our initial aim from God should also qualify our consciousness of purpose. That it, in fact, does so is the widespread testimony of religious men. But we are now asking how it happens that at times what is normally on the extreme fringes of consciousness can come to occupy its center.

My suggestion, in line I believe with Whitehead's intention, is that consciousness of God in any focused sense is usually associated with prehensions of him other than the derivation of the initial aim. Consciousness depends upon contrast and negation,[37] whereas God's role in our

37 *PR* 399.

derivation of the initial aim is unvarying, however much the aim may vary. The weight of atmosphere we constantly experience does not enter into our consciousness, although we would be aware of its sudden removal. In the case of our initial aim, God's abrogation of his constant role would mean our nonexistence; so consciousness by contrast is impossible.

In the remainder of this section we will consider primarily the other way in which God is prehended, that is, as one among the initial data of the human occasion. Even here we see that the constancy of God's presence militates against consciousness of him. In the consciousness of most of us most of the time, God's presence as part of our total actual world functions only as another aspect of our dim and poorly discriminated sense of derivation from a real past. As in the case of the prehension of God's aim for us, the totality of every experience is subject to interpretation with no reference at all to God's presence. But those who interpret it in reference to the constant presence of God find their interpreted experience dimly qualified by that presence. In this case, however, an additional element of difference obtains between those who affirm and those who deny the presence. Where only the derivation of the initial aim is at stake, God's effective activity for each occasion is not altered by belief or disbelief. He confronts believers and unbelievers alike with the ideal possibility for self-actualization. Each occasion continues to receive from him the now relevant ideal, an ideal that takes account of the new situation produced by the relative successes and failures of the past, but is always the best possibility for this new occasion now. But the causal efficacy of a past occasion for the present one in every other respect than the initial provision of the aim is affected by the aim of the new occasion, and in the human occasion the structure of belief affects the aim.

For these reasons, those who deny the presence of God so form their subjective aim as to reduce the efficacy of that presence for them. Since every entity in the world of an occasion must be positively prehended, God is never totally excluded. But God's causal efficacy beyond the provision of the initial aim may be reduced to triviality. On the other hand, those who affirm the presence of God may so form their subjective aims that God's causal efficacy for them may be maximized. It may even impinge upon consciousness in such a way as rather clearly to confirm the belief that facilitates that impingement. Faith can lead to experiential self-validation.

But not all religious experience is a vague, persistent concomitant of the everyday life of the believer. It can also appear in dramatic ways in moments that seem almost wholly discontinuous with ordinary life. There are, for example, intense experiences of the numinous, and ecstatic experiences of union and communion. If we are to understand the occurrence of such experiences, we must consider both the ontological and the ontic bases for their occurrence. In all this we are simply assuming the authenticity of the experience.

The experience of the holy may be considered first. It is widely regarded as coterminous with religious experience. He who dimly experiences the presence of God in his whole life is also dimly experiencing God as holy. The periodic intensification of the experience is at the same time an intensification of the sense of the holy. Indeed, holiness may be identified as the subjective form of the prehension of God in the mode of causal efficacy. Any particular prehension of God may involve other subjective forms, but this one is constant. Hence, God is the Holy One. The element of the holy does not disappear even in experiences of most intimate union or communion.

In Whiteheadian terms, ontological union with God is impossible. Any occasion in a human living person remains such, and God remains God. If at any point there were no member of the serially ordered society constituting the living person, then the human person simply would not exist. That could not be called union with God. Nevertheless, the ecstatic experience often interpreted as union with God can be given strict ontological explanation in the categories of thought developed in this book.

Every occasion in a living person inherits from past occasions of experience of that living person; it inherits from occasions in other living persons; it inherits from the occasions constituting the body of which it is the presiding member; and it inherits from God. When the dominant line of inheritance is that from earlier occasions in the living person, then personal identity is maximized. This identity may or may not be weakened by the occurrence of strong influences from other living persons, but in any case, these influences create intimate interpersonal relations. When the predominant determinants of a human occasion are from the body, the occasion tends to become subhuman and subpersonal in character, for this means that it is doing little more than playing its role in stimulus-response mechanisms of the psychophysical organism.

The fourth possibility is that the becoming occasion inherit primarily from God. That means that the causal efficacy of God for that occasion would exceed in importance for its satisfaction that of all other occasions combined. If this should occur, then the occasion in question is largely dissociated from its identity with the living person, its social relationships with other human beings, and even its interactions with its body. All of these would remain, but they would be reduced to triviality. In that case, the occasion would be constituted largely by its continuity with God. Such an experience could be quite literally described as ecstatic. Experientially speaking, it may well be understood as an experience of union with God, even though, philosophically speaking, actual identity must be denied.[38]

[38] My dogmatic denial may not be warranted on strictly metaphysical grounds. Whitehead notes the possibility that two enduring objects can intersect in a single occasion belonging to both objects. (PR 302.) I do not believe, however, that such intersection can meaningfully be affirmed of living persons.

An experience of communion is differentiated from that of union by the continuing self-identity of the human person. The human occasion continues to inherit from its personal past to an important degree. Its inheritance from God is therefore experienced as the prehension of an Other. However effective that prehension may be in the satisfaction of the becoming occasion, the sense of the distinctness of the living person from what is thereby prehended remains. Thus, the relation is one of intimacy of two persons rather than of unity between them.

It must be stressed again that the ontological possibility of experiences of this sort does not determine whether they actually occur. This is a purely ontic question. On purely ontic grounds there do seem to be reports of experiences susceptible of interpretation in these terms. These reports are also susceptible of interpretation in other terms such as psychoanalytic ones. Hence, they do not constitute proof of the actual occurrence of the ontological relationships described. However, such explanations as the psychoanalytic ones force upon the report an interpretation much more remote from the spontaneous self-understanding of the experience itself. Hence, an initial prejudice in favor of the present interpretation is legitimate. My assumption is that the " natural " or more spontaneous interpretation of an experience is to be preferred to one that imposes on the experience categories not suggested within it.

Granting the occurrence of religious experiences of these sorts, the question of value also remains open. Those who have had these experiences commonly report great intrinsic value. Also, in some cases lasting beneficial results appear to follow. On the other hand, widespread efforts to achieve such experiences may distract from pressing needs and still fail to achieve their distinctive goals. In most religious communities mystical experience is not held up as a goal before all.

We will now consider the conditions most likely to lead to this heightened consciousness of God. We may suppose that whether or not the prehensions of one's own past occasions are drastically deemphasized or downvalued in the satisfaction, at least the prehensions of other living persons and of the occasions of bodily experience must be excluded from any important role. This means, first, that perception in the mode of presentational immediacy must be downvalued. The subject must dissociate himself from sight, sound, and touch. Since we experience God only in the mode of causal efficacy, this usually unconscious side of our experience must be brought into dominant awareness. Then within this unconscious dimension there must be a further downvaluing of the causal efficacy of the body. Finally, many elements in the causal efficacy of the past occasions of the living person must be excluded from importance. Only if vivid awareness can be sustained through this long process of negation, would one expect the prehension of God in the mode of causal efficacy to attain predominance in consciousness.

Thus far the assumption has been made that in the variation of religious experience the variable is man and not God. A great deal of religious thought tacitly or explicitly does assume this, but there is no ontological necessity for this restriction. The causal efficacy of one entity for another is determined both by the subjective aim of the prehending occasion and by that of the prehended occasion.

To varying degrees, an occasion may actualize itself with an aim at the future.[39] Its aim is not only at its own satisfaction but to achieve that satisfaction in such a way as to lay a very specific obligation on its successors. When consciousness is present, this aim to affect the future can and often is conscious.

For example, when I begin to say a word, I place a considerable obligation upon successive occasions constituting my personal life to finish just that word. When I begin to type a sentence, I place a slightly vaguer obligation on my

[39] See above, pp. 180 ff.

successive occasions to finish that sentence. When I sign a contract to write a book, I place a much vaguer but still potent obligation on more remote future occasions. But my aim to affect the future is not only an aim to affect my own future. When I say a word, I usually intend that it be heard and have some effect on the thinking, feeling, or activity of some other person. When I type a sentence, I usually hope that it will be read. When I sign a contract, I intend to bind another party as well as myself.

All this is so evident that its elaboration may seem pointless. But it is important to use these simple illustrations to emphasize that what is prehended depends not only on the prehender but also on the prehended occasion's intention that it be prehended in a certain way. It would be arbitrary to deny to God this freedom to differentiate his relations to particular occasions. Hence, we may suppose that God may well take the initiative in presenting himself to human occasions with peculiar force and specific efficacy prior to and quite independently of their self-preparation or desire for this occurrence. Whether God does so, when, and where, are entirely ontic questions. However, some religious traditions have been so convinced that God does take very particular and decisive initiative that they belittle all attempts of man to attain to an experience of God by his own efforts. Hence, there does seem to be important evidence of the divine initiative.

Thus far in this discussion of religious experience as experience of God, attention has been directed only to that kind of experience in which no sensuous element plays a significant role. Such pure spiritual experiences do seem to occur and to play a critical role in the understanding of religion. But far more of what we ordinarily call religious experience involves the mediation of visual objects, sounds, lighting effects, smells, and bodily movement as means of evoking the awareness of the presence of God and the apprehension of the meaning of God for life.

This suggests that there are sensuous elements in experience that have some association with the prehension of God such that the accentuation of the former accentuates also the latter. Most of these sensuous elements gain their function through a particular history. The cross and the sacraments, for example, receive most, if not all, of their meaning for Christians through the story of Jesus. However, there may be also some natural associations between sensuous objects and the experience of the divine. For example, it may be that any sufficiently mysterious sensuous experience tends to break through our usual structuring of experience so as to allow the inbreaking into awareness of elements not usually conscious. In this way we could understand how some such sense objects might facilitate the consciousness of the prehension of God. Once again, these are purely ontic questions to be studied in the psychology and phenomenology of religion. However, ontic questions are in fact approached very differently according to the categories of description or explanation available to the investigator. In this respect purely hypothetical suggestions such as the ones made here may be relevant to the determination of fact.

All experience of God, whether primarily characterized by the experience of the holy or by union or communion, whether involving or rejecting sensuous symbols, is experience of one who is " wholly other." This expression can mean many things, and some of these meanings are excluded by the doctrine of God formulated in this book. But a doctrine of God that intends to speak of the object of religious experience must come to terms with this experiential fact.

" Wholly other " means, first of all, numerically other. Man is not God. Even in the most extreme case of " union with God," the radical difference between man and God remains. If " union " is actually attained, this can only be at the price of total dissolution of the human self in that which is wholly other to it. This would mean strictly that at some moment there would be no occasion occurring in the serially ordered society that is the human living person. That this is possible is doubtful, but even if it should happen, the numerical otherness of God and man would not be abridged.

More important, God is experienced as qualitatively "other." This otherness is not only otherness to myself but otherness to every other experienced datum. God is not experienced as one-among-others. When one tries to describe what is experienced in the experience of God, the major factor in the description must be one of contrast. Typically this contrast takes such forms as pointing to the invisibility of God as over against the visibility of the things we ordinarily think of ourselves as experiencing.

In Whiteheadian terms, many of these contrasts are much less clear or important than is usually supposed. For example, it is not God only who is invisible. On the contrary, very few if any actual occasions are visible in any simple and direct sense. Enduring objects, which are personally ordered societies of occasions, can sometimes be made "visible" through the use of instruments. But even in this way, it is doubtful that we ever see any single actual occasion. Furthermore, such enduring objects as we do see we can see only because of their predominantly physical character. Living persons, which are enduring objects composed of primarily mental occasions, can never be seen. We never see other persons, only their bodies. We never see past occasions of our own experience, although we may reenact their visual experiences. Hence, God's invisibility is not really so distinctive a characteristic.

It may be argued that in the case of other occasions we can see their bodies, or their brains, or their effects on corpuscular societies, or that we can detect their occurrence by the use of mathematical formulae and scientific instruments, whereas God can be seen in no way. Some difference there surely is, but hardly so clear-cut as this. God's relation to the world is one that makes a difference — indeed, all the difference — in all that is seen. The world has to God a relation dimly analogous to that of the brain to the living person. The clear difference between God and all other occasions with respect to visibility seems only to be that whereas in all other cases we can contrast the state of things in which the entity is absent with that in which it is present, to think of God as radically absent is to think of nothing at all.

What is said here of sight applies equally to the other senses. Our sense organs have evolved for the purpose of relating us practically to complex societies — especially corpuscular societies external to our bodies, and they have only indirect relevance for our relations with individual occasions. Experience in the mode of presentational immediacy, of which sense perception is an important part, arises in late stages of the concrescence of an actual occasion by a process of transmuting the numerous prehensions of individual occasions into a simplified datum that can be projected upon some contemporary region. The foundation of all experience, certainly of the experience of God, lies in the nonsensuous prehension of individual entities.

Although individual occasions do not come to focus in sense perception, they can impress meanings upon us that do rise to consciousness. My own past experiences can have causal efficacy for the present such that elements occurring in them are reenacted in the present occasion. There is cumulative evidence that such impressions do occur also in the relations of occasions in one living person to those in another, as in mental telepathy. Hence, we may speak quite literally of a nonsensuous perception of meanings. If God " speaks " to man, this can be understood according to the same principle of the immediate impression of meanings upon the human occasion, although what is more commonly referred to as God's speaking is a far less immediate effect.

That experience of this sort is nonsensuous does not mean that it may not be accompanied by sense experience. The analogy of dreams may be considered. In dreams new stimulation of eyes and ears by the outside world is not what is productive of the dream experience. The explanation of the content of the dream is to be sought primarily in the unconscious aspects of past occasions of the dreamer's experience, although conscious aspects of those past experiences, immediate bodily influences, the self-determination of the new occasion of dream experience, and still other factors are not to be excluded. Dreams are to be understood as primarily nonsensuous experiences in the sense that they derive from nonsensuous perceptions. Nevertheless, we can and do describe the content of dreams in sensuous terms. The nonsensuous prehension of past occasions is transmuted into a peculiar kind of perception in the mode of presentational immediacy, with many resemblances to, as well as many differences from, that of ordinary waking experience in which the sense organs play a prominent initiatory role.

In the same way, we should recognize that the direct impression of a meaning by God upon the human occasion might stimulate physiological activity such that there would be accompanying experiences of vision or audition. Once again it must be stressed that whether any of the human experiences that have been interpreted as the reception of divine communications have in fact involved such communications is a purely ontic question. At the very least, this account should warn us that in the reception of such divine communication the content of the communication is inevitably intertwined with other contents inherited from one's own past and the environing world. The present analysis is intended only to show the process that would be involved should any such communication occur.

The experience of God is then wholly other from sense experience, but this does not sufficiently characterize its otherness. It is also other than every other type of nonsensuous experience. This otherness is often expressed in the contrast of infinite with finite or eternal with temporal. When these contrasts are pressed radically for their strictest philosophical meanings, they prove misleading and display implications counter to the original religious intention. But short of this finally misleading conclusion, the terms capture something of the uniqueness of the experience of God.

The finite is the limited, that which is here but not there, now but not then. God is wholly unlocalized. He is either everywhere or nowhere, and in some senses both terms must apply. Also, every other occasion depends for its occurrence on a power not its own and not given in preceding creaturely occasions. In each moment God derives the power to be from his own preceding state and is the ground of the being of his own future as of that of all other occasions. In all these senses, God is *not* finite, hence infinite. The term is good and useful as long as it is not taken also to deny that anything which can be said of finite entities can apply literally to God, that God's experience can also be enriched, or that the future which is indeterminate in the world is indeterminate also in God's knowledge.

The temporal is that which comes into being and perishes. God has neither a beginning nor an end. The temporal is characterized by the endless loss of achieved values. In God all that has been attained is forever preserved. In these important senses God is not temporal — hence eternal. But the term " eternal " often carries other connotations. It points to a sphere to which time is irrelevant, a sphere in which process is simply not real. This is, indeed, the meaning of " eternal " for Whitehead as for much of traditional thought. Hence, he speaks of the eternal objects and of God's eternal envisagement of them. But God, although not temporal in the sense of participating in perpetual perishing, is also not eternal. God is everlasting.[40]

Perhaps the experience of God in itself dimly suggests these contrasts of God and other entities, but for the most

[40] See above, p. 187.

part we must recognize that these distinctions depend on highly developed reflection. This reflection arose in history long after the first experiences of God in his otherness. Hence, we must seek a more primitive ground of that otherness in the religious experience itself.

At this point, I suggest that the otherness of God expresses itself, paradoxically if you will, in his absolute nearness. Every other entity can be somehow distanced, either as temporally past or spatially separate, but God's presence is absolutely present. He is numerically other, and qualitatively, incomprehensibly other. But this other is spatiotemporally not distant at all.

In Chapter IV, I presented an interpretation of the relation of God to space-time in terms of which we may think of the extensive standpoint of God as including all the regions comprising the standpoints of other occasions.[41] Such an interpretation in its formulated state depends upon reflection, but it is closely allied to many of the spontaneous expressions of religious experience. If it is correct, then the peculiar character of the otherness of God in prereflective religious experiences can be understood. We are literally in God and God is literally in us — and this in both directions in a way that is absolutely unique.

We are in many other actual occasions in the sense that they prehend us, but we are in no other entity in the sense that our standpoint is included in the region that comprises its standpoint. Many other actual occasions are in us in the sense that we prehend them. Also, there may be actual occasions whose standpoints are included in ours in the way ours are included in God's. But in no other case can we think of another entity as sharing with us our entire standpoint. God is literally present in the region which is also our standpoint. Further, we are not to think of this as meaning only that some small part of God is there present. If we are thinking of the physical pole of God, that understanding may be appropriate. But Whitehead

[41] See above, pp. 194–196.

notes that the mental pole of an occasion and its satisfaction as a whole cannot be divided into parts. The whole is present equally in every physical part. Thus God, and not just part of God, is literally present with me and in me.

Yet this relation of mutual indwelling does not result in a relation of part to whole between myself and God. In its own becoming each occasion retains its privacy and its freedom of self-determination. Only as it becomes past is it included in the other in the sense of being prehended. Regional inclusion does not detract from ontological separateness. This unique relationship of the absolute co-presence of ontologically discrete entities may be understood as productive in part of the utter mysteriousness of the experience of God.

We have now considered at some length the possible forms of man's experience of God. In some cases we have seen that beliefs about God and about the possibility and value of religious experience play a large role in determining whether conscious experience of God occurs and in what form and with what efficacy. There remains another dimension of belief about God which can have and has had profound importance for human experience. This is man's belief that God experiences him.

The major, although not the only, objection to pressing the implications of infinite and eternal in their application to God is that they seem to render meaningless the belief that God knows and loves the world. Knowledge and love that have no effect upon the knower and lover are so remote from any notion of knowledge or love of which our imaginations are capable that the use of the words seems pointless.[42] Whitehead is firmly convinced that in a quite literal sense God knows the world and that man can therefore know himself as known. He is also convinced that man's knowledge that he is known and loved by God and that what he is and becomes is preserved by God is of su-

[42] This point has been made frequently and effectively by Hartshorne.

preme existential and religious importance. Apart from it, the apparent worthwhileness of life would be shattered by reflection. With it, the inmost meaning of each moment takes on importance.

The relation to experience of God of the belief that God knows us, loves us, and preserves our achievements is much the same as that of the beliefs discussed in the early part of this section. There we noted that the belief that God is the ground of our being, our purpose, and the order that sustains us may claim to reflect directly our experience of our own existence in an ordered world. Yet primarily it must be acknowledged as interpretation. In the same way, it may be that our self-experience is dimly tinged by an awareness of its openness to another, but primarily such awareness is a function of interpretation.

When one does understand his experience in this way, not only does the realization of valued satisfaction gain importance, but aspects of experience take on added importance for the experience itself. If we believe that God knows us in such a way that he knows our subjective aim and its relation to the ideal possibility with which he has confronted us, our motivation gains in our own eyes an urgency otherwise lacking. In Biblical terms, it is because God looks on the heart that man becomes aware of the heart as the center of his being. Only then does man's dim awareness of estrangement from what he might ideally be, become a sense of sin requiring forgiveness. Hence, this belief that we are known by God has the profoundest influence upon experience even though it may not be viewed as itself a direct expression of the experience. Once experience is transformed in this way the direct experience of God discussed above may take the quite distinctive form of the forgiveness of sins.

This sketch of the many-sided possible relation of man to God is intended to suggest also the complex relations that can and do obtain between belief and experience. Some religious thinkers may minimize belief on the ground that only firsthand experience is authentic and reliable. Others may minimize experience on the ground that it is too private, too unpredictable, too likely to be illusory. Both sides have their point. Belief can have a profound effect upon our understanding of ourselves even when no conscious experience of God is present, and for the great majority of believers such belief is probably dominant in the formation of their religious lives. But belief not tested at any point against experience is both arid and untrustworthy. Likewise, the experience of God may be for some so vital that all interpretation and reflection seem invalid by comparison. But in the long run, it must be recognized that both the fact and the manner of the occurrence of the experience were not unaffected by preexisting categories of thought and expectation. Experienced interpretation and interpreted experience need each other for their mutual completion and correction.

3. THE RELIGIOUS AND THE ETHICAL

In the preceding section matters of ethical concern appeared incidentally from time to time. Also in Chapter III, there was extended treatment of ethics. Nevertheless, there is still need for additional consideration of ethics from the perspective gained in the discussion of God.

Many leading representatives of the great religions of mankind oppose preoccupation with conscious experience of God. They hold that man's destiny and call, at least in this life, lie not in turning from the natural and the human to God, but in accepting the natural and the human as the proper spheres of his service. In extreme cases the call to service of the fellowman may be wholly dissociated from any belief in the divine, but more commonly it is held that it is just in concern for fellowman that right relation to the divine is achieved.

In Whiteheadian terms this view may be stated as that God's ideal aim for each human occasion is directed toward a satisfaction that contributes to the strength of beauty of his fellowmen. Right relationship to God means the realization of the aim provided by him. Hence, the right relationship to God is established when the decision of the human occasion is oriented to the service of humanity.

In further development of this doctrine that man's call is to the need of his fellow, one may move either toward a highly rational ethic or toward a total emphasis upon love. The inevitable tension between these two elements was discussed in Chapter III.[43] There it was argued that no simple inclusion of one of these principles within the other is possible. If there is final resolution, it must be in an impartial but personal love of all men — a superhuman ideal. We can now see that fundamentally the same result can be achieved by the love of God. If God is truly loved, then all that comes from him and returns to him must be loved also for its own sake. The love of God must involve the impartial love of all and each. But even here the tension between spontaneity and reflective concern for the right distribution of goods is not entirely resolved.

In Chapter III it was noted that there is another element in Whitehead's thought that may point toward an ideal solution of the ethical problem. To every occasion there is given an ideal aim. This ideal aim is formed in terms of all the factors relevant to that situation, most of them beyond the ken of the occasion itself. If in each decision that ideal aim is simply affirmed, then the ethical tensions can be surmounted. In the light of the discussion of God in Chapters IV and V, we can now add that the ideal aim is the gift of God. In conformity to God's aim the ethical problems of rational reflection and spontaneity of concern would be transcended. Ideal religion would be the fulfillment of ethics without loss of its distinctively religious character.

Let us assume that perfect conformation to God's aim for the occasion is the one norm transcending all tensions and all the differences of time, place, and circumstance. Does this provide any genuinely relevant basis for life? Or

[43] See above, Ch. III, sec. 5.

when we return to ask the question of what God's aim may be, must we simply revive all the ethical and religious problems? I believe that the natural deduction from Whitehead's thought and the experience of saintly people closely approximate each other in their answer to these questions.

I have suggested that we consider the initial aim of each occasion as a composite of the aims for it of all those entities in the past that have had specific aims for it.[44] These entities would be past occasions in that living person, occasions in other living persons, subhuman occasions, and God. Of these, only the person's own past and God have sufficient importance to detain us. We may consider, therefore, that in the initiation of each new occasion there is a complexity of aim due to the influence of these two sources. There is the aim at the fulfillment that one's own past has aspired toward and there is the aim at that fulfillment which is offered the occasion by God. So long as these two aims are in tension with each other, we may suppose that in the decision by which the subjective aim is finally determined, there will be some compromise between them. This compromise will determine the aim that will be inherited from that occasion by its successors.

In Chapter III, I suggested that Whitehead's doctrine that the aim at the ideal constituted the entire initial aim of the occasion might be interpreted as calling for a certain passivity in the becoming occasion so that in its decision it would not deviate from the ideal. Even there I argued that this conclusion need not be drawn.[45] However, with the alternate assumption that the initial aim is composite, including God's aim but not exhausted by it, the inappropriateness of passivity is much clearer. There must be some resolution of conflicting aims. Mere passivity might lead to a common denominator between them, but would fall far short of either.

The process whereby the subjective aim is formed is for

[44] See above, pp. 182–183.　　　　[45] See above, p. 130.

the most part somewhere beneath the threshold of consciousness. Nevertheless, consciousness is dimly qualified by the sense of some "rightness in things, partially conformed to and partially disregarded." [46] This is the impact upon consciousness of the ideal aim given by God and the failure of the subjective aim finally to accord with that possibility. The consciousness of the difference between what is and what might be, and the sense of the rightness of what might be, can grow. A conscious desire may emerge that the conformity toward rightness be increased. A part of the aim of occasions for the future members of the living person to which they belong may be that the ideal aim in those occasions may be more fully realized. An occasion that inherits from its predecessors the aim to maximize the realization of the ideal aim has far greater possibilities of reaching a decision in which the ideal aim will be more adequately affirmed.

I assume that temporal occasions, even when in their clearly focused consciousness there is predominance of desire that the rightness in things be conformed to, also contribute to their successors more limited aims. Furthermore, I have argued that personal identity is maintained by the unmediated inheritance from still earlier occasions of experience of the living person. Hence, I suggest that no conscious decision to subordinate aims inherited from temporal occasions to that inherited from God will have immediate and total effect. Quite the contrary, it must function against almost insurmountable odds. Nevertheless, such conscious decisions can serve gradually to shift the balance from the determination of the new subjective aim by the person's past to its determination by God. Perhaps, even, more sudden alterations are possible in extreme instances. In any case, the cumulative result of repeated and constantly renewed decisions to be open to and determined by God's ideal aim can lead to a situation in which God's aim for the occasion does achieve a kind of natural and un-

[46] *RM* 66.

forced dominance. This condition we may describe as saintliness.

Even in the saint, I assume, tensions remain and conscious effort must still be made. Yet there does seem to be a transcendence of the need for constant reflection as to the moral good. There is a spontaneous conformity to the rightness in things that exceeds the saint's own ability to foresee or explain. There is an inner directive agency for which the saint takes no credit but on which he profoundly relies. There is, in other words, the providential guidance of God.

I suggest, therefore, that there can be and is a kind of passivity in the saint that is wholly inappropriate in others. He can be passive because there is no duality in the aim that operates within him. His will is genuinely to do the will of God. But for the man who only in some moments wills to do that will, there is no alternative but to reflect upon the total ethical situation. He may, of course, attempt to begin the cultivation of that sensitivity which flowers in the saint, but he must emulate the saint's depth of willing and not his passivity before the inner promptings. There is in the religious a transcending of the tensions of the ethical, but it lies at the end and not at the beginning of the road.

As to how a greater conformity to the ideal aim may be attained, that is a question which must be left to those who are expert in the direction of souls. Perhaps for some it may involve disciplines of introspection and contemplation. Perhaps for others the act of worship may be of chief importance. Perhaps for still others obedience in each new act to the best that they know may be the way.

The discussion of ethics in a religious context has brought us to the idea of providence. Some senses of this doctrine must simply be rejected. There cannot be in Whiteheadian terms some one goal for a man's life set before his birth and unchanging through all the vicissitudes of time. The goal must be adjusted to every time and circumstance, to the decisions already made both by the man in question and by all those others whose decisions impinge upon his life. But there is a principle of guidance that is not subject to the limits of understanding in the person guided. And that principle works in harmony with itself also in other persons and things. Men are instruments of purposes they do not comprehend.

Unfortunately, the doctrine of providence has often been allowed to suggest that God has willed just that course of events which has in fact transpired. A doctrine of providence based on Whiteheadian concepts must deny that emphatically. Much that occurs is profoundly contrary to that at which God aims. The guidance of God is often, if not usually, thwarted. His purposes are therefore frequently ineffective. Yet God is not, for that reason, finally defeated. He constantly readjusts his aim to the partial successes and partial failures of the past so that some new possibility of achievement always lies ahead. The effectiveness of God's providential concern depends upon the receptivity and responsiveness of man, yet the outcome is not simply the product of human effort.

In this last section we have been considering how the ideal aim received from God by which he exercises his providence for us resolves in principle the ethical tensions of human existence. We have been assuming that indeed it is in man's concern for his fellowman that man fulfills God's aim for his life and not in the quest for religious experience of God such as was treated in the preceding section. But it may be too simple to reject that quest in the name of ethical passion. Perhaps God's purposes are more varied than that. Perhaps there are times and places at which for some persons at least the ideal aim must be at communion with God of an ecstatic kind. The task is to learn to discriminate the divine impulse from that inherited from one's own past. It is finally only in that discrimination, and not in any principles, ethical or supraethical, that man can find his true end.

VII

The Theological Task

1. CHRISTIAN NATURAL THEOLOGY

In *Living Options in Protestant Theology,* I argued that there is need for a Christian natural theology and that the philosophy of Whitehead provides the best possibility for such a theology. Critics quite reasonably complained that I did not develop such a theology in that book or even provide adequate clues as to what shape it would have. This book is my attempt to fulfill the obligation I imposed on myself by making that proposal. It intends to be a Whiteheadian Christian natural theology. This expression needs clarification.

By theology in the broadest sense I mean any coherent statement about matters of ultimate concern that recognizes that the perspective by which it is governed is received from a community of faith.[1] For example, a Christian may speak coherently of Jesus Christ and his meaning for human existence, recognizing that for his perception of ultimate importance in the Christ event he is indebted to the Christian church. In this case, his speech is theological. If, on the other hand, he speaks of the historic figure of Jesus without even implicit reference to Jesus' decisive importance for mankind, his speech is not theological. Also, if he claims for statements about Jesus' ultimate signifi-

[1] In this section I am following Tillich in using "faith" and "ultimate concern" interchangeably.

cance a self-evidence or demonstration in no way dependent upon participation in the community of faith, he
would not intend his statements to be theological in the
sense of my definition.

Most theological formulations take as their starting
point statements that have been sanctioned by the community in which the theologian's perspective has been nurtured, statements such as creeds, confessions, scriptures, or
the fully articulated systems of past theologians. But according to my definition of theology, this starting point in
earlier verbal formulations is not required. One's work is
theology even if one ignores all earlier statements and begins only with the way things appear to him from that perspective which he acknowledges as given to him in some
community of shared life and conviction.

Definitions are not true and false but more or less useful.
Hence, I shall try to justify this way of defining theology
as being helpful in understanding what actually goes on
under the name of theology. First, it distinguishes theology from the attempt to study religion objectively —
from the point of view of some philosophy, some branch of
science such as psychology or sociology, or simply as a historical phenomenon. There are those who wish to erase
this distinction and to identify theology with, or as inclusive of, all study of religion.[2] However, the normal use
of the term points away from this extension. The psychologist who studies religious experience, perhaps quite un-
sympathetically, does not think of himself as a theologian.
Those who do think of themselves as theologians, on the
other hand, do not concern themselves primarily with discussing religion. For the most part they talk about God,
man, history, nature, culture, origins, morality, and destiny. The beliefs of the community that has nurtured them
may be called religious beliefs, but for the most part they
are not beliefs *about* religion.

[2] See, for example, John A. Hutchison, *Language and Faith* (The
Westminster Press, 1963), Ch. IX.

Second, my definition suggests that theology cannot be distinguished by its subject matter from all other ways of thinking. It is so distinguished from many of them because it limits itself to questions of importance for man's meaningful existence, but it can claim no monopoly on such topics. Philosophers also discuss them as do psychologists and artists. The line of distinction here is very vague, for theology may extend itself into questions of less and less obviously critical importance for man's existence. This may be the result of more or less idle curiosity on the part of the theologian, of the conviction that his authorities are also normative with regard to such matters, or of the belief that all truth is so interconnected that he must concern himself with everything. However, almost everyone agrees that a classification of plants is less " theological " than a discussion of man's true end, even if the plant classification is based more directly on Biblical texts than is the discussion of human destiny. Furthermore, the work of the theologian can be distinguished from that of some philosophers only to the degree that the theologian acknowledges, and the philosopher resists, dependence on any particular community of ultimate concern for his perspective. Since the theologian may, in fact, be quite independent and original, and since the philosopher may in fact recognize that some of his ideas arose from a culture deeply influenced by a particular community of faith, no sharp demarcation is possible. We can only speak in some instances of the more or less theological or philosophical character of some man's thought. But this may not be a fault of the definition, since it seems to correspond to common practice and to help clarify that practice. Philosophical theology, as theology that makes extensive and explicit use of philosophical categories, merges by imperceptible degrees into a philosophy that denies dependence upon any community of faith as the source of its insights.

Third, my definition makes no reference to God. This is terminologically strange, since " theology " means reasoning about God. But we must be cautious about understanding words in terms of their roots. " Theology " as doctrine of God still exists as a branch of philosophy with this original meaning, such that one may quite properly speak of Aristotle's " theology." Likewise " theology " as doctrine of God exists as a branch of theology as I have defined it. As long as the two meanings are clearly distinguished, the term can and should be used in both senses. The branches of thought and inquiry they designate are overlapping. There can be, and is, extensive discussion of the question as to whether or not God exists that is not theological in the sense of my definition, and there is a great deal of theological work in the sense of my definition that does not treat of God.

One important advantage of defining theology as I have done, rather than as reasoning about God, is that it makes possible the recognition of the close parallel between the efforts to articulate Christian faith and similar efforts in such movements as Buddhism. In some forms of Buddhism there is with respect to God only the doctrine of his nonexistence. Thought in the Buddhist community focuses upon man and his possibilities for salvation or illumination. According to my definition, there need be no hesitancy in speaking of Buddhist theology as the thought arising out of the Buddhist community.

A more questionable feature of my definition is that it makes no reference to the holy or sacred. The communities out of which has arisen what we normally call theology are communities in which the power of the sacred is alive. This is just as true of Buddhist atheism as of Christian theism. The reason for omitting all reference to this element is that many leading Christian thinkers today deny that Christianity essentially has anything to do with the sacred. Christianity, they tell us, is not a religion. The correlation of God's act in Christ with Christian faith is absolutely unique and not to be compared with religious experience. Some of these theologians, and others as well,

believe that Christian theology is most relevantly compared
with doctrines about the meaning of life that are usually
called secular, such as communism, fascism, romantic naturalism, and rationalistic humanism. Christianity is held
to be worthy of adherence because of its superior illumination of the questions also treated by these movements,
which do not think of themselves as religious or as having
to do with the sacred. To define theology as having to do
with the sacred, or as expressive of a perspective formed in
a community that has apprehended the sacred, would be to
rule out much of the work being done by men today who
regard themselves, and are generally regarded, as theologians.

The price paid for this breadth of definition is that the
term " theology " must then be extended beyond the limits
of its most common application. This extension is already
widely occurring for just this reason, so such extension is
not an eccentricity; nevertheless, it reflects only the recent
history of the use of the term. According to this definition
we must speak also of communist, fascist, naturalist, and
humanist theologies. However, a major qualification is preserved in this respect. If the Communist insists that his
doctrine is purely scientific, that his view of history is a
function of purely objective rational inquiry unaffected
by the community of which he is a part, then his work is
not theology but bad science. Others who are not persuaded that the Communist thinker in question is really
so free from the influence of his community may of course
insist that his thought is covertly theological. But I have
defined theology in terms of the *recognition* of indebted-
ness to a community of faith, and this element may be
lacking. Other Communists, more honest than this, may
recognize their work as theological in the sense of the definition. Naturalists and humanists, on the other hand, may
find that the community that mediates and supports their
perspective is extremely diffuse. They may claim, more
reasonably than most Communists, that they have come to

their convictions relatively independently and have only then found some support in a wider community. To whatever extent this is the case, their thought is less theological by my definition. Again, we must recognize that we are dealing with a question of degree and not with a clear either/or.

A final feature of the definition is that it excludes from theology the work of the originator of a community. Of course, it may be his theological reflection as a member of an earlier community that has led to the new insight or religious experience. But insofar as there is real discontinuity, insofar as the apprehension of the holy is direct and not mediated by the community, or insofar as the understanding of the human situation is the result of radically independent reflection, we have to do with a prophet, a seer, or a philosopher, rather than with a theologian. Again, the distinction may be a matter of degree. Many of the originators of communities have understood themselves as recovering authentic traditions from the past rather than as initiating something new. To that degree their thinking is theological. But the *radically* originative element is not. The greatest religious geniuses have *not* been theologians!

Once again let me emphasize that other definitions are perfectly legitimate. They will draw the lines of inclusion and exclusion differently. One may approve or disapprove theology in any one of its meanings. It is better not to begin with an assumption either that theology is good or that it is bad, and then to arrange a definition that supports this contention. One may identify theology with dogmatism in the sense of blind appeal to authority and refusal to be honest about the facts. In such a case he may and should despise it. But then he should also be willing to learn that most of the men who have been thought of as theologians have not done the kind of work implied in his definition. He must be willing to try to find some other term by which he will refer to those whom others call theologians. Or one may identify theology as speaking in obedience to the Word of God. But then he must recognize that only those who believe that there is a " Word of God " can believe that there is a theology. To those on the outside, the great majority of the human race, what he calls theology will appear at best the confession of the faith of one community among others. He will also require some other term to describe what is done in other communities where the " Word of God " is not obeyed.

The definition of theology here employed is relatively neutral on the question of its virtue or evil. Those who believe that the only fruitful thinking is that which attempts strenuously to clear the slate of all received opinion and to attain to methods that can be approved and accepted by men of all cultures, will disapprove of the continuance of a mode of thought that recognizes its dependence upon the particularities of one community. On the other hand, those who believe that there are questions of greatest importance for human existence that are not amenable to the kind of inquiry we associate with the natural sciences, will be more sympathetic toward theology.

My own view is that theology as here defined has peculiar possibilities for combining importance and honesty. Practitioners of disciplines that pride themselves on their objectivity and neutrality sometimes make pronouncements on matters of ultimate human concern, but when they do so they invariably introduce assumptions not warranted by their purely empirical or purely rational methods. Usually there is a lack of reflective awareness of these assumptions and their sources. The theologian, on the other hand, confesses the special character of the perspective he shares and is therefore more likely to be critically reflective about his assumptions and about the kind of justification he can claim for them. If in the effort to avoid all unprovable assumptions one limits his sphere of reflection to narrower and narrower areas, one fails to deal relevantly with the issues of greatest importance for mankind, leaving them to be settled by appeals to the emotions. The theologian insists that critical reflection must be brought to bear in these areas as well as in the rigorously factual ones.

In the light of my definition of theology, we can now consider what *natural* theology may be. Some definitions of natural theology put it altogether outside the scope of theology as I have defined it. This would be highly confusing, since I intend my definition of theology to be inclusive. However, we should consider such a definition briefly. Natural theology is often identified with that of theological importance which can be known independently of all that is special to a particular community. In other words, natural theology, from this point of view, is all that can be known relative to matters of ultimate human concern by reason alone, conceiving reason in this case as a universal human power. This definition is, of course, possible, and it has substantial continuity with traditional usage. It is largely in this sense that Protestant theologians have rejected natural theology. A consideration of the reasons for this rejection will be instructive.

In principle, natural theology has been rejected on the ground that it is arrogant and self-deceptive. It is argued that reason alone is not able to arrive at any truth about such ultimate questions. When it pretends to do so it covertly introduces elements that are by no means a part of man's universal rational equipment. Every conviction on matters of ultimate concern is determined by factors peculiar to an historically-formed community or to the private experience of some individual. Since no doctrine of theological importance can claim the sanction of universal, neutral, objective, impartial reason, what is called natural theology can only be the expression of one faith or another. If Christian thinkers accept the authority of a natural theology, they are accepting something alien and necessarily opposed to their own truth, which is given them in the Christian community.

The last point leads to a consideration of the substantive

or material reason for the rejection of natural theology. The philosophical doctrines traditionally accepted by the church on the basis of the authority of philosophical reason have, in fact, been in serious tension with the ways of thinking about God that grew out of the Old and New Testaments and the liturgy of the church. The philosophers' God was impassible and immutable whereas the Biblical God was deeply involved with his creation and even with its suffering. Brilliant attempts at synthesis have been made, but the tensions remain.

My view is that it is unfortunate that natural theology has been identified substantively with particular philosophic doctrines. There is no principle inherent in reason that demands that philosophy will always conclude that God is impassible and immutable and hence, unaffected by and uninvolved in the affairs of human history. Philosophers may reach quite different conclusions, some of which do not introduce these particular tensions into the relation between philosophy and Christian theology.[3] The modern theological discusssion of natural theology has been seriously clouded by the failure to distinguish the formal question from the substantive one.

On the formal question, however, I agree with the rejection of natural theology as defined above. The individual philosopher may certainly attempt to set aside the influence of his community and his own special experiences and to think with total objectivity in obedience to the evidence available to all men. This is a legitimate and worthy endeavor. But the student of the history of philosophy cannot regard it as a successful one. It is notorious that the ineradicable ideas left in Descartes's mind after he had doubted everything were products of the philosophical and theological work, or more broadly of the cultural matrix, that had formed his mind. There is nothing shameful in this. Descartes's work was exceedingly fruitful. Neverthe-

[3] That this is so is fully established by the work of Hartshorne. See especially *The Divine Relativity*.

less, no one today can regard it as the product of a perfectly neutral and universal human rationality. If one
should agree with him, he should recognize that he does
so decisively because his fundamental experience corre-
sponds to that of Descartes. He cannot reasonably hope
that all equally reflective men will come to Descartes's
conclusions.

To put the matter in another way, it is generally recognized today that philosophy has a history. For many centuries each philosopher was able to suppose that his own
work climaxed philosophy and reached final indubitable
truth. But such an attitude today would appear naïve if the
great questions of traditional philosophy are being discussed. Insofar as philosophers now attempt to reach final
conclusions, they characteristically abandon the traditional questions of philosophy and limit themselves to
much more specialized ones. In phenomenology, symbolic
logic, and the analysis of the meaning of language, attempts are still being made to reach determinate conclusions not subject to further revision. These attempts are
highly problematic, and in any case questions of ultimate
concern cannot be treated in this way. If natural theology
means the product of an unhistorical reason, we must reply
that there is no such thing.

However, responsible thinking about questions of ultimate human importance continues to go on outside the
community of faith. Furthermore, many of the members of
the community of faith who engage in such thinking consciously or unconsciously turn away from the convictions
nurtured in them by the community while they pursue this
thinking. It is extremely unfortunate that the partly legitimate rejection of natural theology has led much of Protestant theology to fail to come effectively to grips with this
kind of responsible thinking. Some theologians have ideal-
ized a purity of theological work that would make it unaffected by this general human reflection on the human
situation. They have attempted so to define theology that

nothing that can be known outside the community is relevant to its truth or falsehood, adequacy or inadequacy. I am convinced that this approach has failed.[4]

In almost all cases, the theologian continues to make assumptions or affirmations that are legitimately subject to investigation from other points of view. For example, he assumes that history and nature can be clearly distinguished, or that man can meaningfully be spoken of as free. He may insist that he knows these things on the basis of revelation, but he must then recognize that he is claiming, on the basis of revelation, the right to make affirmations that can be disputed by responsibly reflective persons. If he denies that science can speak on these matters, he thereby involves himself in a particular understanding of science that, in its turn, is subject to discussion in contexts other than theology. He must either become more and more unreasonably dogmatic, affirming that on all these questions he has answers given him by his tradition that are not subject to further adjudication, or else he must finally acknowledge that his theological work does rest upon presuppositions that are subject to evaluation in the context of general reflection. In the latter case he must acknowledge the role of something like natural theology in his work. I believe that this is indispensable if integrity is to be maintained and esotericism is to be avoided.

The problem, then, is how the theologian should reach his conclusions on those broader questions of general reflection presupposed in his work. The hostility toward natural theology has led to a widespread refusal to take this question with full seriousness. Theologians are likely to accept rather uncritically some idea or principle that appears to them established in the secular world. For exam-

---

[4] In *Living Options in Protestant Theology*, I have tried to show in each case how, whether recognized or not, theological positions depend systematically on affirmations that are not private to theology. I acknowledge the brilliance of Barth's near success in avoiding such dependence.

ple, a theologian may assume that modern knowledge leads us to conceive the universe as a nexus of cause and effect such that total determinism prevails in nature. Conversely, he may seize the scientific principle of indeterminacy as justifying the doctrine of human freedom. Or he may point to the dominant mood of contemporary philosophy as justifying a complete disregard of traditional philosophy. My contention is that most of this is highly irresponsible. What the theologian thus chooses functions for him as a natural theology, but it is rarely subjected to the close scrutiny that such a theology should receive. It suffers from all the evils of the natural theologies of the past and lacks most of their virtues. It is just as much a product of a special point of view, but it is less thoroughly criticized. In many cases it is profoundly alien to the historic Christian faith, and yet it is accepted as unexceptionably authoritative.

If there were a consensus of responsible reflection, then the adoption of that consensus as the vehicle for expression of Christian faith might be necessary. But there is no such consensus that can be taken over and adopted by the Christian theologian. Hence, if natural theology is necessary, the theologian has two choices. He may create his own, or he may adopt and adapt some existing philosophy.

If the theologian undertakes to create a philosophy expressive of his fundamental Christian perspective, we may call his work Christian philosophy in the strict sense. There can be no objection in principle to this undertaking, but historically the greatest philosophical work of theologians has never been done in this way. Many philosophies have been Christian in the looser sense that their starting points have been deeply affected by the Christian vision of reality. But the conscious recognition of this dependence on a distinctively Christian perspective has been rare.

Practically and historically speaking, the great contributions to philosophy by theologians have been made in the modification of the philosophical material they have adopted. Augustine's work with Neoplatonic philosophy and Thomas' adaptation and development both of Aristotle and of Augustinian Neoplatonism are the great classical examples. Both Augustine and Thomas were superb philosophers, but neither undertook to produce a new Christian philosophy. They brought to the philosophies they adopted questions that had not occurred to the philosophers with comparable force. In the process of answering these questions, they rethought important aspects of the philosophies. In doing this they did strictly philosophical work, appealing for justification only to the norms of philosophy. But even in making their philosophical contributions they were conscious that the perspective that led them to press these questions arose from their Christian convictions. This source of the questions does not lessen the value of their work as philosophy, but it does mean that their philosophical work was a part of their work as theologians. Theology is not to be distinguished from philosophy by a lesser concern for rigor of thought!

If, then, we are today to follow in their footsteps, our task will be to adopt and adapt a philosophy as they did. I suggest that in implementing this program the theologian should accept two criteria for the evaluation of available philosophies.

First, he should consider the intrinsic excellence of the structure of thought he proposes to adopt and adapt. The judgment of such excellence may be partly subjective, but it is not wholly so. Despite all the irrationalism of the modern world there remains the fact that consistency and coherence where they are possible, are to be preferred over inconsistency and incoherence. A theory that proposes to explain many things must also be judged as to its success in doing so. If a few broad principles can unify a vast body of data, the employment of many *ad hoc* principles is to be rejected. Criteria of this sort have almost universal practical assent, so that it is always necessary to give special reasons for their rejection. If a particular position that claims philosophical authority is markedly inferior by these criteria, there can be no justification for adopting it to serve as a natural theology.

Second, there is no reason for accepting as a natural theology a position hostile to Christian faith, if another position more congenial to faith is equally qualified according to the norms suggested above. The study of the history of thought suggests that there is a plurality of philosophical doctrines, each of which can attain a high degree of excellence by all the norms on which they agree in common. This does not mean that any of them are wholly beyond criticism, but it does mean that the finally decisive criticisms stem from a perception of the data to be treated in philosophy that is different from the perception underlying the philosophy criticized. Diverse visions of reality lead to diverse philosophies and are, in turn, strengthened by the excellence of the philosophies to which they give birth.

For example, there are persons to whom it is wholly self-evident that sense data are the ultimate givens in terms of which all thought develops and who are equally convinced that the only acceptable explanation of the way things happen follows mechanical models. These convictions will lead to a particular philosophical position. Against this position it is useless to argue that there are data that this philosophy does not illumine, and that mechanical models capable of explaining the processes of thought have not been devised. The philosopher in question does not agree that there are other data and assumes that the lack of adequate models is a function of continuing human ignorance.

The particular position I have described would be a caricature of any major philosophical thinker, but it does point to a type of mentality that is not rare in our culture. When I realize that the particular conclusions generated by the serious reflection that arises from such assumptions have only the authority of those assumptions, then I feel free to turn to another philosophy that includes among its data human persons and their interactions; for my perception of reality is such that these seem to me at least as real and ultimate as sense data and mechanical relations. I cannot prove the truth of my vision any more than the sensationalist can prove the truth of his, but this does not shake me in my conviction. I may well recognize that my way of seeing reality has been nurtured in the community of faith, but this provides no reason for accepting as my natural theology the conclusions derived from the sensationalist-mechanist vision. On the contrary, it provides excellent reasons for choosing the conclusions of a personalistic philosophy, always providing that as a philosophy, measured by the appropriate criteria of that discipline, it is of at least equal merit. Every natural theology reflects some fundamental perspective on the world. None is the pure result of neutral, objective reason. Every argument begins with premises, and the final premises cannot themselves be proved. They must be intuited. Not all men intuit the same premises. The quest for total consensus is an illusion, and indeed there is no reason to accept majority rule in such a matter if the majority does not share one's premises. Hence, a Christian theologian should select for his natural theology a philosophy that shares his fundamental premises, his fundamental vision of reality. That philosophy is his Christian natural theology, or rather that portion of that philosophy is his natural theology which deals most relevantly with the questions of theology. It would be confusing to include under the heading of natural theology all the technical aspects of philosophy, but, on the other hand, no sharp line can be drawn, and the coherence of the whole is of decisive importance for selection.

In the sense now explained, natural theology is the overlapping of two circles, the theological and the philosophical. Natural theology is a branch of theology because the theologian in appropriating it must recognize that his selection expresses his particular perspective formed in a community from which he speaks. On the other hand, it is also philosophy because it embodies thinking that has been done and judged in terms of philosophical norms.

There may seem to be some tension here. Philosophy is critical, imaginative, and comprehensive thinking that strives to free itself from the conditioning of particular traditions and communities, whereas a criterion for the selection of a philosophy by a theologian should be its sharing of a basic vision of reality. But there is no contradiction. The philosopher does not set out to show how the world appears from the perspective of a community of faith, and to some degree, he can free himself from such perspectives. Even if he is a Christian, for example, he can set aside all the particular beliefs about Jesus Christ, God, miracles, salvation, and eternal life that he recognizes as peculiar to that tradition. He can and should refuse to accept as relevant to his philosophical work, any data that do not appear to him to be generally accessible. He will begin with ordinary language, or the findings of science, or widespread experience of mankind, rather than with the special convictions of his community. This starting point will lead the philosopher to the consideration of many questions ordinarily not treated by Christian theology and to the omission of many questions usually treated by theology. It will also lead to the consideration of overlapping questions.

However, beyond this level of conviction, life in a community also produces a primary perspective, a basic way of understanding the nature of things, a fundamental vision of reality. It is at this level that the philosopher cannot escape his perspective.[5] He can, of course, reject a per-

---

[5] Whitehead saw the work of the creative philosopher in terms of the novelty of his perspective. The philosopher " has looked at the universe in a certain way, has seen phenomena under some fresh aspect; he is full of his vision and anxious to communicate it. His value to other men is in what he has seen " (*Dial* 266) . Whitehead also recognized that the philosopher's vision is affected by the historic community in which he stands. " Modern European philosophy,

spective that he may have at one time accepted, but he can do so only in favor of some other perspective. And it should be said that changing perspectives in this sense is not simply a voluntary matter. Conscious decisions may affect the process but they do not in themselves constitute it. The decision on the part of the Christian theologian as to where he should turn for his natural theology should involve the judgment as to whether the vision of reality underlying the philosophical system is compatible with that essentially involved in the Christian faith.

In this book, I am proposing a Christian natural theology based on the philosophy of Alfred North Whitehead. Whitehead's philosophy was, I believe, Christian, in the sense of being deeply affected in its starting point by the Christian vision of reality. To some extent he himself seems to have recognized this fact. Furthermore, Whitehead's most important philosophical work grew out of his Gifford Lectures, a lectureship in natural theology. Hence, the judgment that Whitehead's philosophy provides us with a suitable Christian natural theology is not altogether an alien imposition upon him. One might well simply select the relevant doctrines in his thought and treat them as the appropriate natural theology.

Nevertheless, I see the relation of the Christian theologian to Whitehead's philosophy as analogous to that of theologians of the past to the philosophies they have adopted from the Greeks. Whitehead's work is obviously already Christianized in a way Greek philosophy could not have been. Hence, it proves, I am convinced, more amenable to Christian use. Nevertheless, the questions in the foreground of concern for the Christian theologian were on the periphery of concern for Whitehead. Philosophy of

---

which had its origins in Plato and Aristotle, after sixteen hundred years of Christianity reformulated its problems with increased attention to the importance of the individual subject of experience, conceived as an abiding entity with a transition of experiences." (*RM* 140.)

science, epistemology, ontology, logic, and mathematics, along with broad humanistic concerns, dominated his thought. He never organized his work extensively around the doctrine of man or the doctrine of God. Hence, the theologian approaches Whitehead's work, asking questions the answers to which are not readily available. He must piece together fragments from here and there. Furthermore, at certain points, more crucial to the theologian than to Whitehead, the questions are simply unanswered or are answered in ways that do not seem philosophically satisfactory when attention is focused upon them.

For these reasons, the present book is a development of my own Christian natural theology rather than simply a summary of Whitehead's philosophy in its relevant aspects. It is *heavily* dependent on Whitehead. Much of it is simply borrowed from him. But I have also entered into discussion with him as to how some of the doctrines might better be formulated.

It should be reemphasized that the work of Christian natural theology does not involve an unphilosophical imposition of conclusions on recalcitrant materials. At no point in previous discussion have I intended to replace philosophical argument by dogmatic assertion or to distort Whitehead so as to render him more amenable to Christian use. My attempt has been to make the philosophical doctrines conform more fully to the philosophical norms, especially to Whitehead's own norm of coherence. The role of my Christian point of view has been to focus attention upon certain questions. If indeed, beyond this it has dictated solutions that are philosophically inferior to available alternatives, I ask only to be corrected. A Christian natural theology must not be a hybrid of philosophy and Christian convictions. It must be philosophically responsible throughout. Where my philosophical work is poor it is to be judged simply as poor philosophy and not justified by my Christian convictions.

The choice of Whitehead as the philosopher on whom

to base a Christian natural theology requires only brief comment. Obviously I have chosen him because I am persuaded by him. But I can speak more objectively. If there has been any great philosopher in the twentieth century who stands in the tradition of comprehensive syntheses of human knowledge, that philosopher is Whitehead. Beside him every other candidate seems specialized, and in my view, less profound. Although many have given up the effort to understand him, and others have rejected his whole enterprise, most of those who have worked through his philosophy with care recognize its excellence by all the standards normal for the evaluation of a philosophy.[6] I cannot prove that excellence here, yet I hope that even my presentation of fragments of his thought has evoked some sense of its coherence, adequacy, and power.

Whether I judge rightly as to the appropriateness of Whiteheadian thought for Christian use is for the reader to decide. Clearly there is no overwhelming consensus among Christians as to what the faith is. For this reason no unanimous agreement on the suitability of any natural theology is conceivable. Yet I believe that in Whitehead we have an excellent philosophy unusually free from the tensions with Christian faith characteristic of other philosophies that Christians have tried to employ.

2. RELATIVISM

In the preface and elsewhere in the book, I have indicated my conviction that a cosmology inspired by the natural sciences has played the dominant role in undermining Christian understanding of both God and man.

---

[6] As an exception, note Blyth, *Whitehead's Theory of Knowledge*. Blyth argues that there are fundamental inconsistencies in Whitehead's position. The difficulty arises chiefly from Whitehead's frequent unfortunate references to mutual prehensions. If taken literally, this terminology implies that contemporary occasions prehend each other, a doctrine explicitly repudiated by Whitehead. Sherburne's explanation of Whitehead's probable meaning handles most of Blyth's criticisms. (Sherburne, pp. 73–76.)

I have developed at some length aspects of a Whiteheadian cosmology which, I believe, both does more justice to the natural sciences and creates a new possibility of Christian understanding of man, God, and religion. But there is another factor that has contributed to the decline of faith in modern times, which has not yet been seriously considered. This is the historical study of culture and thought. This study has led to the view that every kind of human activity and thought can only be understood as an expression of a particular situation, that all value and " truth " are culturally and historically conditioned, and that this means also that our attempts to find truth must be understood as nothing more than an expression of our conditioned situation.

In the foregoing discussion of Christian natural theology I expressed my own acquiescence in this relativistic understanding to a considerable degree. It is because no philosophy can be regarded as philosophically absolute that the Christian can and should choose among philosophies (so long as they are philosophically of equal merit) the one that shares his own vision of the fundamental nature of things. But if so, then are we not engaged in a fascinating and difficult game rather than in grounding our affirmations of faith? If we can pick and choose among philosophies according to our liking, what reason have we to suppose that the one we have chosen relates us to reality itself? Perhaps it only systematizes a dream that some of us share. The problem of relativism is fundamental to our spiritual situation and to our understanding of both theology and philosophy. Before bringing this book to a close, I want to confront this problem directly, and, though I cannot solve it, perhaps shed some light upon it as Whitehead helps us to see it.

Few philosophers have recognized as clearly as Whitehead did the relativity of their own philosophies.[7] Yet in Whitehead's vision the relativity of philosophies need not

[7] *ESP* 87.

have so debilitating an effect as some views of the relativity of thought suggest. He understands the relativity of philosophies as closely analogous to the relativity of scientific theories.[8]

In the field of science the fundamental principles now applied are remote from the fundamental principles of the Newtonian scheme. Nevertheless, the Newtonian scheme is recognized as having a large measure of applicability. As long as we focus attention upon bodies of some magnitude and upon motion of moderate velocity, the laws of science developed by the Newtonians hold true. They have, therefore, real validity, and those who accepted them were not deceived. These laws did not cease to be true when science passed beyond them to the investigation of elements in the universe to which they do not apply. What happened was that heretofore unrecognized limits of their truth came to light. Certainly the Newtonian apprehension of nature was conditioned by history and culture, but it was also substantiated in its partial truth by centuries of patient thought and experimentation. That thought and experimentation are not discredited.

Whitehead believed that the situation in philosophy is similar. No philosophical position is simply false. Every serious philosophy illumines some significant range of human experience. But every philosophy also has its limits. It illumines some portion of experience at the cost of failure to account adequately for others.[9] Also, science and history keep providing new data of which philosophy must take account. The task of the philosopher in relation to the history of philosophy is not to refute his predecessors but to learn from them. What they have shown is there to be seen. A new philosophy must encompass it. Where there are apparent contradictions among philosophers, the goal must be to attain a wider vision within which the essential truth of each view can be displayed in its limited validity.[10]

[8] *PR* 20–21.   [9] *FR* 70–71.   [10] *PR* 11–16.

There are, of course, sheer errors in the work of philosophers. These can and should be detected, but this has nothing to do with the problem of relativism. Indeed the possibility of showing errors presupposes a nonrelativistic principle at work. And no philosophical position is built upon sheer error. The more serious problem arises at the point at which philosophers draw inferences based on the assumption that their systematic positions are essentially complete. These inferences will prove erroneous, because in the nature of the case no system of thought is final. All must await enlargement at the hands of the future.

If Whitehead is right, and surely he is not entirely wrong here, then we should employ a philosopher's work with proper caution. We should never regard it as some final, definitive expression of the human mind beyond which thought cannot progress. But we need not suppose that the entire validity of his work depends upon the chance correctness of some arbitrarily selected starting point. What the philosopher has seen is there to be seen or he would not have seen it. His description may be faulty, and what he has seen may have blinded him to other dimensions of reality. He may have drawn inferences from what he has seen that he would not have drawn if he had also seen other aspects of reality — perhaps those other aspects dominating the work of another philosophical school. But when all is said and done, we may trust philosophy to give us positive light on problems of importance.

Whitehead's excellence is impressive when judged by his own principle. Within the total corpus of his thought one can understand the truth of Plato, the truth of Aristotle, the truth of Descartes, the truth of Hume, the truth of Kant, the truth of Dewey, the truth of Bradley, and many others. From the broad perspective he grants us, we can grasp the aspects of reality that dominated the thought of each of these men, can see the limited correctness of the inferences they draw, and can note how the work of the others is needed to correct and supplement what each has done. Whitehead looks forward to a future when a still more comprehensive vision can be attained in which his own work will be seen as also fragmentary in its grasp of reality. We too may look forward to that time, but we should not expect it imminently. The work of great philosophers is rarely superseded rapidly. And Whitehead is a great philosopher.

Whitehead also recognized and insisted upon the relativity of values. There is not one good. In the primordial vision of God there is an appetition that all possible values be realized. No one pattern of excellence is finally preferred.[11]

But this does not mean that values are not worth achieving. It does indeed mean that our contemporary ideals are not absolute and that no pattern of mores, however fine, can be anything other than one among many. There is no natural law, if that would mean an eternal sanctioning of one such pattern. But there is an objectivity of value. There is real better and worse. There are criteria by which various achievements, even achievements in various cultures governed by diverse visions of excellence, can be judged. The relativity of values does not mean that values are not real.

On both of these points Whitehead has dealt with the problem of relativity seriously and has removed from it its nihilistic sting. There is no human attainment of final truth, but there are more and less adequate approximations. There is no human value that is eternally sanctioned for all times and places. But there are real excellences to be achieved in many ways, all eminently worth achieving. Can we rest with this solution to the problem of relativism?

On this point I, for one, am deeply torn. I find Whitehead's thought so powerfully persuasive, and I find it so comprehensively illuminating of the history of thought, that I am for the most part disposed to act and think of it

[11] This has been discussed above, p. 104.

as just what it claims to be — the most adequate approach to philosophic truth yet found. In these terms the fact that we know it is not final, that the future will supersede it by showing its limitations, is not disturbing. We must in any age act upon the truth that is given us.

But at the same time that I find Whitehead's thought so deeply satisfying, I realize that there are others, more intelligent and sensitive than myself, who see all things in some quite different perspective. Can I believe that they are simply wrong? From my Whiteheadian perspective I can usually understand why they adopt the view they hold, what factors in the whole of reality have so impressed themselves upon them that they allow their vision to be dominated by those factors. But is there not an ultimate and unjustified arrogance in supposing that my perspective can include theirs in a way that theirs cannot include mine? Must I not reckon more radically with the possibility of sheer error in my own vision?

Here I think we must come to terms with an aspect of the modern sensibility that we cannot transcend. Just because we humans can transcend ourselves, we can and must recognize the extreme finitude of all our experiences, all our judgments, all our thoughts. Every criterion we establish to evaluate our claims to truth must be recognized as itself involved in the finitude it strives to transcend. From this situation there is no escape. We must learn to live, to think, and to love in the context of this ultimate insecurity of uncertainty.

This may suggest to some theologians that the whole enterprise of natural theology is, after all that has been said, misguided. It seeks support for theology in a philosophy that cannot transcend relativity and uncertainty. These theologians may hold that Christian theology should remain faithful only to the Word of God that breaks through from the absolute into the relative. But there is no escape here. I can be no more sure of the truth of the claim that the absolute has shown itself than of the truth of the philosophical analysis. However certain the absolute may be in itself, it is mediated to me through channels that do not share that absoluteness. If the appeal is to some unmediated act of the absolute in the believer, there must still be trust beyond certainty that the act has truly occurred and been rightly interpreted. Faith does not free us from involvement in relativities any more than does philosophy.

Yet, in another sense, faith is the answer to the human dilemma of being forced to live in terms of a truth that one knows may not be true. Perhaps even here Whitehead can help us or at least we can sense in him a companion in our struggles.

One of the enduring problems of philosophy is that of the relation between appearance and reality. For our present purposes we may consider appearance to be the world given us in sense experience and reality to be those entities treated in the physical sciences that seem to be the agencies by which experience is aroused in us. Whitehead developed a penetrating analysis of this process that takes full account of physics and physiology and is effectively integrated into his account of human experience. But Whitehead's account left unsettled the kind of relation that might actually exist between the objects in the external world and the sense experience of them. Is there some meaningful sense in which the grass is really green, or does the conformity of our experience to that of the entities that we prehend go no farther than the occasions of experience in the eye? Certainly it would be strange to say that the light that mediates between the grass and the eye is also green. Yet man's instinctive belief that the outside world really possesses the qualities it arouses in him is so deep, that Whitehead is reluctant to regard this belief as wholly illusory. At this point philosophical analysis breaks down. It cannot assure us that the whole of our aesthetic experience is not fundamentally deceptive.

Whitehead's discussion of peace has already been treated twice in this volume, but it has not been exhausted. One element in particular remains. Ingredient in peace, for Whitehead, is an assurance that ultimately the vision of the world given in sense experience is true.[12] This is the assurance that reality does not ultimately deceive. It is an assurance that exceeds rational demonstration. It is faith.

In the context of the present discussion this faith must be that the necessity to live and act by a belief whose truth we cannot know is accompanied by an assurance that as we do so we are not wholly deceived. We will not pretend to a privileged apprehension of reality as a whole. We will not suppose that those who disagree with us are therefore wrong. We can only witness to the way that our best reflection leads us to perceive our world. But we can and must believe that in this witness also, somehow, the truth is served.

3. THE OTHER TASKS OF THEOLOGY

Insofar as the theologian appeals for the justification of his statements to the general experience of mankind, he is engaged in Christian natural theology. He may have gained his insight from special revelation, but he is asking that it be accepted on its own merit as illuminating the human situation. Much of the work that has been done, even by those who have most vehemently attacked natural theology, is Christian natural theology in this sense. But there is another dimension to the theologian's task. He must also witness directly to what is peculiar to his own community and to that revelation of truth by which it is constituted. At this point he is engaged in Christian theology proper.

There is no one way of carrying out this theological enterprise. Men equally responsible to their faith and to their community approach their task of Christian reflection in many different ways. Of these we will consider a few briefly, without any intention of disparaging still other approaches.

First, there is interpretation of the text. Especially in

[12] *AI* 377 ff.

Protestantism the community has attributed a normativeness to the Bible that makes its exposition and proclamation central to the theological task. This point of view has been maintained with special effectiveness in those Continental European traditions which have provided the greatest intellectual leadership in the nineteenth and twentieth centuries. Here, especially in the contemporary scene, the theologian is not sharply distinguished from the Biblical scholar. Instead, they share the one task of understanding and making relevant the message found in the text. The Biblical scholar may focus more narrowly on the understanding, the theologian on the relevance, but even this division of labor is hardly maintained. In recent years it has often been the Biblical scholars rather than the systematic theologians who have done the most creative and influential theological work and who have been most effectively engaged with the question of relevance to the modern situation.

In this country this near identification of theology with interpretation of the text is sometimes confused with conservatism. It may, of course, be conservative in spirit and is so at least to the extent that it begins with the assumption that the Scriptures remain normative for the church. But the radicality with which the criticism of Scripture has been carried out in terms of modern historiographical methods, the intense concern to find within the Scripture that meaning and message which is of vital relevance in our situation, should warn us that the distinction of conservative and liberal is not relevant to the distinction between this approach to theology and others.

Second, the theologian may take as his approach to the proper task of theology, confession based on reflection on what has occurred and continues to take place in the community. This will involve him in considering the role of Scripture in the community and in employing Scripture as a source for determining the formative events of the community. Nevertheless, the role of Scripture and its interpretation is quite different in this confessional approach to theology from that discussed above. Here the community rather than the Bible is taken as the point of reference.

The first approach to theology discussed above is characteristic of the Reformation and the theological currents that have maintained closest continuity with it. Biblical study in the tradition of the Reformation is distinctively theological by virtue of its assumption that truth for man's existence is to be found in the text. A scholar who approached the Bible without any conviction of its existential importance might contribute to the discipline of Biblical scholarship and indirectly to theology, but he would not himself be engaged in the theological enterprise. Similarly in the confessional approach, only if the man who speaks of what has taken place and now takes place in the community does so as a believing participant, is his work theological.[13] An outsider might discuss the same topics, and the theologian might learn much from him. But the work of the outsider will be history or sociology and not theology.

The confessional theologian reflects upon the history that has formed the community of which he is a part and that has given him the meanings in terms of which he sees all of life. He confesses the redemptive and revelatory power of the key events in this history. He speaks of the meaning and nature of that faith by which the power of the events becomes effective in the believer. Again, he does not attempt to describe this faith as a psychologist might. He speaks of it in its living immediacy as a power effective in the community and shared by him. He explains how it seems to arise and how it affects the whole quality of life and action. He discusses the response that is appropriate

---

[13] A borderline case is that of the man who enters empathetically into an alien perspective and imaginatively presents its convictions. I would say that in this sense a Buddhist can write a Christian theology.

to it and how it binds men together in fellowship. Beyond this there is the life and practice of the community. This too must be described from within in its peculiar meaning for its members. There are preaching and sacraments to be understood and interpreted in their relation to the revelatory events and the faith of the believer. There is the understanding of historical continuity and discontinuity to be worked out, the role and limits of innovation. There is the attempt to understand how God is peculiarly at work in all of this and how his present work is related to his work in the revelatory events.

In principle, confessional theology makes no affirmations with application beyond the community or subject to verification outside of it. But theology proper may take a third form which I will call, quite arbitrarily, " dogmatic " theology. The dogmatic theologian makes claims of truth which are relevant to all men whether or not they are within the community. He may speak of the human situation as such, and not just of the situation of the believer. Insofar as the theologian appeals to the general evidence available to those both within and without the community for the vindication of such affirmations, he is involved in Christian natural theology. But insofar as he makes affirmations about the universal human situation that are not warranted in general experience but only in the revelatory events by which the community lives, he is in my terms a dogmatic theologian. For example, the dogmatic theologian may affirm on the grounds of the resurrection of Jesus that all men will be resurrected, without supposing that there is other evidence for this truth or that objective proof is possible.

I suggest that in working out these approaches to theology proper, Whiteheadian categories will prove hardly less useful than in the formulation of a natural theology. The presence of God in Jesus Christ, the way in which the Christian is bound to him in faith, the nature of the new being in him, the sacraments, the present working of the Holy Spirit — all these are subject to clarification and illumination by the use of Whiteheadian concepts. That task still lies ahead of us.

But in our day the encounter of Christianity with the other great world religions renders questionable the continuing work of Christian theology in any of its forms. This encounter is not new, but as the world draws together politically, economically, and culturally, the divisiveness of organized religions all continuing to confess their several faiths, becomes increasingly intolerable to many. It is, of course, possible to continue business as usual. But the knowledge that there have been other great revelations by which communities have lived cannot simply be set aside. The work of the theologian must be set in a new key. The inner tension of Christianity, between its particularism and its universalism, expresses itself again in the responses to this situation.

One response is to attempt to distance ourselves from all the particular traditions and communities in order to be able to study each impartially and to accept only what is common to all. But what each shares with the others may be that which is least valuable rather than that which is best. The highest common denominator of all religions may prove to offer nothing by which man can find meaning in life. Hence, others insist that that procedure is impossible. They believe that it is from the perspective given by one community in which we are genuinely and committedly involved that we can learn most effectively from other communities. Believers from the several traditions can engage in a dialogue from which all can learn, although there can be no expectation of agreement or conversion. A third response is to give up what I have called Reformation and dogmatic theology and to limit theology proper to the confessional form. By claiming no special knowledge about man as man but only about the believer as believer, this confessional theology refuses to engage in controversy with other faiths. A fourth response is to deny that the several communities are on the same level at all. One community is claimed to be founded upon the one truth given uniquely to it. Hence theological reflection within that community is the only responsible way of articulating universal truth.

Can natural theology help us here? It cannot help in the sense once supposed when it was thought that human reason could reach conclusions on matters of theological importance that transcend all the relativities of religion and perspective. I have argued that the theologian must select a philosophy according to its compatibility with his fundamental vision as well as according to its philosophical excellence. He cannot then suppose that adherents of other faiths should simply accept his choice as a common basis for joint reflections.

Yet what is remarkable about Whitehead's extraordinarily comprehensive and original philosophy is that it has also many points of contact with the East. The emphasis on immanence, the rejection of any substance underlying the succession of experiences, the relation of man to nature, the primacy of aesthetic categories in the understanding of ethics, all have affinities to this or that Asiatic philosophy or religion. I have tried to suggest in the preceding chapter how several forms of religious experience more fully developed in the East than in the West can be understood in their genuineness in Whiteheadian categories. Hence, the judgment that finally Whitehead's philosophy favors the Judeo-Christian concern for persons and interpersonal relations, its monotheism, and its belief that there is meaning in the historical process, does not mean that Eastern thought is simply rejected. Indeed, it might be quite possible for a Buddhist to develop from Whitehead's philosophy a Buddhist natural theology almost as reasonably as I have developed a Christian one.[14] Whitehead certainly would not object.

Whether or not Whitehead might provide a natural

---

[14] Hartshorne has emphasized the affinities of Whitehead's philosophy with some forms of Buddhism, e.g., *The Logic of Perfection* (The Open Court Publishing Company), p. 273; Kline, p. 25.

theology common to East and West, he can offer great aid
to the West in its task of rethinking its faith in the light
of the reality of the great religions of the East. What has
made the encounter so often painful has been the sense
that where the religions differ, if one is right, the others
must be wrong. Ultimately, at some points, this may be so.
But if we can learn to see the multiplicity of authentic
types of religious experience, if we can see also the truth
that is present in so many different ways of apprehending
the nature of things, then we can begin by confronting the
truth in each faith with the truth in others. At some points
each tradition must learn to state its truth more carefully
to avoid the falsehood that arises from exaggeration, or
from insensitivity to the fragmentariness of every human
apprehension. The points of conflict will recede as this is
done. Each can believe the truth of the other without becoming less convinced of the truth of that which has been
revealed to it.

I do not mean to suggest that we can solve our problems
of religious diversity simply by adding together the beliefs
of all faiths. I do mean to suggest that we can begin by
assuming that what each claims to be true — claims with
greatest confidence based on its primary revelation and
surest intuitions — *is* true. The experiences it affirms do
take place. The benefits it has found are real. But men
cannot individually encompass all the multiplicity of religious experiences. If a man attempts to enrich his life
with all the possible blessings, he will gain few indeed.
Life requires a definiteness, a decision, a focus. The final
question between the religions of the world must be one
of value. Granted the truth each apprehends, where ultimately can man's final need be met?

When that question is asked with utter honesty, none of
the great religious communities of our world can provide
the answer. Each has identified itself with doctrinal and
cultural elements too specialized to speak to the condition
of man as man. A greater purity and therefore a greater

universality of relevance can be found in the great classical figures of the religious traditions. But among them also, relativity remains. The Buddha's vision of reality is not that of the Christ, and both differ profoundly from that of Socrates.

Nevertheless, it may be that all are not in the end on the same plane. It may be that man's *final* need finds its answer only in one. What the Christian dare not claim for himself or for his church, he may yet claim for Jesus Christ, namely, that there the universal answer is to be found. The task of vindicating such a claim lies before us as Christians, both in the challenge of personal witness and in the demand for theological reflection.

Index